Reading between the Lines

READING
FORM AND CONTENT IN
BETWEEN
LEVINAS'S TALMUDIC READINGS
THE LINES

ELISABETH
TRANSLATED BY RACHEL KESSEL
GOLDWYN

DUQUESNE UNIVERSITY PRESS
Pittsburgh, Pennsylvania

Copyright © 2015 Duquesne University Press
All rights reserved

Published in the United States of America by
Duquesne University Press
600 Forbes Avenue
Pittsburgh, Pennsylvania 15282

No part of this book may be used or reproduced, in any manner or form whatsoever, without written permission from the publisher, except in the case of short quotations in critical articles or reviews.

Library of Congress Cataloging-in-Publication Data

Goldwyn, Elisabeth, author.
[Revah ben ha-otiyot. English]
Reading between the lines : form and content in Levinas's talmudic readings / Elisabeth Goldwyn ; translated by Rachel Kessel.
    pages cm
Includes bibliographical references and index.
  ISBN 978-0-8207-0483-8 (pbk.)
1. Lévinas, Emmanuel. 2. Talmud—Criticism, interpretation, etc. 3. Talmud—Philosophy. 4. Jewish philosophy—History—20th century. I. Kessel, Rachel, translator. II. Title.
B2430.L484G6513 2015
296.1'206092—dc23

2015025976

∞ Printed on acid-free paper.

To my friends and colleagues
with whom I am lucky to study Torah.

Contents

Abbreviations	ix
Introduction	1
1. What Is the *Midrash?*	11
2. *Midrash* and Prophecy	33
3. Levinas's Attitude to the Interpreted Text	60
4. The Relationship between Exegesis and Reality	88
5. Interpretive Pluralism	115
6. Unique Features of Levinas's *Midrash*	138
Afterword	189
Notes	195
Index	214

ABBREVIATIONS

The following abbreviations of Levinas's primary works are used in this volume. Any other abbreviations used in individual essays for non-Levinas works are indicated at the beginning of the endnotes for those essays.

BV	*Beyond the Verse: Talmudic Readings and Lectures.* Trans. Gary D. Mole. Bloomington: Indiana University Press, 1994
DF	*Difficult Freedom: Essays on Judaism.* Trans. Seàn Hand. Baltimore: Johns Hopkins University Press, 1990.
EI	*Ethics and Infinity.* Trans. Richard A. Cohen. Pittsburgh: Duquesne University Press, 1985.
EN	*Entre Nous. Thinking-of-the-Other.* Trans. Michael B. Smith and Barbara Harshav. London: Continuum, 2006.
GCM	*Of God Who Comes to Mind.* Trans. Bettina Bergo. Stanford, CA: Stanford University Press, 1998.

HO	*Humanism of the Other.* Trans. Nidra Poller. Chicago: University of Chicago Press, 2006.
ITN	*In the Time of the Nations.* Trans. Michael B. Smith. London: Continuum, 2007.
NT	*Nine Talmudic Readings.* Trans. Annette Aronowicz. Bloomington: Indiana University Press, 1994.
NTR	*New Talmudic Readings.* Trans. Richard A. Cohen. Pittsburgh: Duquesne University Press, 1999.
OB	*Otherwise than Being or Beyond Essence.* Trans. Alphonso Lingis. Pittsburgh: Duquesne University Press, 1998.
PN	*Proper Names.* Trans. Michael B. Smith. Stanford, CA: Stanford University Press, 1996.
TI	*Totality and Infinity.* Trans. Alphonso Lingis. Pittsburgh: Duquesne University Press, 1969.

Introduction

Emmanuel Levinas, one of the twentieth century's greatest philosophers, often engaged in Jewish thought and talmudic exegesis as well. From my very first encounter with his talmudic readings their style and form drew my attention and interest. As one who loves, studies, and teaches Talmud, I found the content of his commentary bold and fascinating, its methods creative and original.

Levinas often wrote about the study of Torah; about its value as a practice to be pursued, with all of its ethical and religious meanings; and about its role in the shaping and rejuvenation of Judaism in times of crisis, for example after the Holocaust. He emphasized the Torah's universal appeal, the human values it teaches, and the responsibility of Jews to translate these values into a language comprehensible to everyone, to promote them in the world. His talmudic readings are first and foremost Torah study, the practical application of these values. This study process uses a method associated with the Jewish tradition of Torah study, and in his writings Levinas often infuses the principles of study with meaning that exceeds their form. His many comments on methodological issues show that not only was he completely aware of the principles guiding his learning, but he also perceived the method as strongly connected to the content, as a matter worthy of consideration. This volume sets out to clarify the interpretive method utilized by Emmanuel Levinas and its association with the content that is conveyed.

Levinas's commentary on the Talmud is philosophical in content and affiliated with his philosophical writings. They direct philosophical questions at the text and see every detail taught in the text, whether *halakha* (Jewish law), stories, the process in which a statement was conveyed over the generations, or verses cited, through this prism. Hence, learning these interpretations demands prior knowledge of his philosophy.

The difficulties that many have encountered when learning the talmudic readings of Levinas stem in part from the dialogue they generate between two cultures, two languages, and two different modes of expression—between philosophy and Talmud. His writing is distinctly interdisciplinary and it demands proficiency and familiarity with two different domains.[1] These difficulties may be why existing research on Levinas's talmudic readings, research produced predominantly by Jewish scholars and mostly in Hebrew, is meager.[2]

Nevertheless, I believe that there is good reason to persist in analyzing this talmudic commentary, created in the specific context of French Jewry in the latter half of the twentieth century. Its basic assumption that the Talmud is a text with meaning for every person at any time also transforms it into an efficient basis for debating many existential questions that concern Jews at the beginning of the twenty-first century. We have not yet overcome the trauma of the Holocaust. Moreover, we are also occupied with fundamental identity issues, questions of assimilation versus singularity, the meaning of Israel's existence, as well as the relationship between religion and ethics, religion and politics, and religion and science.

Many current-day Jews do not see themselves as observant Jews and are not committed to any type of Jewish law, but they do identify themselves as Jews. Whereas in the past, faith was an essential and obvious identity component of people in general and of Jews in particular, this is no longer so.

Furthermore, the existence of the State of Israel—where a considerable part of the world's Jews live in a sovereign, democratic state, one that declares its recognition of the equal rights of all its citizens regardless of faith, race, and sex—is unprecedented in Jewish history.[3] Jews have never before been a majority governing non-Jewish minorities and recognizing their equal rights. Moreover, Jews have never before been equal citizens in other democratic countries where anti-Semitism is illegal, as are most diaspora Jews today.

These new circumstances create a need and an opportunity for renewed thinking, for creating new Jewish dimensions. Just as after the destruction of the Second Temple there was a need for a new *midrash* (homiletical exegesis) to translate Jewish tradition for the post-temple era, today it is necessary to create a *midrash*, or to be precise *midrashim* (the plural form), to translate Jewish tradition for an era in which reality has been irrevocably transformed. It is necessary to reshape Judaism so that it can adapt to this reality.

Levinas's talmudic commentary proposes a humanistic Judaism that is both connected to its roots and immersed in Western culture, albeit from a critical perspective. This is one important alternative among the many current diverse voices within the Jewish world. This is a new *midrash* of the type we need today, a study of Torah that is connected to life's most urgent questions and that offers deeply meaningful answers.

The *midrash* was generated as a tool for coping with circumstances of crisis. Once the Jewish faith lost its spiritual-religious center when the Temple was destroyed, a significant change in Jewish culture was necessary. The sages formed postdestruction Judaism by means of creative Torah study, redesigning worship and liturgy while maintaining a discourse with the texts that had shaped everything that had preceded them. Through the *midrash*, for example, regular prayers were designed, to replace the perpetual daily sacrifice (*korban hatamid*), and repentance was established to replace the ritual order (*seder ha'avodah*) practiced at the Temple on the Day of Atonement. Moreover, in response to sociological and economic transformations, charity was offered as a replacement for the agricultural gifts to the poor (*matnot aniyim*). This was made possible by holding on to the holy text while maintaining almost total interpretive freedom. The *midrash* made it possible.

I do not mean to review the entire history of Jewish culture, but Levinas's *midrash*, similar to Torah study at Rosenzweig's *Jüdische Lehrhaus* (Free House of Jewish Learning)[4] and at present-day pluralistic *batei midrash* (houses of learning), emerged in response to dire circumstances. Rosenzweig was reacting to World War I, Levinas to World War II and the Holocaust. The reality in Israel encompasses unprecedented Jewish innovations, but notwithstanding the positive aspects of this reality, we are also coping with challenges that may be considered crises. The pluralistic *batei midrash* in Israel emerged 25 years ago in response to a deep identity and cultural crisis. These three examples of Torah study have in common a point of departure that is not associated with tradition and with a continuity of Torah study, but, rather, they evolved disconnected from the yeshiva world. Rosenzweig was raised in an assimilated family and first studied Torah as an adult. His *beit midrash* was established in response to the need of educated and assimilated Jews to connect with their Jewish identity by learning Torah. As they were educated but not in the study of Torah, a new type of Torah study was needed and Rosenzweig presents its foundations in the inaugural speech of his *Lehrhaus*. Levinas did receive a basic Jewish education, but he only began studying Talmud as an adult after World War II. He never studied at a yeshiva. In his talmudic commentary he appeals to an audience of whom many lacked any Jewish education and which was also in the midst of an identity crisis following the Holocaust. In the case of the pluralistic *batei midrash* in Israel, the situation is slightly more complex. The founders of these institutions, reminiscent of Rosenzweig and Levinas, arrived at the study of Torah as the result of an identity crisis and in the understanding that in order to connect with their Jewish identity they must study Talmud. These *batei midrash* attracted men and women of a secular background and observant women who had mostly been barred from studying the Talmud previously. (Talmud study in Israeli state religious schools for girls commenced at about the same period as the first pluralistic *batei midrash*—the late 1980s. Only a few women had studied Talmud in academic institutions prior to that time.) Male yeshiva graduates joining these *batei midrash* often did so in discontent with the Torah learning to which they had become accustomed or because they wanted to experience the different type of Torah study pursued at these centers. The common ground of all these people was a Jewish identity crisis along with the hope that Torah study would prove useful for Jewish renewal.

This point of departure allowed and still allows a great deal of interpretive freedom, leading to a similarity in the study goals and methods formulated in order to reach them. Rosenzweig wrote: "It is a learning in reverse order. A learning that no longer starts from the Torah and leads into life, but from the other way round: from life, from a world that knows nothing of the Law, or pretends to know nothing, back to the Torah."[5] Learners bring their urgent questions to the study and seek a response in the text, using creative interpretations that bridge the centuries separating the text from their own time and in the hope that this learning will have an effect on their way of life. The learners come from different domains. Most are educated but not necessarily Torah scholars. Learners' diverse fields of knowledge and occupations produce a wide range of interpretations, as envisioned by Rosenzweig, evident in Levinas's interpretation with its mutual ties to his philosophy, and also in the pluralistic *batei midrash*. This movement from the external to the internal and back again has an impact on the perspectives displayed by the learners as well, as they bring universal values to their learning and find support for these values in the texts that are studied. Learning in the *beit midrash* does not aim to separate learners from other realms but, rather, to ally with these realms, inspire them, and become enhanced by them. For this reason, the *batei midrash* are constructed in such a way that learning is partial and does not demand all-consuming dedication.

In this type of Torah learning the approach is organic and synchronic, meaning that every part or level of the text may be relevant to any other part and to any question asked, and all areas of life are relevant to the study of Torah. Rather than attempting to see the text in its original context of time and place, inquiries focus on its possible meaning in the here and now for specific learners occupied with current issues.

Little meaningful research has been conducted to date on the pluralistic *batei midrash* in Israel and their study methods.[6] Studying Levinas's method of interpretation can teach us quite a lot about these *batei midrash* due to their similarities. Furthermore, Levinas has much to offer these *batei midrash,* both with regard to method and content. I shall do my best to prove these claims in this work. Most of the publications discussing Levinas's talmudic readings focus on their content and deal with them mainly as philosophical texts.[7] His interpretive method and its basic concepts have also attracted some scholarly attention.[8]

As I studied and taught these talmudic readings, I grew to understand them as a type of *midrash,* and for this reason I thought that incorporating tools used in the research of the rabbinic *midrash* and *agaddah* would enhance and inspire their study. This research, originating as it does from a literary discipline, deals with issues of form, language, editing, and genre, and with the connection between all of these and the content. The *midrash* is indeed an interpretation of the Torah, and Levinas's talmudic readings interpret sections of the Babylonian Talmud; but the research of *midrash* and *agaddah* serves as a sound theoretical foundation on two levels of study: first concerning Levinas's attitude to the Talmud, its approach to the Scriptures and to reality—which resembles that defined as *midrash;* and second, the interpretive method that derives from these features, reflecting these same principles. Levinas clarifies these principles in his writing and applies them in his commentary. Maintaining tradition from a perspective of renewal and regeneration is the essence of the classical *midrash,* and it is also the essence of this talmudic commentary.

Levinas addressed the matter of compatibility between style and content in his philosophical works as well. One of his major critiques of Western philosophy targets its conceptual language. Concepts reflect generalized thinking, which has no room for details. As a result, this type of language facilitates and even demands disengagement from reality, since reality is comprised of distinct, diverse details. Furthermore, thought that relates to its objects as concepts eliminates their otherness and transforms them into part of the self, part of one's consciousness. This may be beneficial and logical in the case of inanimate objects. The problem is when humans find themselves generalized as objects, when a person becomes merely an incidental example of the human race, with little personal significance. In this case, total generalized thinking is inadvertently transformed into totalitarianism and violence. Human beings are subjects rather than objects. Their essence can never be encompassed into generalized concepts as each person is infinite. Although Levinas had no recourse but to use concepts as the essential structure of language and of philosophical thought, he sought a way to express transcendent thought, as content that reflects an opening up to the other, a language that does not grasp others as objects but makes room for them as subjects. He tried to create a language with spaces that leave room for otherness and for the unique multiplicity of what, and particularly who, the concepts comprise.[9] This writing contains an unsaying (*dédire*) of that which was written, including spaces, doubts, and question marks, making it a unique type of philosophical writing.

The issue of adapting form or language to content is also evident in Levinas's talmudic commentary. Time and again he indicates the difference between the language of the Talmud, which never departs from concrete reality, and conceptual language. When choosing to remain close to the textual continuity he is interpreting even when the text deviates from its primary topic—he does this consciously and often comments on it. This has to do with the capacity of talmudic language to include spaces of otherness, as mentioned. Hence, the lesson proffered to readers, with its structure and style that deviate from what is customary and largely reflect the strange style of the object of interpretation, is a far-reaching attempt to adapt the form of writing to its content. This results in talmudic lessons written in a style that is open to the otherness of the talmudic text and attentive to its multiple levels. It was this thought that formed the grounds for examining whether and how the style and methodological features of his commentary suited the content they convey.

A method of study that emphasizes not only the content of the text but also its form and unique rhythm helps to uncover levels of meaning and content in Levinas's talmudic readings (and not only in the talmudic text) that exceed those generated by philosophical readings. Of course, this interpretation does not supplant other interpretations or diminish their significance. I have no doubt as to the value and the need for interpretations that focus on the thematic subtleties of the talmudic readings, their philosophical meanings, and so on. The method suggested here, however, has the capacity to expand the scope of interpretation, to recognize other dimensions of these texts. This approach, which presumes that the text's form and design are significant and therefore it should be studied in its entirety, including its rhythm and alleged detours—exposes the text's abundance and uncovers meanings that could not be revealed otherwise. This may be a way of unsaying the text, of connecting to its intrinsic inspiration and finding in its spaces other meanings that are merely part of the infinity contracted into the written letters. This path invites the learners to become partners in the study process, to ask questions about their lives and about the topics that occupy them through all dimensions of the material studied. Such learning constitutes a living Torah.

As stated, the current approach to Levinas's talmudic readings is based on research, but it is primarily an interpretation of his lessons that resembles his own interpretation of the talmudic discussions. The purpose of this volume is not only to present a theory but mainly to allow readers unfamiliar with Levinas's philosophy and with the literature of the *midrash* to understand his talmudic interpretations and apply them to themselves and to their lives. Readers are invited to take part in this *beit midrash* where Talmud and Levinas's writings are studied and where current-day reality is considered from their own perspective. Have I managed to create a *midrash* on Levinas's *midrash* on the Talmud?

Chapter 1 defines the term *midrash*. It lays the foundation for the debate and describes the characteristics of the traditional *midrash agaddah* based on the research in this field and hermeneutical theories. The next chapters focus on central features of the *midrash* as defined in this first chapter and examine them within the talmudic interpretation of Emmanuel Levinas. This structure presumes that finding midrashic features in Levinas's commentary on the Talmud corroborates the claim that the commentary is indeed a type of *midrash*.

Chapter 2 explores Levinas's perception of Torah study and interpretation as part of a revelation versus the rabbinic conception of their enterprise as replacing the work of the prophets.

Chapter 3 examines various aspects of the relationship between this talmudic interpretation and the interpreted text, such as its view of the Torah's holiness and of midrashic methods. This chapter attempts to distinguish between Levinas's talmudic readings and his other writings and to compare these readings to features of midrashic biblical exegesis.

Chapter 4 considers the relationship between the exegesis and circumstances external to the text. These circumstances constitute both the origin of questions addressed to the text and also the purpose of the commentary. This aspect, shared by the traditional *midrash* and Levinas's commentary, has a crucial effect on their common hermeneutical theory.

Chapter 5 discusses the pluralism and interpretive freedom common to the *midrash* and to Levinas's talmudic commentary, as well as their significant differences in this regard.

Chapter 6 deals with the following unique features of Levinas's *midrash:* consistent focusing on interpersonal aspects of the text, even when it seems to be occupied with other matters; translating the unique language of the text into its universal implications; using philosophical tools and terms as part of the interpretation; and insisting on interpreting the full text with all its elements and details.

Occasionally I shall consider Levinas's contribution to the current reality of Jewish life in general and to the pluralistic *batei midrash* in particular.

In my writing I choose to extensively quote the Talmudic readings and to interpret large textual segments. In this way, I attempt to match the form of my words to their content and the outcome of the learning to its object—namely, more learning of the lessons and less writing about them. From time to time, and in order to explain things in their correct context, sections from Levinas's philosophical works shall be cited as well.[10]

I have no presumptions of an objective relationship between a writer and the object of her writing. Therefore, I find it important to clarify my point of departure as well as my connection to Levinas's talmudic readings.[11] I grew up in a home that endorsed the conviction whereby Judaism should impact our lives as moral people in the world, people who act to promote good in the world and, therefore, act to apply this conviction in practice. In Levinas's writings I found a similar point of departure—words, descriptions, and thoughts that added a fascinating and empowering dimension to that instilled in me as a child by my mother and father, Janine and Lucien Lazare.

As a woman, I first obtained access to the Talmud in the academic world, which provided me with the necessary tools and foundations for its study. Learning and teaching Talmud for years in study groups consisting of Torah enthusiasts in a pluralistic *beit midrash*[12] taught me the value of studying in a group, where partners join to create interpretations that converse with their personal and group life. This type of learning is in fact a way of practicing human interrelations, and it integrates the personal reality of each learner and the circumstances common to all learners. The Talmud is a text that deals with life, draws from it and inspires it, and connects people to the sound box of their culture but also to current issues occupying them. In the *beit midrash* I learned the potential and value of adapting the method of learning to the content learned.

In the context of learning Talmud, exploring the connection between the method of learning and its content indeed derives from this point, from the awareness that original forms of learning facilitate learning processes organically connected to life. I take at face value Levinas's invitation to all learners to join him in the process of learning, and I attempt to discern how this invitation is manifested, beyond the declaration of intent, in the commentary itself and in its style of writing.

May my words be acceptable. (*Yihyu leratzon imrey fi.*)

Chapter 1

What Is the Midrash?

∼∞∼

The term *midrash* denotes a way of interpreting a canonic text, one that makes it possible to generate other meanings in addition to the plain meaning (the *pshat*). *Midrash* is also the designation of a group of books constituting collections of biblical interpretations that follow the way of the *midrash*, for example: Midrash Bereshit Raba.[1] The current discussion will focus on the *midrash* as a method of interpretation, as this is the topic of the book. I shall not be dealing with collections that bear this name.

Assuming a basic understanding of the text, the *midrash* is a way of identifying other meanings within the interpreted text.[2] The distinction between *pshat* and *drash* or *midrash* already appears in early rabbinic literature, although in many cases it is hard to identify the precise boundary between the plain meaning of the text and the *midrash*. Midrashim are commonly divided into *midrash halakha* and *midrash aggadah:* when the purpose of the *midrash* is to learn a law (*halakha*) it is considered a *midrash halakha*. Anything that is not *halakha* is considered *aggadah,* which includes the learning of ideas, behavioral codes of conduct that are not laws, expanding biblical stories and filling in gaps, stories and parables, justifications of religious commandments, and more. When these are learned from and in reference to a canonic text they are considered *midrash aggadah*.

Research of the *midrash* often deliberates on how to define its object of study. Some define the *midrash* narrowly, as distinctly related to rabbinic literature, with well-defined formal features; others extend the definition to include midrashic interpretations from different periods, with more flexible formal features. My attempt at characterizing the *midrash* refers to existing definitions but is affected by the question of whether Emmanuel Levinas's talmudic readings are a type of *midrash*. Should they be included within an interpretive tradition, to which they add their own unique dimension? Levinas's talmudic commentary, even when discussing halakhic sections, is not occupied with *halakha* as an attempt to determine laws. It is always an aggadic interpretation that aims to extricate the fundamental-theoretical (philosophical) meaning of the interpreted text. Hence, the discussion of whether his talmudic commentary is a type of *midrash* centers on *midrash aggadah*.

The *midrash* as a method of interpretation is a major component of rabbinic literature, distinguishing it from other traditions of biblical exegesis generated at the same time, previously, or subsequently.[3] This literature was produced orally and was only written down in later periods. The Mishna was not written in a midrashic form, but its content resembles the *midrash halakha* and *midrash aggadah* of its time (the *tannaitic midrashim*), and the same sages are mentioned in both. Therefore, the Mishna may simply consider the same content under a different method of redaction, arranged in a thematic order that facilitates memory formation. Since this was the Oral Law—that is, material that did not exist in written form—any redaction that aided memory had a very significant role. This is probably also the grounds for the style of the Mishna, with its propensity for short decisive language, usually with no explanations and no lingering over the study process (the *midrash*), although it does include a few *midrashim*.[4]

The Talmuds, arranged to follow the order of the Mishna, include many *midrashim* and may even be perceived as *midrashim* on the Mishna. In the time of crisis subsequent to the destruction of the Second Temple, the sages realized that contemporary religious life had changed, and that religious worship as shaped by the Bible and the prophets was no longer relevant. They studied the biblical text using midrashic techniques, with the aim of redesigning Judaism to fit their world. In this way, the *midrash* served as the main tool used by the sages to effect major changes in Judaism until it reached the form familiar to us. For example, once the Temple was destroyed sacrificial offerings were forbidden, as in previous eras they were not permitted outside the Temple. In their stead and through homiletical interpretations (*drashot*) based on biblical verses, the sages determined that prayers would be an appropriate substitute.

The method of the *midrash*, implied in the biblical text but further developed and established by the sages, was utilized as a form of Torah study throughout subsequent generations as well.[5] Can Jewish cultural history be conceived of as a developing and diversifying tradition of *midrash*? This may be one way, among many others, of understanding Jewish cultural continuity and the common element linking different types of Jewish texts. Examples of the latter are the biblical interpretation devised by Philo of Alexandria, the Zohar literature,[6] techniques of halakhic ruling throughout the generations, and modern exegesis, as well as Levinas's commentary on the Talmud. There is no denying that there are other Jewish ways of studying the Bible and the Talmud (which will be discussed further below), but tracing the different types of *midrash* throughout the generations might form a portrait encompassing the significant common features of all types of *midrash*—that is to say, a portrait of a homiletical tradition. The diversity and uniqueness of the various types of *midrash* are the evolving element in this tradition. Indeed, the tension between tradition and innovation is one of the constitutive tensions of the *midrash*: the traditional text receives new meaning through the *midrash*.

The Relationship between the Commentator and the Text

Hermeneutical theory distinguishes between three figures affiliated with the written text and asks about their relationship. These are the text, the author of the text, and the reader/commentator. The author of the holy text, be it God or Moses, are not here to explain the text. In this respect, the holy text resembles any text whose author is no longer alive or who is distant from his work. The *midrash* does not deal with the author's intention.[7] It deals with the relationship between the commentator and the text, and in this respect it is based on a hermeneutical theory that quite surprisingly resembles twentieth century hermeneutics.

The *midrash* is a relationship between the commentator and the text, one characterized by their mutual dependence: the text receives new meaning previously unknown to it, and the *darshan* (learner) learns something previously unknown about his or her own world and him- or herself. Furthermore, the text has no meaning if there is no commentator to learn it and to give it meaning; however, the commentator is also dependent on the text, both as a platform for the commentator's words but mainly as a result of the premise that the text has the power to teach the learner what he or she could not otherwise learn. Therefore, the text and the commentator teach each other and need each other. This method is essentially different from that of other interpretive methods. It differs from those approaches that award the text higher authority than that of the commentator, whose role is then merely to expose the meaning of the text; and it also differs from research methods in which the commentator has the authority to determine which of the text's versions is correct and what is its "real" intention. Awarding the text and the commentator equal status, based on a dialectical attitude of mutual dependency, seems to resemble Gadamer's *Horizontverschmelzung* (fusion of horizons). The commentator brings to the text premises, language, values, and anything that shapes his or her understanding of reality in general and of the specific text in particular, while the text brings with it the world from which it was produced, including its premises, language, and values. The encounter between the commentator and the text creates a fusion of horizons, where the commentator learns something new from the text, and thus expands his or her horizons, while the text also receives a new interpretation and expands its horizons of meaning. Gadamer stresses that the purpose of the interpretation is not only to understand the "truth of the text" but also to learn from it something that is meaningful and valid for the commentator.[8] This approach differs in essence from Derrida's deconstruction, which gives the interpreter absolute authority regarding the text.[9] Ruhama Weiss, who compares the study of Torah to the act of lovemaking, describes the relationship that exists within the *midrash* in figurative terms: "The learner thinks of the Torah and of his life, and the Torah too thinks of itself and of the learner. The study of Torah, according to this image, is not the learner's effort to interpret a given Torah but rather a joint effort at mutual interpretation by learner and Torah alike."[10]

The *midrash* as a dialectical relationship between the commentator and the text encompasses and maintains different tensions: between tradition and innovation,[11] between past and present, between the Written Law and the Oral Law, between the single text and its many meanings, between the demand, the theory—and the real world and those who act within it, and between the general and the personal. Below I shall examine other features of the *midrash* and analyze how they contain these tensions. I shall primarily discuss the rabbinic *midrash,* which is indisputably the classical, most typical *midrash*.

The Midrash and the Interpreted Text

As stated, the *midrash* is an interpretation of a canonic text, which it quotes and to which it openly refers, even when this relationship is complex and uses methods that take apart the interpreted text and give it a new and different meaning than its plain one. The *midrash,* which is of course familiar with the *pshat* of the text,[12] chooses to find in the text new meaning or meanings. Possible motivations for offering a new meaning might include a *pshat* that is problematic from a moral viewpoint; the passage of time that renders the *pshat* irrelevant or uninteresting for the commentator; the assumption that the text has more than one meaning and that the commentator's job is to expose as many meanings as possible; a question brought by the commentator to the text in search of an answer; or a topic occupying the commentator, with which the text converses and for which it suggests a new perspective. Even when the text is problematic in some way the *midrash* does not disassociate from it; rather, it continues the conversation. What could perhaps have been said in another, lecturing mode, remains in a setting that refers to the text, albeit in order to draw away from its plain meaning.

This approach, which in any case is unwilling to distance itself from the text and assumes that the text can be retained even when its *pshat* arouses difficulties, demonstrates a deep respect for the interpreted text. The *midrash* exists in the tension between holding on to tradition and the holy text, on the one hand, and innovation, a new interpretation that gives the ancient text additional meanings, on the other. In order for tradition to remain relevant for those who have held on to it for generations, and despite significant changes in life circumstances and values, it must develop mechanisms of adaptation and change, or else it shall become irrelevant and maybe even corrupt. Then again, change and innovation might lead to disengagement from tradition. The *midrash* is a mechanism whereby this tension can be maintained and managed, committed as it is to the canonic text while giving it new meaning; or as Barry Zimmerman says, the *midrash* uses old words to say something new.[13] In this way, a text formed in the distant past converses with the present. The homiletical interpretation allows itself to incorporate its own concepts within the renewed meaning of the text. Hence, the *midrash* makes it possible to maintain cultural continuity without relinquishing the wish and the need for change, for creative updating of the old text to fit a different era.

Here, for example, is a short well-known *midrash* from Bamidbar Raba: "'The tablets were the work of God, the writing was the writing of God, engraved on the tablets' (Exod. 32:16). Do not read *charut* (engraved) on the tablets, but rather *cheirut* (freedom), for the only one who is free is one who is involved in Torah study."[14] The *midrash* quotes the biblical verse, knowing that its plain meaning describes the tablets before they were shattered by Moses. The letters were engraved on them by God. When reading the verse, the term "the writing of God" seems unclear. The *midrash*, indirectly answering this query, wishes to say something more about that which was engraved on the tablets—about the Israelites who rejected the Torah and committed the Sin of the Golden Calf, about anyone who forsakes the Torah, and perhaps about those listeners who do not engage sufficiently in the study of the Torah in the opinion of the *darshan*. According to the *midrash* the Torah, with its engraved letters, is intended to underlie the freedom of all who engage in its study. One of the understandings of this *midrash* is that the engraved letters do not limit one's freedom to read and interpret; on the contrary, they invite the study of Torah as open dialogue between the commentator and the text. Learners are called upon to face the Torah, to try and understand its meaning for them by utilizing their unique intelligence and personality. They practice independent thinking and learn that they must obey without becoming enslaved. This freedom contrasts with enslavement to idolatry, being swept along by fervent passions as part of a rapturous crowd, as in the Sin of the Golden Calf.[15]

In this context, idolatry may be characterized by passion, by acting on impulse as in pagan worship. Studying Torah, as a system of laws that must be obeyed without becoming enslaved to them, is the exact opposite. It is a comparison between meaningful freedom versus passionate impulses. This is the meaning of freedom based on the Torah, a meaning that remains relevant to the life of each and every one of us in the present. We are exposed to our passions, to the inclination to become easily enslaved and addicted. Learning the Torah, which limits passion while nurturing self-control and obedience, is the very substance of our freedom, as it is derived from that which is engraved and inscribed upon the tablets.

This is an educational principle as well: boundaries and laws do not contradict freedom; rather, they are its foundation. People who lack laws are not free but are the slaves of their desires. Educators are responsible for teaching their disciples boundaries and laws.

This *midrash* would be meaningless without the verse quoted and without understanding its *pshat*. The essence of this *midrash*, of any *midrash*, is that it openly refers to the biblical verses and adds to them its own layer of meaning.

Midrash and Prophecy

The *midrash* is situated within a religious context. God's words are expressed in written form in the canonic text. These words are, according to the narrative of the Torah and the words of the prophets, the words of God, as conveyed directly to the prophets who transmitted the message to the people and wrote it down. God's will, instructions, and demands were conveyed through this direct channel. The conclusion of the prophetic era created a void, which the *midrash* aims to fill.[16] The *midrash* assumes that God's word as recorded in the Scriptures holds meaning for all times and for all people, and therefore interpreting the text is a way of learning

God's message and demands for his followers, while updating them to contemporary times. In this way, the study of Torah has taken the place of the prophecies.[17]

Here is an example that expresses this consciousness of the *midrash* as a way of clarifying God's instructions to humankind: "R. Joshua b. Levi said: three things were enacted by the mortal court below, and the heavenly court on high agreed to their action. Who has gone above [to heaven], has returned [and reported]? Only, we [obtain these points by] interpreting the texts; and, in this instance too, we so interpret the texts."[18]

The Gemara asks: How does R. Joshua b. Levi know that the heavenly court agreed to the rulings of the mortal court? The question is formulated sarcastically: who went up to heaven and returned to report the will of God? The answer is that the homiletical interpretation based on biblical verses is the source from which we can learn that the heavenly court agreed to the rulings of the mortal court, just as it can teach us the rest of God's demands for humankind. Indeed, R. Joshua b. Levi then proceeds to use further interpretations to explain his statement that the Scriptures, as the word of God, are eternally valid and that it is necessary to develop methods of interpretation in order to connect and mediate between the Scriptures and God's followers.[19] The *midrash* sees itself as a replacement for the prophecies, an authoritative successor that is also inspired, although its inspiration is less direct than that of the prophecies.

A more critical or scholarly view of this *midrash* is also compatible with this approach. From a phenomenological perspective, it is clear that the *midrash*—both *midrash halakha* and *midrash aggadah*—was the major tool shaping Jewish culture in the constitutive stage of the rabbinic period. Later as well, and throughout the centuries, Torah study and interpretation had a significant effect on Jewish culture, with all its various forms and emphases, and the way of the *midrash* was a customary method of study, although not exclusively so.[20] Hence, from a cultural point of view the void formed with the conclusion of the prophetic era was indeed filled by the *midrash*.

Midrashic Methods

As early as the rabbinic era, the sages attempted to define the methods of the *midrash*, or, how *midrashim* are formed. This is a difficult task, particularly in light of the interpretive freedom assumed by the *darshanim* (plural of *darshan*), who produced quite a number of *midrashim* that do not fit any definition or order. I shall now try to characterize several foundations of the various midrashic methods, relevant for both *midrash aggadah* and *midrash halakha*.[21]

Every Detail in the Text Is Meaningful

This premise serves as the basis for a number of approaches to the text, including the following: (1) letter-based homiletical interpretations (the biblical division of letters into words is not binding; each letter has a life of its own and letters can be joined to form new words using various techniques, such as acronyms, assigning numeric values to Hebrew letters [*gematria*], dividing words in two, etc.); (2) word homilies (use of double meaning, taking a word out of its context and etymology, changing vocalizations, changing the spelling, transferring between languages, etc.); (3) homilies based on parts of verses and whole verses (linking distant verses that have a word in common, changing the logical ratio between different parts of the verse, or taking a verse out of its context); (4) verbal analogies (*gzeira shava*); and (5) *pitra* (the verse is understood to refer to some other figure or event). No detail in the text is superfluous; on the contrary, any detail can serve as the basis for or source of a *midrash*.

The Unity of the Bible

The Torah does not follow any chronological order. *Darshanim* are familiar with the entire Bible and relate to it as a synchronic text. In other words, any matter may have relevance for any other matter and any verse may have relevance for any other verse that is unrelated to its original context. For example, many *midrashim* presume that the Patriarchs observed the commandments given at Mt. Sinai, although chronologically the Patriarchs preceded the Revelation at Mt. Sinai. The *midrash* utilizes formal similarities, thematic connections, and any other means of linking remote issues. Another presumption involving the Bible's unity is the meaning attributed to the order of the different episodes. The absence of any visible connection between sections serves as justification for a *midrash* regarding *smichut parshiot* (adjacent episodes).

Gaps in the Text Invite a Midrash to Fill Them

There are many different kinds of gaps in the biblical text. The *midrash* does not stop at attempts to understand the text as it is; rather, it sees itself invited to fill these gaps. For example, the *midrash* asks the following: What did Cain say to Abel when they were in the field (Gen. 4:8)? What happened between Abraham and Isaac on the three-day walk to Mt. Moriah on the way to the Binding of Isaac (Gen. 22:4)? Which forms of work are prohibited on the Sabbath (Exod. 20:10)? The *midrash* has different ways of answering these queries.

Organic Thinking

Organic thinking, which is at the foundation of the *midrash*, is a way of thinking that sees life with all its facets as a whole in which each detail is worthy of attention, rather than only generalizations.[22] Intricacies of work in the Temple, for example, inapplicable for most of the sages living as they did after the destruction of the Temple, were transformed into meaningful indicators for their world. For example, from the biblical reference that the shewbread must be "before me always" (Exod. 25:30), they learned the diligence required for the *mitzvah* of Torah study, a *mitzvah* that they themselves had prescribed. Hence, the *midrash* deals with all areas of life, from the most abstract theological questions to the most concrete human needs, such as food and bodily excretions. The exact measure required to observe a religious commandment is accorded the same gravity as questions concerning the essence of truth.

Isaak Heinemann, who coined the term "organic thinking" as characteristic of the rabbinic *midrash*, perceived it as a primitive type of thinking, or at least prescientific, as it offers no clear definition of its area of practice and uses a range of tools that are not all rational and methodical.[23] In my opinion, organic thinking is capable of containing the complexity and variety of human reality; this is part of its underlying value and of the meaning it holds for all people in all times.

For instance, when the Talmud deals with an abstract matter such as repentance—the mechanism through which sins and transgressions are rectified—after a short theoretical discussion of the significance of the matter, it brings stories that show the considerable difficulties involved in rectifying and repenting from a sin committed between people, stories of real people who wronged others and were wronged themselves and who have a hard time rectifying their transgressions. Thus, we are exposed simultaneously both to the important value of repentance and to the difficulty of carrying it out in practice.

MIDRASH AND LIFE

A most important feature of the *midrash* is its aim. Learning God's message is not only an intellectual occupation. It is intended to instruct those engaged in learning how to live, what to do and what not to do, and even to answer existential questions such as those dealing with the administration of the world, the place of evil in the world, God's role with regard to his followers, and so on.[24] The *darshanim* try to learn from the text something that will impact their lives and the life of those to whom they address their *midrash* (a community of learners or those studying with them in the *beit midrash*).[25]

The aim of the exegesis, in its customary plain meaning, is the text itself—to facilitate correct understanding of its intent. But for the *midrash*, for exegesis directed at life and at shaping modes of thinking and behavior, the text becomes concurrently a means and a teacher. The *darshanim* use it to legitimize and validate their words. This usage is not necessarily manipulative. They make an effort to adjust their words to the spirit of the text, to its deepest aims as perceived by them. The aim affects the content of the interpretation as well as the methods used in its generation. Real life, with its demands, occupies the center of attention. Thus, the learners not only ask the text "What are you saying?" but also and primarily questions such as, "What are you saying to me about my life?," "What are you demanding of me?," "What are you telling me about this subject?," and "What is your connection to my situation?" The commentators have questions that arise from their reality, a reality that they are interested in influencing, and it is those questions that they ask the text.

Since the *midrash* is an interpretation that relates to the real world, understanding it requires one to discover the question that it is trying to answer, what occupied the *darshan,* and what is the aim of the *midrash*.[26] For example, at the Revelation on Mt. Sinai, when the Israelites were preparing to hear the Ten Commandments, the text says: "Then Moses led the

22   *Reading between the Lines*

people out of the camp to meet God, and they stood at the foot of the mountain" (Exod. 19:17). This verse poses no difficulty; it is comprehensible and logical. "The foot of the mountain" describes the place where Moses placed the Israelites in preparation for the anticipated ceremony. However the *darshan* wished to learn something else from this verse, and thus, says: "'And they stood at the foot of [*betachtit*, also: underneath] the mountain': R. Abdimi bar Hama bar Hasa said: This teaches us that God suspended the mountain above them like a barrel and said: 'If you accept the Torah, good. If not, there will be your burial place.'"[27]

What seems to be a simple description of where the Israelites stood, at the foot of the mountain, is transformed into a divine threat, an intimidating picture of a mountain about to collapse on top of them. This picture is not necessary in order to understand the verse. The *darshan* wanted to use this verse in order to say something about commitment to the Torah at the time it was given and in his era (and ours) as well. This is not a case of a free, easy choice. The Israelites were coerced into observing the Torah, preceding their free choice. This interpretation does not aim to clarify the verse but, rather, to convey a message that is enhanced by means of the verse's figurative illustration and that has implications for its recipients' perceptions of reality. Obeying the Torah's precepts is an existential exigency. Those who adopt this perception are first and foremost people who are commanded and thus responsible for their deeds. The question posed by this *midrash* does not arise from the text; it arises from reality, from an existential problem debated by the *darshan* and his generation, which the text thus interpreted seems to answer.

Here is an example of a *midrash* that stems from a difficulty arising from studying the text—an interpretive question—but the answer it gives refers one to real life:

> R. Nahman ben R. Hisda expounded: what is meant by the text, "Then the Lord God formed [*va-yitzer*] man" (Gen. 2:7)? [The word *va-yitzer*] is written with two *yods* [וייצר] to show that God created two inclinations, one good and the other evil.... In truth [the point of the two *yods*] is as stated by R. Shimon ben Pazi; for R. Shimon ben Pazi said: Woe is me because of my creator [*yotzri*—if I follow my inclination], woe is me because of my evil

inclination [*yitzri*—if I combat it]! Or again as explained by R. Jeremiah ben Elazar; for R. Jeremiah ben Elazar said: God created two countenances in the first man as it says, "Behind and before you have formed me (*tzartani*)." (Ps. 139:5)[28]

The creation of humankind is described using the verb "va-yizer" written with two *yods* (Gen. 2:7), while the creation of the other animals is described a few verses later using the same verb written with one *yod*. This is the grounds for the question "Why was the same word written differently to describe the creation of humankind and the creation of the animals?" The various answers given in the *midrash* try to characterize the difference between humans and other animals: between the good inclination and the evil inclination, between the evil inclination (*yetzer*) and spirituality (*yotzer*), and between male and female (who according to the *midrash* had not yet been separated at this stage of Creation). The human experience is one of tensions, divisions, and duality, as manifested in the verse in the form of the double *yod*. The *midrashim* answered the textual question, but did so mainly by referring to human nature and its uniqueness. Here too it is evident that there is no need for one correct answer. On the contrary, the multiple answers to the question only enhance the discussion of human complexity and of the conflict between body and soul, emotions and reasoning, human will and obligation, good and evil, and male and female human dimensions. In this way our understanding expands and grows, and with it the meaning of the text.

Now we can see that the methods employed by the *midrash*—which are creative and take the liberty of doing almost whatever they wish with the text, so much so that it is very hard to characterize them—are linked to the aim of the *midrash*. Since the *midrash* observes life outside the text, significant discrepancies between the text and reality call for creative resolutions. Schematically, this can be described as follows:

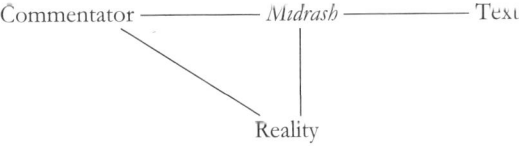

In other words, sometimes questions arise from real life and the commentator brings them to the text in search of answers; other times studying and interpreting the text teaches the commentator something about the real world even though this was not the original intention. In any case, there is a relationship between the holy text and reality; the text aims to influence the world, and thus, it presumably refers to the world. But this relationship is completely dependent on the commentator's actions, on the *midrash*. Without this mediation the text is merely a dead letter.

Another aspect of the relationship between the *midrash* and real life is its concrete, substantive attention to details and life situations rather than only to principles and concepts. This can be explained through R Abdimi's aforementioned *midrash* on the mountain as a barrel suspended above the heads of the Israelites. This *midrash* raises essential philosophical questions, for example, concerning human freedom and the relationship between freedom and obligations, the source of authority with regard to obligations and the law, and the tension between free human choice and God's providence over the world. All this is manifested in the concrete illustration given in the context of a constitutive event familiar to us all. Namely, due to the centrality of the Revelation on Mt. Sinai within popular cultural consciousness, this illustration of the mountain as a barrel draws the learners, in an almost direct manner, to all of these questions. The use of such a strong and tangible picture immediately invites me as a learner into the discussion: if the mountain is suspended above my head, what does this say about my Torah, about my freedom, and about the nation for whom this forms a constitutive event?

Conceptual language defines the object of its investigation and deals with it on the most fundamental abstract level. The *midrash* uses nonconceptual language; it does not define concepts and does not generate them. Its discussion, even when occupied with abstract fundamental questions such as human freedom versus moral commitment, remains grounded in details, in actuality, and in the complex multiplicity that is reality. Its commitment is not to systematic consistency, to generalizations that are invariably true, or to true-and-false dichotomies. Rather, its commitment is to human reality and experience with all its complexity, multiplicity, and confusion. The truth of the midrashic world depends on the perspective of the person voicing the *midrash,* and this truth has many faces.

THE MIDRASH IS FORMED THROUGH ORAL INSTRUCTION

As stated, the *midrash* is the study and interpretation of a canonic text. The canonization process usually ends once the holy text is fixed in written form that cannot be changed and that is itself holy. Midrashic study is the oral study of a holy written text, and it takes the form of a live conversation between a teacher and a student or between study colleagues. In this process the written letter, which is limited by its very form, constituting as it does a contraction of the original thought and inspiration within a permanent shape, gradually expands, becomes alive and meaningful for those studying it, and thus reconnects students to its sources of inspiration. Sometimes the ongoing study process is summarized in writing and then we can study it repeatedly. The rabbinic *midrashim* that refer to the biblical text assumed a written form in the Talmud and in the *midrash* collections. From the moment they were written down they themselves became the object of other *midrashim*. (For example, the Zohar literature served as the basis for the homiletical interpretations of those who gathered around Rabbi Isaac Luria [the Holy Ari] of Safed, whose writings too served as a basis for the homiletical interpretations of Hassidic leaders.)

The research literature widely agrees that rabbinic literature — the collections of *midrashim,* the Mishna, the Tosefta, and the Talmuds as we know them — constitute the writing and redaction of material produced and transmitted orally between the generations.[29] The central place of this awareness is evident in the term "Oral Law" used to designate rabbinic literature, and it is compatible with the narrative of these texts. For example, the first chapter of the Tractate Avot describes the chain of transmission of this Oral Law, from Moses to the major sages who produced the Mishna and the *tannaitic midrashim*.

The redacted form of these texts provides many indications that this was an Oral Law written down only post factum. For instance, sometimes different traditions are evident concerning the source of a law, story, or *midrash*. Some discrepancies are not the result of redaction but, rather, appear to be authentic arguments where the sages involved held a live debate, which found its way into the written version. Different versions in parallel sources may depict the same event, although errors sometimes seem to be the result of scribal mistakes in subsequent stages of transmission rather than differences in oral transmission.[30] Other examples are collections of interpretive *midrashim,* which appear to be a later conscious redaction of ancient materials, including multiple homiletical interpretations of the same verse, repeating a source in different contexts, and so on. Yet others are (homiletical) *midrashim* arranged by topic, which some scholars identify as having rhetorical features characteristic of oral discourse.[31] Furthermore, the Mishna and the Talmuds include redactions that can only be understood as being intended to help remember the text.[32]

Therefore, the *midrash* is an oral reference to the text (whether articulated in the synagogue or in the *beit midrash*),[33] and it was only written down at a later stage. This is typical of the *midrash* in contrast to other types of written biblical commentary, such as the *pesharim,* pseudoepigraphy, philosophical-allegorical interpretations (such as the Rambam's commentary), and *pshat* commentaries.

Hence, the *midrash* was formed as the result of a relationship, of discourse between people, and of studying in a group. Indeed, the Rabbis adamantly object to autodidactic Torah study:

> R. Jose b. Hanina said: What is the meaning of the words "A sword on the *badim* and they shall become fools" (Jer. 50:36)? May a sword fall upon the necks of the scholars who sit and engage in the study of Torah each for himself (*bad b'vad*); and not only this, but they become also foolish and they also become sinners.... Rabina said: He who loves to teach many, has the fruit of knowledge. And this is what Rabbi said: I learned much from my masters, more, however, from my colleagues, and still more from my disciples.[34]

A Torah scholar who studies alone (*bad b'vad*) becomes a fool and a sinner. The implications are obvious.

Does the significance of oral debate have anything to do with the aim of the *midrash,* the wish to influence the real world where people encounter, relate to, and influence each other? Is it a consequence of how the *midrash* relates to the truth, which is always complex and requires different points of view? Even when the live debate left no trace in the subsequently written text, the *midrash* seems to have been addressed to different people; and even when it was uttered as a public sermon it allowed people to ponder its message and agree or disagree with it, whether openly or covertly.

Pluralism and Interpretive Freedom

The *midrash* does not purport to have arrived at the one true interpretation of the interpreted text; rather, it offers an interpretive option in which the *darshan* has some interest. The basic premise of this approach is that "the Torah has seventy faces"—the written Torah can be understood by different people in different ways, and all are correct. Each new interpretation uncovers another aspect, another truth embedded in the text, enriching one's ability to understand what is written and to learn from it. The encounter between the eternal text and the commentator is unique, and the circumstances of this encounter expose a facet of the truth that only that commentator could have revealed. Any wise person may suggest an interpretation. The truth is context dependent (depending on time, place, person, etc.) and multifaceted, just as real life is complex and multifaceted.[35]

Any person who studies the Torah is entitled to form an interpretation as he or she sees right, even if it seems very far from the plain meaning of the biblical text. The *midrash* is, as Yona Frankel says, "a consequence of the search, study, and free thinking of the *darshan*,"[36] and as long as the *darshan* explicitly and consciously refers to the interpreted text there seem to be no limitations. Moreover, it is possible, as Ofra Meir claims, that "specifically by maintaining the biblical point of departure could the imagination of the *darshan* take wing and leave behind the limitations that might apply to unrestrained acts of creation."[37] Nonetheless, there is a caveat: interpretations can only be offered by Torah scholars who study with certified teachers, are situated within a Torah environment, and engage in study-oriented dialogue concerning the Torah. The *midrash* is not produced in a void.

Hence, interpretive freedom is based on a clear association with the biblical text, on the presumption that the Scriptures are addressed to people, be whom they may, and that they have more than one meaning; therefore, they hold meaning for the learners in their context and time. The *darshanim* bring to the interpretive act their own world, opinions, and issues of interest, and they have full legitimacy to discuss these with the text.[38] The freedom is so extensive that sometimes the *midrash* even reverses the meaning of the *pshat*. When the plain meaning is unacceptable on moral, apologetic, theological, or other grounds, the text is given a homiletical interpretation.[39] This is a common and prominent practice among halakhic *midrashim,* and I will demonstrate it through an example from the issue of the stubborn and rebellious son. The Bible says:

> If a man has a stubborn and rebellious son who does not obey the voice of his father or the voice of his mother, and though they chasten him does not heed them; then shall his father and his mother take hold of him, and bring him out to the elders of his city, to the gate of his place. And they shall say to the elders of his city: "This our son is stubborn and rebellious; he does not obey our voice; he is a glutton and a drunkard." Then all the men of his city shall stone him with stones, that he shall die; so shall you put away the evil from among you, and all Israel shall hear and fear. (Deut. 21:18–21)

The talmudic discussion of the stubborn and rebellious son, in Tractate Sanhedrin chapter 8, is influenced by *midrashim* that reduce the force and authority of the biblical law to the degree of an absurdity. This, however, is not all: "There never has been a stubborn and rebellious son and there never will be. Why then was the law written? That you may study it and receive reward."[40]

This is not a distinct homiletical interpretation, but the discussion of these verses leads to the conclusion that this law is inapplicable and that it is not valid in any concrete situation. Reading the *midrashim* formed with regard to this statement shows that this law was unacceptable to the sages for moral reasons and thus, through consistent midrashic debate, they neutralized it and transformed it into a theoretical issue, a mere subject for study, ultimately reaching this explicit statement.[41] Commitment to the biblical verses means that they cannot be disregarded or nullified, and therefore they become an object of theoretical study. Such study can focus on educational problems involving teenagers and their complex relationship with their parents, indicating that the biblical text indeed holds value for all times and places, although not as a law that allows society to execute its sons for disciplinary reasons. It is true of a halakhic issue, and all the more so in the case of aggadic issues. Here, for example, is a *midrash* on Cain and Abel: "R. Shimon b. Yohai said: It is difficult to say this thing, and the mouth cannot utter it. Think of two athletes wrestling before the king; had the king wished, he could have separated them. But he did not so desire, and one overcame the other and killed him, and he was crying out 'Let my case be pleaded before the king!' Thus, 'The voice of your brother's blood cries out against *me*' (Gen. 4:11)."[42]

This is a difficult *midrash* from a theological point of view. It holds God responsible for the first murder because he did not intervene and prevent it, and it understands the words, "The voice of your brother's blood cries out against me" as uttered by Cain. R. Shimon b. Yohai stretches the limits of the text's meaning and manages to reverse the plain meaning, since the plain meaning is that God holds Cain responsible for Cain's crime. This *midrash* derives from a theological-existential question that arises with regard to injustice committed by people against each other without divine intervention.[43] Thus, the interpretive freedom is almost unlimited, so long as a straightforward explicit attitude to the text is retained.

A term characteristic of the pluralism expressed by the *midrash* is "another thing" (*davar aher*), indicating another *midrash* on the same verse. Many collections of *midrashim* are arranged in clusters of "another thing,"[44] and they bring a variety of different *midrashim* on the same verses. The redactor who quotes them does not choose between them. This multiplicity is perceived as an asset rather than a problem,[45] in the sense of "these and also those are the words of the living God."[46] The redactor does not see fit to choose the suitable *midrash* or the correct interpretation of the verse but quotes the existing *midrashim* side by side. Each *midrash* adds an entire context of understanding and important truths to the interpreted verse, thus holding a different conversation with different people, each according to their needs, worldview, inclinations, and life circumstances.

Midrash scholar Yona Frankel states, "The sages were free to interpret using all languages and on all linguistic levels, in the belief that there is no language or manner of expression that is not insinuated in the biblical text."[47] Thus, the freedom is not only in the content of the *midrash* but also in the means used. The assumption that the Scriptures contain everything, all truths as well as all manners of expression, facilitates such a degree of daring. Moreover, as Frankel says, "There is no connection between the form of the homily and the idea that the *darshan* wishes to express. *Darshanim* used any homiletical form available to them in order to express their ideas in this way."[48] As part of the *darshan*'s commitment to the verse, the learner is given full freedom to say whatever one wants through the exegetical means chosen. On the one hand, the *midrash* with its free creative content demands diverse and bold interpretive techniques to maintain its creativity. This is the aspect of adapting the form—the interpretive methods—to the content. The many methods of the *midrash* and their diversity constitute an adaptation of form to the unfettered content. On the other hand, the content of a certain homiletical interpretation is not necessarily compatible with its form; any method that leads to the desired result is legitimate.

The *midrash* is also not committed to the continuity of the interpreted text: it can choose one part—several verses, a single verse, part of a verse, or even a single word—in order to convey its message.[49] This is because it is not the text that is at the center but, rather, the exegetical idea in the context of the text and in association with it. The issue here is the search for the text's instruction and for its answer to the questions posed by the *darshan*. This is particularly conspicuous when studying sections of *midrash* collections, such as Bereshit Raba, where in many cases the connection between the various *midrashim* is flimsy, or even nonexistent. *Midrashim* that contradict each other appear side by side, without joining to form a single idea or an interpretive continuity.

Conclusion

The *midrash* seems to be based on its own hermeneutical theory, although one that is close to Gadamer's hermeneutical theory. It does not interpret the text as an aim but as a means of instruction in order to influence the life of its learners and the real world. One manifestation of its commitment to the text is the fact that no part of the text is dismissed as a "later addition" or an "implant" that has no room in the text. On the contrary, the *midrash* chooses to interpret that which seems puzzling, incomprehensible, or even unacceptable from a theological, moral, or ethical viewpoint. In other cases the *midrash* chooses to focus on something that can serve as a good way of conveying an important message. Thus, even when the *midrash* interprets only one word in the text and takes it out of context, this does not mean that it is emending the text or suggesting a more correct version. The text is a given and the *midrash* chooses its point of focus in order to converse with the learners. In this way, for example, the two stories of the Creation in

Genesis are expounded as bearing significance for the essence of Creation and of humanity from different perspectives.

As long as the text is present in the *midrash* the means of interpretation are almost unlimited. The attitude of the *midrash* to the truth of the text is pluralistic, enabling, and even inviting multiple interpretations in a constantly regenerating interpretive process. The text will never have one true interpretation; the commentator will always be able to say something new about the text, to add another interpretation, and to consider another aspect of meaning not previously considered. Thus, in an active study-oriented dialogue between people, many different interpretations of the one text are formed. Nevertheless, the text does not dissolve or come apart in the process of interpretation. It remains in the position of a teacher to its students, the Torah learners. This method produces a unique interpretive language and a major means of shaping the Jewish tradition in its constitutive phase.

Emmanuel Levinas, in his methodical comments on the Talmud's interpretation of the Bible, refers to the features listed here and describes the uniqueness of the *midrash* as an interpretive method. Is Levinas's talmudic commentary itself a *midrash*? What is the significance of his choosing a unique form of writing for his talmudic readings, one that differs from his essays and philosophical writing? Is his choice of a similar genre to that employed by the object of his interpretation conscious or intuitive? What are the aims and intentions served by this form of writing? Assuming that the *midrash* is a constitutive means of rabbinic Jewish culture, is Levinas's interpretation a link in this homiletical tradition? If so, what characterizes this *midrash* and gives it its uniqueness versus the classic *midrash*? The next chapters will deal with these questions. Each chapter will refer to one feature of the *midrash* from those presented in the current chapter and explore whether and how it appears in Levinas's commentary and its meaning therein. I shall examine how he treats the inspiration of the text and the relationship between this inspiration and his commentary. I shall analyze how he relates to the text, his approach to the real world as the interpretation's point of departure and aim, the pluralism built into his method of interpretation, and the unique aspects of his midrashic method.

Just as the *midrash* perceives itself as part of the discourse with the Written Law rather than an external observation, and just as Levinas perceives himself as part of the discourse with the Torah and the Talmud and not as an external observer, I too perceive myself as part of the discourse with Levinas, the Talmud, and the Torah—rather than merely an external observer. From time to time I will ask how all of this is reflected in Israeli reality and in the Torah study taking place at present in Israeli pluralistic *batei midrash*.

Chapter 2

Midrash and Prophecy

As seen in the previous chapter, the sages viewed the *midrash* as a type of substitute for the prophecies, an alternative means of contact with heaven. In the absence of direct messages conveyed by God to the prophets, and thence to the rest of humankind, the remaining option was to interpret the biblical text and generate homiletical interpretations. Does Levinas see a connection between biblical interpretations and prophecy? If so, what is the essence of this connection?

Levinas's conception of God is abstract. God is not a figure who operates within the world, similar to the human course of action. Therefore, according to Levinas, the story of the Revelation on Mt. Sinai as an actual event in which God gave Moses the Torah that included the Oral Law, this story in which God descends to the mountaintop and delivers the tablets, constitutes a problem for modern man. How does all this fit in with the abstract concept of divinity, an infinite divinity? An abstract God cannot be depicted as descending to the mountaintop, writing on tablets, or meeting Moses.

Preoccupation with the transcendent, with that which is beyond and completely other than the self, is indeed a basic motive of human thought and existence (*TI* 30–35). Humans seek a relationship with the transcendent, but a relationship with infinity cannot resemble any other relationship, as the existence of infinity does not resemble any other existence. Therefore, to the degree that the concept of revelation has content and meaning, it cannot be the merely plain meaning depicted in the Bible when it describes the Revelation on Mt. Sinai. The question is, then, what meaning can this story have for those who hold an abstract (philosophical) conception of divinity?

Levinas writes: "It is nevertheless true that for modern Jews—and they are the majority—to whom the intellectual destiny of the West, with its victories and its crises, is not borrowed clothing, the problem of the revelation insistently arises and demands new conceptions.... The ontological status or regime of the Revelation is thus worrying essentially for Jewish thought, and its problem should come before any presentation of the contents of this revelation" (*BV* 131; see 102–03, 129, 143). Levinas is obviously speaking of himself as well here, as a philosopher, expressing his own need to voice the religious terms differently, philosophically rather than mythically, in a manner more suited to his worldview:

> Those present for the first time at this session of talmudic commentaries should not stop at the theological language of these lines. These are sages' thoughts, not prophetic visions. My efforts always consist in extricating from this theological language meaning addressing themselves to reason.... It consists, first of all, in a mistrust of everything in the texts studied that could pass for a piece of information about God's life, for a theosophy; it consists in being preoccupied, in the face of each of these apparent news items about the beyond, with what this information can mean in and for man's life. (*NT* 14)

He seeks to discuss the theosophical terms that seem to provide information about God from the perspective of their consequences for humanity, from their ethical perspective. At the same time, he does not relinquish the concept of revelation.

Hence, this discussion is based on an interpretive question: how does one interpret and provide a homiletical interpretation of the biblical story, of God's revelation in the world and of receiving the Torah, without getting into a conflict with Levinas's worldview and view of divinity, which is shared by many contemporary Jews? The question thus posed is based on the shared premises of the *midrash* and of Levinas's interpretive method: the productive tension between tradition and renewal, between the Written Law and the Oral Law, between past and future, and between theory and reality. The *midrash* is the link that connects these contrasts. In order to resolve the discrepancy between the text and the worldview, a *midrash* is called for.

Since God is abstract, it is also not possible to speak of the "word of God" or of prophecies in their plain meaning. That being said, what is revelation? Revelation is the relationship between infinity and the person, the finite self. Human beings are finite, but they are not entities enclosed within themselves whose entire world is merely an object of themselves, of their consciousnesses or actions. Moving out of one's self, enclosed as it is within itself, is a revelation.

How does revelation occur? According to Levinas, revelation occurs in the encounter between oneself and another person. The encounter with the other person is special and differs from any other encounter, since this person, as a person, is not contained by my power of perception. The Other is not merely an object that I observe or use but, rather, is a subject that I meet who articulates what he or she has to say. But even before the person speaks, the face of the other constitutes a demand: "You shall not murder"—you shall not murder in its plain meaning, and you shall not murder the incomprehensible uniqueness of the other. These are the contents of the revelation.

The encounter with the other person, in which I am inherently commanded to be responsible for the other, for his or her life, is called a revelation. What is the source of this demand? The gaze of the person observing me says, prior to any other saying, "You shall not murder." The infinity that I encounter in the gaze of the other person commands me. In my encounter with the face of the other, at the same time I encounter infinity.

The subject who encounters the other—who experiences a revelation in the form of an obligation of responsibility for the other—is an essential partner in formulating the contents of this revelation. This is prophecy, and in this respect all people are prophets. God does not speak. God's traces, the traces of infinity, are revealed in the face of the other person, in the command, "You shall not murder," and in order to carry out this obligation I must clarify my duty and responsibility for the other. In the absence of a human act the revelation has no content. As Levinas says:

> The transcendence of the revelation lies in the fact that the "epiphany" comes in the saying of him that receives it. The order that orders me does not leave me any possibility of setting things right side up again with impunity, of going back from the exteriority of the Infinite, as when before a theme one goes back from the signified, or as when in a dialogue one finds in "you" a being. It is in prophecy that the Infinite escapes the objectification of thematization and of dialogue and signifies as *illeity*,[1] in the third person. This "thirdness" is different from that of the third man. (*OB* 149–50)[2]

Infinity is manifested in human beings by "saying"—by facing another person from a position of responsibility rather than as a perceivable object about which knowledge can be accumulated (*EN* 219–22). Being that God is transcendent, single, and infinite, God cannot be a subject of study and reflection. God cannot be defined, and that is why we know so little about God. The only possible affirmative statement about God is that "God comes to mind,"[3] or to be exact, that the infinite descends or contracts into the finite. The human consciousness has within it something that is beyond the limits of its grasp,[4] something that is infinite, which is called God. God is the creator and the source of the principle of justice (*BV* 25). Levinas also speaks of a metaphysical desire,[5] which is a desire for a relationship with the completely Other, with transcendence. It is a desire that is different from meeting needs, as it is not vital for one's existence. And there are traces, traces of God, encountered in both the face of the other person (*HO* 38–44) and in the Scriptures, in the form of demands.

Levinas writes, "The infinite transcends itself in the finite, it *passes* the finite in that it orders the neighbor to me without exposing itself to me.... One might give the name '*inspiration*' to this intrigue of infinity in which I make myself the author of what I hear" (*GCM* 75–76). Inspiration is listening and being open to the Other, or obeying a demand to be responsible for the other person whose face I encounter as a trace of infinity. But I am the one formulating the contents of the revelation, transforming the saying, the gesture of approach, to the said, to speech. What allows one to encounter otherness is, in a certain respect, the prophetic dimension that exists in every person.[6] Regarding this, Catherine Chalier writes, "When thinking of human spirituality as prophecy, Levinas is interested in this event of speech that forever disrupts one's peace of mind, because it firmly recruits the 'self' of the hearer, who therefore cannot resume his previous affairs, as though from that moment on the voice of the heavenly will exist within him."[7] This prophetic event is formulated in words said between people, between myself and the other person I encounter.

Studying and interpreting the Scriptures constitutes an opening up to the commanding voice heard through the written text. Chalier continues, "Studying requires a similar state of mind to that which once enabled certain men and women to become prophets, because it requires, at the moment of study, a willingness to hear the words read, reviewed, and learned as though they originated from God's mouth and as though they are directed at me."[8] Being open to otherness is the common foundation, the essential similarity, between prophecy and the study of Torah. As prophecy is formulated by the prophet who receives it, the *midrash* is formulated in the words of the *darshan*, in the effort to understand the Torah, the commandment underlying the written words. Despite the concurrence between Levinas and the sages on this issue of the relationship between the *midrash* and the prophecies, it is precisely at this point that the difference between them emerges. The sages see the *midrash* as distinct from the prophecies: the former replaced the latter in their role of connecting God and humankind. The *midrash* fills the void that appeared when the prophecies reached their conclusion. In Levinas's view, however, interpretation and *midrash* are prophecy. They involve an openness to the transcendent Other and are a formulation of the contents revealed in the encounter with otherness.

The course taken by Levinas in his reinterpretation of the prophetic concept is reminiscent of Maimonides in his *Guide for the Perplexed*, where he redefines prophecy as the pinnacle of all spiritual virtues on a scale informed by Aristotelian concepts.[9] Levinas redefines prophecy differently than Maimonides, but he uses a similar method of reinterpretation, based on a system of concepts and values that does not follow the simple meaning of the biblical text but is affected by a philosophical system of concepts and values.[10]

This course of thought, which does not forego the Revelation on Mt. Sinai but does not accept it in its simple form, and which seeks its meaning beyond humanism yet with no mythology, allows me to discover how I, as a rational person and a daughter of the Jewish People, fit into the story without renouncing my own system of beliefs and opinions. The figure of God emerging from the biblical stories in their simple form constitutes a challenge for many people, both observant and nonobservant. The option suggested here is intriguing even if one does not accept it in this precise form. It can serve as a model for a method of reasoning and interpretation. Instead of disregarding the figure of God, the text is asked what this figure teaches us, in the here and now, which we would not have otherwise known.

The Contents of Revelation

Levinas says nothing explicit about the source of the Torah and how it came to be. He refers to this question indirectly, for instance in his talmudic lesson on the passage in Tractate Megillah 7a (*ITN* 55–75). There, following the talmudic passage, he attempts to unravel the criteria leading to the inclusion of the scroll of Esther in the Bible. Though he does not say so, this careful discussion of the criteria for including a certain book in the Bible may reflect the route taken by other books prior to their inclusion in the biblical canon. This possibility is apparent from talmudic discussions on the holiness and inclusion of other books in the Bible, such as Ecclesiastes, Song of Songs, and Job (but never any of the five books of the Pentateuch).

Elsewhere Levinas states that classical literature—any classical literature, that of other nations as well as the Bible—carries messages that remain relevant for all time, and invites renewed interpretations (*BV* xi, 111, 171; *NTR* 68–69). This implies, though not stated explicitly, that the Bible's process of sanctification was an ongoing human process similar to the classicization of other literary texts. Hence, in this respect the Bible is no different from any classical literature: it was written with great love and imbued with timeless human wisdom that appeals to people of all eras, and it invites interpretations that have implications and relevance for the reader's world.

If so, what distinguishes the Bible from all other classics? Levinas answers that the Bible is unique, holy, given "from heaven," by virtue of its contents: "The Torah is transcendent and from heaven by its demands that clash, in the final analysis, with the pure ontology of the world. The Torah demands, in opposition to the natural perseverance of each being in his or her own being (a fundamental ontological law), care for the stranger, the widow and the orphan, a preoccupation with the other person" (*ITN* 61). If so, the uniqueness and holiness of the Torah are not necessarily derived from its origins or from how it reached us but from the messages embodied in it and from the ethics it represents. Now we can return to the story of Mt. Sinai and expound it: Torah given from heaven symbolizes the breaking into the world by that which is outside ontology, that is, outside natural existence and its order, and even a breaking into the human world of laws that contradict ontology. The natural law of an entity is the concern of the Same with the perseverance of its being. All creatures, humans included, are guided first and foremost by the interest of preserving their being. Responsibility and caring for another person—ethics—contradicts this rule. The Torah commands one to care for another person, commands one to behave ethically, and in this respect it derives from an origin that is outside being, from heaven, from God.

Revelation facilitates and even demands that one leave the concern for preserving one's own existence and face the other, to bear responsibility for the needs of another person. A person cannot escape this closed existence under his or her own power. Ethics must come from outside, from infinity. This is the content of revelation. The Torah's stories, commandments, and words of wisdom are intended for everyone and are intended to direct the learner to the other person. Every person has an active part in the Torah's ability to command him or her to care for the other, as this act of direction is predicated on study and interpretation of the Torah.[11]

The Interpreter (*Darshan*) and Revelation

The central place of the *darshan*'s role in facilitating the Torah's act of teaching ethics, as well as articulating and mediating revelation, is a topic often discussed by Levinas. For example, in his talmudic lesson "The Will of God and the Power of Humanity" (*NTR* 47–77), he explains this idea while implementing it and taking part in the revelation. As a result, this lesson becomes a *midrash* on the talmudic passage, a *midrash* on a *midrash*.

The passage in the Babylonian Talmud (Makot 23b) forms a link and a comparison between the role of the human court of law in applying divine justice to human beings and the interpretation of the Torah's words, thus revealing the divine will. In both cases a transcendent source generates values that humans are unable to produce within themselves, values that have to do with their mutual relationships. Both in the court of law and in the *midrash,* people embrace values learned from transcendence, and then, formulate and implement them. This is their prerogative and their responsibility.

The mishna states: "All those who are liable for excision (by celestial intervention), if they have submitted to whipping, are exempt from excision. For it is written 'Your brother would be debased in your eyes' (Deut. 23:3). Once sanctioned, he is as your brother. Such is the opinion of R. Hananiah ben Gamliel." The Torah mentions many transgressions that are punished by excision (*karet*), meaning the death of the sinner and all his descendants by the hands of heaven. This is an absolute punishment. In a certain respect, it rescinds one's humanity, one's place in human society, since it is carried out by God, as though human justice is incapable of dealing with a person who commits such a transgression. R. Hananiah ben Gamliel rules that a person who commits such a sin, and for whom a human court of law has decreed and carried out a punishment of whipping, is exempt from the punishment of excision. Despite the disputations on this matter, which appear in the mishna and in the associated gemara, the Talmud rules that the final decision shall follow the opinion of R. Hananiah ben Gamliel. Hence, in this case a human court of law assumes the previously divine authority to inflict punishment. Although the punishment of excision appears to reflect a type of justice that is beyond the human world, beyond that which human beings are authorized to handle, Jewish law transfers this authority to human hands.

Levinas writes the following about this mishna:

> Defined here by concepts as unpleasant as whipping, human justice substitutes itself for the rigorous verdict of the Absolute: "He will be excised from his people" (Num. 9, 13). Excision from life, but also from Israel, which is to say from the human order, from the order of true humanity, from true society.... R. Hananiah breaks with the gloomy mythological fatality whose eventuality would indicate a religious tyranny, in order to proclaim

that with regard to heaven fault does not exist which—between men and in clarity—one could not expiate or make expiatable. The court, an assembly freed of the blind pulsions of existence, elevated to disinterestedness, would be the place where regenerative divine will manifests itself—in the form of the fraternal, a paternal initiative. (*NTR* 57)

Levinas emphasizes the divine source of human justice—a fraternity stemming from a "paternal initiative." Justice comes from heaven, from the heteronomic law deriving from the divine order rather than from human intellect. This is the paternity of the initiative. But the application of justice, of this value with its transcendent source, is an act of fraternity, a matter given to humans to work out between themselves. Therefore, the punishment of excision draws an uncrossable line. It penalizes the perpetrator for an act that in essence detracts from the perpetrator's humanity, so much so that he loses the right to be part of human society; and in the absence of human rectification of this punishment it is the equivalent of dark mythological fatalism and might lead to nihilism.[12] A person who loses the right to and the hope for atonement has no reason or desire to endeavor to do good. There is nothing to save him from becoming immersed in evildoing. His fate is no longer under his control or his responsibility. Nonetheless, one question remains: in what way is whipping an act of fraternity?

Levinas continues, "But it depends on the earthly judge, on man, on the brother of the guilty, to restore the neighbor to human fraternity. Being responsible for his brother right up to being responsible for his freedom! Which can only occur by means of violence in the pain that awakens, that is to say, instructs and educates and tests" (*NTR* 58). The judge's responsibility is endless; he is responsible for the freedom of the other, since without the atonement that follows from serving the sentence the sinner remains devoid of free choice. No matter what he or she does, the sinner is irreversibly sentenced to elimination. When someone who has been sentenced to excision is punished by human hands, receiving a commuted sentence, the person gains freedom at a painful cost (in all respects). But serving the sentence allows the perpetrator to reenter human society with all that this encompasses: it expresses the sinner's responsibility for his or her actions and a wish for change, for repentance, indicating a subservience to laws shared by human beings. This is an act of rectification. The suffering associated with the punishment is a moment of opening up to the Other, even if only passively and forcibly. It is an encounter with surrounding human society with its laws and norms, and in this respect it constitutes a return to human fraternity. It is as if the whipping has the power to arouse one from the persistence of the individual's existence, from the concern for oneself which disregards others and causes one to commit destructive acts toward them.

If we were to interpret the whipping as a metaphor rather than an actual physical punishment, Levinas provides us with a first-rate educational guideline. Setting limits that are not to be crossed under any circumstance, limits that are imposed on one and are not a matter of choice, is one aspect of this guideline. The point of departure is not freedom, but freedom is preceded by basic norms of not harming others. Nevertheless, since according to this approach one is perceived as having the freedom to choose and the responsibility for one's deeds, particularly severe acts require painful rectification. Pardon is not granted automatically; there is a need for an act of rectification between people, between a judge and a defendant, between the offender and the offended, and sometimes between an educator and a disciple.

R. Hananiah ben Gamliel's statement in the mishna is so bold that, unsurprisingly, it aroused objection. Who gave a human judge the authority to change a heavenly verdict? The talmudic passage goes even further by equating the heaven-earth relationship, with regard to the punishment of excision and the role of the human court, with the relationship manifested in the *midrash* in the form of human interpretation of the Torah. R. Joseph's question, as portrayed in the Talmud, also questions the authority of the *darshan* to interpret the heavenly Torah. Levinas refers to this: "All this is certainly suggested by the question of R. Joseph: 'Who has gone above, has returned and reported?' Can the Mosaic revelation itself, as an historical fact, bear up against this? Who attests after all to its authenticity? R. Joseph's question goes that far. It is then that Abaye, taking up again a saying of R. Joshua b. Levi, confers on the interpretation of Scriptural verses, on hermeneutics, on *Midrash,* the power to force the secret of transcendence" (*NTR* 67). R. Joseph questions the authority of the commentator to interpret the divine will. Levinas extends R. Joseph's question to include the very authenticity of the Torah, its transcendent source. Judging by the plain meaning of the Talmud this does not seem to be R. Joseph's question. Why does Levinas interpret it thus? The only recourse is to recognize it as Levinas's question, a question that occupies him as a twentieth century scholar. Presumably, some of the readers may identify with this question. Expounding the text in light of issues that occupy the *darshan*, from his perspective, is an established midrashic method. His treatment of R. Joseph's question resembles the mishna's treatment of the punishment of excision: the mishna takes the liberty of turning a heavenly punishment into a human punishment, whereas Levinas takes the liberty of imbuing R. Joseph's question with a meaning that concerns him in the present and transforms it into a question of his own on the divine source of the Torah, on its origins in heaven.

Levinas is, of course, well aware of this, and he stresses the logical shortcoming of the answer to this question: "How can such answers—planted in the bosom of a downright *petitio principii*—measure up against the radicalism of R. Joseph's question? It is certainly permitted to understand them as the expression of a position. The biblical canon invested with an exceptional authority, without requiring new revelations, would contain, for he who knows how to interpret its verses, an answer to everything" (*NTR* 68). This is, first and foremost, the expression of a position. But is this enough? If we were to be satisfied with this, it would be an expression of traditional religiosity, which cannot satisfy intellectuals used to questioning all truths and utilizing their intellect. Is this not a primary motive of Levinas the *darshan*? More is needed.

Levinas continues, writing, "The verses commented upon, instead of resting on the authority of Scripture, are they not meant to establish it? In fact, the adventure of the Midrash, the very possibility of hermeneutics, in its rigorously formal advance, do they not already belong to the very way in which another voice is heard among us—the very way of transcendence, as one says in terms of the school? Doesn't this enhance the argument's cyclic effect?" (*NTR* 68). The reading suggests that the *midrash* itself is a reference to that which is outside the intellect of the thinking person. The *midrash* that encompasses the willingness to obey is by its very nature an opening up to the Other, a statement of "here I am"; it is a willingness that facilitates the emergence of transcendence. The *midrash* is a relationship of mutual, dialectical dependence between commentator and text, where each side both learns and teaches. Levinas stresses here the position of the commentator as a student of the text, as one who is willing to listen to its voice and to learn about himself or herself and his or her obligations. Is the *darshan* also speaking of the congruence between the form of study and its contents? Indeed, opening up to that which is said by the text and to its otherness indicates being open to the other person. This seems to be the meaning of the phrase, "the very way in which another voice is heard among us."

But just as the commentator has need for the text, the text also has need for the commentator:

> The expression of signification belongs to its very significance, to the strange fecundity of the intelligible, through which there is spirit, that is, inspiration. As if the sense of a thought were carried—meta-phor—beyond the end which limits the intention of the thinker. It is said farther than his Said. It is said outside of the sayer. Its folded wings or the germ of innumerable lives promised in it—seminal reasons—are also lodged in the letters of the text—metaphors of a thought exceeding what it thinks. This whole literature...awaits or inspires the reading. The verses cry out: "Interpret me." Such is the inspiration of all authentic literature, defining the book as book—it guides the history of nations. (*NTR* 69)

The book contains meaning that is beyond the intention of its writer. This is what Levinas calls inspiration. The inspiration encompassed in the written letters, by virtue of being written, is an invitation to interpret, to hermeneutics. Writing as saying, as approaching the Other, contains by virtue of this approach more than what is said in it.[13] And in order that it be exposed and heard, the meaning—namely, the interpretation or different interpretations—must find expression. Yet if this feature is true of all "authentic literature," does it not imply that Levinas is taking the sting out of the question of the Torah's divine source? Can we really accept that any classical book justifies a *midrash,* that its status is equal to that of the Torah, that the voice of transcendence is heard in all such books? Is not this a diminution of the Torah?

> Interchange from one person to the other, irreducible to the transmission of data, assuring the coherence of an order of things, is produced, to be sure, in the interpretation of a meaning. But all literature does not go back to the

primary ground of meaning, is not the foundation of meaning. Where does this foundation occur? Would this not be the privilege of the Scriptures to which Abaye referred? Is there a sense or story, a said, a fable, that does not tell of the relation of man to man? Is there a relation of man to man which does not take the ego out of itself, which does not break the identity of the identical through which the living clutch their being? Is there a relation of man to man which is not ethical? The ethical is not a region or an ornament of the real, it is of itself disinterestedness itself, which is only possible under the traumatism in which presence, in its impenitent equanimity of presence, is upset by the Other. Upset or awakened. To prove the authenticity and value of this traumatism is again to return to this very traumatism, to that transcendence or wake fullness where all these "notions" signify for the first time for us. (NTR 69–70)

The answer to this question is given on two levels. First of all, the uniqueness of the Torah is in its establishing of meaning, that is, in the very generation of the ethical foundation. Responsibility for the other person is learned first and foremost in the Torah, and that is its distinction. But on the second level, Levinas does not appear to balk at stating that any story, any said, contains the voice of transcendence, being as it is a manifestation of the relationship between one person and another. Any text is in its very being an encounter with the Other, a saying of "here I am." But another premise is added here: any relationship between one person and another is an ethical relationship. Is every relationship between one person and another indeed an ethical relationship, that is, a relationship in which one assumes responsibility for the other? Perhaps this is not a description of an actual state of affairs but of its potential—any relationship between people is an opportunity for an ethical relationship. And maybe we can only understand this if we treat the word "relationship" with all due respect, as a proper relationship, a relationship that draws one out of oneself and introduces one to the other and his or her needs. This interpretive perspective is learned from the Torah and can be applied to the interpretation of any classical text.

Is this a legitimate perspective? Does all literature have ethical content? The answer to this question is no simple matter. Does Levinas attribute the intention to form a relationship of commitment toward the other in the literary attempt to describe human situations or to introduce the reader to human figures? Or is this potential opening up to a relationship of responsibility inherently located within every work and every reader-text encounter? Is there a hidden assumption here whereby writing is derived from the trauma of opening up to the other, and therefore, revives this trauma? Is this the meaning of the emphasis that "the ethical is not a region or an ornament of the real"—namely, that it is always possible to return to the traumatic moments of opening up to the other and of accepting the responsibility afforded by the encounter through learning the text? Or perhaps this is an interpretive perspective, one interpretive focus among many options—an ethical position that seeks the ethics in any text. Such an interpretive focus is based on a hermeneutical theory that puts aside the author's intentions and focuses on the text, the commentator, and the relationship between them. All this said, is there not writing that is an expression of the Same, of the consciousness that is enclosed within itself and converses with itself?

After quoting the talmudic passage that brings three examples of the Holy Spirit appearing in a human court of law, Levinas adds:

> The avowal of he who recognizes his injustice, the unanimous testimony of a people, the wisdom of the judge, are they not explicable by pure reason? Yet nonetheless the final word consists in referring to a tradition attesting to the "heavenly voice." Does not the Gemarah thus suspect an insurmountable ambiguity in the exercise of pure reason? Every logos would require inspiration! There would be difference and traumatism, teaching and wakefulness in every evidence! A paternal "Other," which does not alienate, in every identity! Thus we link up with the initial theme of transcendence at the bosom of the court's decision, penetration of the divine within the world across human propheticism, or conservation of the divine measure of excision, and the difference between divine will and human will, in the very humanization of divine strictness. (NTR 73–74)

The Talmud is aware that all of its examples of the "heavenly voice" (*bat kol*) appearing in a court of law can also be understood differently, through regular interpretation. Each of these stories can be understood with no need to involve a "heavenly voice." The Talmud chooses, however, to conclude the discussion with the words "but this is our tradition," that is, to base its words in this matter on the common tradition that a heavenly voice appeared in court and that this was not a regular logical procedure. This is the point of departure of what Levinas is saying. The need for heavenly inspiration in court derives from the limits of human intelligence and from the concern that, in the absence of inspiration, we may expect to encounter the commonplace aggression and violence often found when one person wields control over another. If at first the passage, and consequently the commentator, stresses the human role in meting out justice, its conclusion stresses the role of inspiration, of heaven, in this enterprise. In the text's terms, the power of the court to mitigate the punishment of excision and to commute it to one of whipping does not eliminate the excision; it only adapts it to human terms.

Levinas does not trust humanism when left to its own means. The autonomous individual is not a sufficient foundation from which ethics can be derived. The autonomous individual is completely immersed in sustaining the self's own existence unless the self opens up to a transcendent voice. Through the text and through this interpretation, Levinas is asking those reading these words in the present—you and me—whether we constitute the exclusive source of our moral conceptions.

Another level inherent in this statement is epistemological. Levinas objects to common philosophical theories (from Plato to Husserl) that conceive of knowledge as an act in which consciousness becomes equal to itself. In his opinion, knowledge is a departure of consciousness from itself and an exposure to that which is outside it. This is the inspiration within all thoughts, the dissonance that remains within each certainty.[14] This is the "heavenly voice" that exists within the biblical verses and in their interpretation.

With regard to the *midrash,* there is therefore a need for a tradition that will direct the interpretation. Tradition recognizes that the proper interpretation of the course of events in these three courts derives not only from human-legal logic but also from a "heavenly voice." The Gemara does to the interpretation what the heavenly voice does to the judgment—it proclaims the voice of transcendence. Tradition is that which makes itself known to the commentator outside of his or her consciousness, that which does not come from within the self, that which arouses and directs the commentator toward the other person. The *midrash* is not an intellectual exercise with no practical implications; it is intended to direct each and every one of us toward the other person. This is Levinas's basic premise concerning the function of the interpretive tradition.

The passage circles back to the topic with which the discussion began by perceiving in these three biblical stories the appearance of a "heavenly voice," something that is beyond plain human rational judgment. This is an interpretive choice with regard to the biblical stories; they can be interpreted differently. The interdependence between the heavenly and the human in the act of justice is learned and realized through a *midrash* of the verses. The *midrash* is the human action that makes it possible to hear the divine voice. The talmudic passage expresses this in its own way and voice, and Levinas stresses and enhances this statement in his commentary.

But despite this strong relationship between the human and the divine, there remains an essential difference, a distinction and insurmountable distance. The heavenly dimension does not merge with the human dimension, even though they are connected through prophecy or inspiration:

> In concluding, may I ask you to admire once again the marvelous audacity of the sentence which serves as the very hinge of our text: "Who has gone up there, returned and reported it?" The end of a certain theology and of a certain religion. The whole liberation, but also the whole gloomy ennui—a matter to overcome—of modern humanity. Lucidity which renders quite intolerable the discourse in which one speaks in an infantile way as if someone had really returned from over there to tell us what happens there, as if the myth of Er of Pamphylia which Plato relates in Book X of *The Republic* were a travel story.[15] But, above all, as if transcendence were only an exchange of data with an other-world where once again an experience occurs in the beyond, coming to augment the baggage of our knowledge and to keep us as an identical being, the same, consolidated in its identity through its experiences, synthesized and synchronized as experience. (*NTR* 74)

Previously, Levinas mainly stressed the transcendent dimension of the *midrash* and the human application of justice. Now he proceeds to argue against theology or a religious approach that suggests there is a truth in heaven, that information is supposed to reach earth in some way. His approach rejects any essentialist definition of religion and Jewish law. He quite surprisingly links classical hermeneutics and epistemology with a very popular theology: they all assume that the essence of the relationship with transcendence involves the conveying of information and, hence, the empowerment of the identical being, the Same, as a receiver of knowledge.

Levinas claims that, similar to philosophy, theology that seeks transcendence in heaven (e.g., speaks on behalf of "God's will," "the truth of Judaism," or "Jewish law" as an entity from heaven) instead of searching for it in the text or by producing a *midrash,* is merely another type of ontology, a reinforcement of the Same. If the meaning of transcendence is merely information, then from the moment knowledge is acquired it becomes an object of the subject that knows it, knowledge that serves to perpetuate its own existence. However, the relationship between heaven and earth is not the conveying of information but a relationship of inspiration. It is a call upon the Same to open up to that which is outside it, to an Otherness that does not become an object of consciousness but, rather, remains in its Otherness and invites the Same to relate to it by opening up rather than generalizing, by stroking rather than grasping. Inspiration constantly questions the Same and undermines its serenity. This is a process that never reaches its full potential; the self always tends to return to its closed state, and time and again inspiration calls upon the self to leave this state. For this reason it is not a body of knowledge that can be fully realized but, rather, a process of learning and listening. It involves asking questions and attempting to answer them, without letting go of the questions, without unreservedly and unquestioningly accepting the answers—a *midrash.* Levinas continues:

> And what profound ambiguity in the response which refers us to the commentary of Scripture! Is not the response as ironic as it is pious? Would the relation of transcendence push its path through human effort? For the extraordinary Sinaic revelation, for the voice of God resounding in thunder but which would no longer be persuasive, one substitutes a pedantic commentary, possibly duped by all the impostures of the century, a flood of paper! Are the impenetrable heavens going to be ripped open on the benches of the *yeshiva* where one comments on commentaries of commentaries referring precisely to the revealed text to which Rabbi Joseph's question applies, and about which other sages will have for a long time suggested its contingency in terms of vicissitudes and experiences of the story which it would be the document? (*NTR* 75)

The audacity is emphasized here by means of irony: referring those who seek "God's will" to a certain type of interpretation of the biblical verses, to a *midrash,* might seem like contempt. Can sitting on the benches of the *beit midrash* serve as an adequate replacement for the Revelation on Mt. Sinai? Can the *midrash* serve as a replacement for prophecy? Can we—and do we want to—believe in a historical event such as the Revelation on Mt. Sinai? Do we want to believe in the words of the prophets as though God speaks through them? As we have seen, as far as Levinas is concerned the Revelation on Mt. Sinai is not a description of a historical event but a text that requires a *midrash* in order to be meaningful. Thus, the words of the prophets also reveal their inspiration in contents that require a *midrash*. His *midrash* on the Revelation on Mt. Sinai and on prophecy may be new in its content but not in its approach. Levinas acts as the sages did in interpreting the written text to mediate between it and their values and contemporary needs.

Levinas says further on: "And destroyed in it is the humanism of a Renaissance man, the superior natural being, welcoming and contesting supernatural experience. In this ambiguity a humanity appears whose spirit and inspiration is prophecy. Prophecy which is not some happy accident of the spirit, a 'genius,' but its very spirituality:[16] an affection of self and others stronger than the receptivity which waits for it, a listening, an understanding surpassing the capacity of hearing, impossible possibility—or miracle—the most hidden, of human existing and perhaps the manner in which the spirit penetrates nature" (*NTR* 76–77). In this paragraph, which concludes his talmudic lesson, Levinas once again speaks of prophecy as the "impossible" capacity to hear the absolute other. Prophecy is a human quality and not an exceptional talent. It is a potential in all people; it is human spirituality. This thought offers an alternative to the customary conceptions of the human as a creature whose spirituality is intelligence, that is, conceptions that acknowledge the human as the source of knowledge, law, and ethics. Prophecy subjects the judge to ethics despite the pressures applied by good lawyers and the media. And the *midrash* is a prophecy, because it constitutes human listening and the formulation of a voice that originates outside human beings.

Levinas's understanding of the *midrash,* prophecy, and their relationship is strongly related to their conceptions in this passage of the Talmud. His interpretive method realizes and applies this approach to the interpreted text. Thus, his approach to the text seeks not an accumulation of knowledge but an attentive encounter with the text—with both its intricate structure and at times seemingly unrelated connections between issues. This approach to the text does not arrive at decisive statements but offers questions, suggestions, and several interpretations among many others; it is a *midrash* on a *midrash*.

In this way he is attentive to the inspiration within the talmudic text that opens up to the Other. Can this effort, this midrashic practice, be grasped as preparation for an opening up of the Same to the Other? Perhaps through this explanation he is inviting us, each of us, to join in such an effort, to interpret the Torah, the Talmud, and maybe even his own words. Is not this a personal summons extended to each one of us to experience moments of inspiration, to that which may lead us to take responsibility in our encounter with the other person? This may indeed be his intention.

Connection to the Origins of Language — Inspiration

In his later writings, Levinas refers to speech and written language as a "contraction of the infinite in the finite" (*BV* viii). What does he mean? Even before speech there is the testimony or the saying (*dire*), a gesture that involves facing the other person, which inherently means assuming responsibility for the other. This is a close relationship even before the formulation of language, an intent whose contents are "here I am"—a consciousness of commitment even before clarifying its content. This is the inspiration that underlies language, any language.[17] The verbal translation, the said (*dit*) or the written text, is always a contraction of inspiration, of the gesture of commitment that was in its origin. The said is a final form that contracts and reduces the saying. This approach differs from those that see language as a tool mainly aimed at describing the contents of consciousness or of the real world as precisely as possible. Language is intended, first and foremost, to connect between people. Therefore, the foundation of language is not the contents of consciousness or concepts (although these are indeed roles fulfilled by language) but, rather, a saying or facing, an infinity, the subject's moving out of the self by the approach of the Other—inspiration.

The written language and the spoken language are manifestations and formulations of the saying, but by their very essence they are limited forms, a contraction of the infinity of saying. Words, whether written or said, are incapable of expressing the full inspiration that they were meant to express. This discrepancy is implicit in them. Language is a limited tool that endeavors to express the unlimited; it is a translation of infinite meaning into letters or words, and similar to other translations it too does not produce a perfect replication of the original.

Nonetheless, it is necessary to distinguish between the said and writing. The said is a living testimony by the speaker who is capable of clarifying his or her intentions; the speaker and the hearer can hold a conversation. In contrast, the written text is separate from the writer. The written letter remains a mark on paper, and in the absence of a reader or learner it is a dead letter. Levinas explains the role of interpretation in bridging the gap between saying and writing, its role in reviving the text and re-expanding it from its written form to its source of inspiration:

> But this coming and going from the text to the reader and from the reader to the text, and this renewal of meaning, are perhaps the distinctive feature of all written work, of all literature, even when it does not claim to be Holy Scriptures. The meaning that arises in an authentic expression of the human exceeds the psychological contents of the writer's intention, whether he is a prophet, philosopher or poet. In expressing itself, intention cuts through currents of meaning objectively carried by language and the experience of a people. These currents ensure the balance, success and echoes of what is said. The act of saying causes a vibration of something that precedes whatever is thought within it. Interpretation draws it out and is not just perception, but the formation of meaning. From this point of view, every text is inspired: it contains more than it contains. The exegesis of all literature stems from the way in which the plain meaning suggested by the letters is already situated in the unthought. The Holy Scriptures, admittedly, have another secret, an additional essence that purely literary texts have perhaps lost.[18] But they are literary texts nevertheless. And it is because all literature is inspired that religious revelation can become text and reveal itself to hermeneutics. (*BV* 171)[19]

The revelation, the inspiration underlying the said or written text, depends not only on the writer or speaker but also on the recipient of the message. The said depends on the relationship between the speaker (or writer) and the hearer (or reader). Two sayings are necessary, two appeals, in order to create meaning: the saying of the speaker and the saying of the hearer (*BV* 97). The speaker is not present in the written text; that which is written receives a constant form, one that is even fixed in letters, a form in which infinity, contracted in writing, might disappear. There is a discrepancy between the written letters and the saying, and this discrepancy only grows with time and the geographical distance from the writer. The written text might lose its saying. The interpretive discourse, in which the written is transformed back into conversation, revives the saying in the written text and its appeal to the reader (see *TI* 73, 96–97, 182–83; *ITN* 94–95). A reconnection with the revelation within the text, with the inspiration at its basis, is made possible through the presence of people who speak to each other.

Exegesis is a saying of the hearer or reader. As Levinas sees it, interpretation of a written text exposes deep levels that exist within it and are borne by language, not necessarily consciously. The inspiration, the saying, underlies literary, theological, and philosophical texts. Their interpretation constitutes taking part in their saying and from this respect it is an exposure of their inspirational dimension, a partaking in their inspiration.

The saying of the text exceeds that which is said therein. Hence, the purpose of exegesis is not to reveal the writer's intention, as the text exceeds the author's intentions. But how does exegesis allow one to take part in the inspiration of the text? There are "currents of meaning objectively carried by language and the experience of a people" (*BV* 171). The very use of language is based on a common element, one that is meaningful but not always conscious. Moreover, exegesis is not passive; it is not a response to the text but an active conversation with it, and in this way it creates meaning.

How can that which was not said be revealed in the said? That is the task of the commentators. They must not only understand the written text, but they must also make an effort to expose that which is beyond the words—namely, the spirit that underlies the text, its deep intention, its source of inspiration. On the contrary, Levinas assumes that every text has an intent, a saying, and he presupposes its content—the inspiration whose content consists of facing the other. However, he invites learners of the text to serve as commentators, to set in motion their creativity in order to understand a fuller meaning of the text, the messages inherent in it beyond the words. Theoretically, these are opposites: the content of the saying with which every text is imbued is predetermined, but each person is invited to try and expose it, taking interpretive license. In this way, the commentator's freedom is limited by the spirit of the words, by the premise that the text's intention is ethical. In the quote below, Levinas speaks of the Talmud's interpretation of the biblical text, which he sees as a model of all interpretation:

> Interpretation essentially involves this act of soliciting without which what is not said, inherent in the texture of the statement, would be extinguished beneath the weight of the texts, and sink into the letters. An act of soliciting which issues from people whose eyes and ears are vigilant and who are mindful of the whole body of writing from which the extract comes, and equally attuned to life: the city, the street, other men. An act of soliciting which issues from people in their uniqueness, each person capable of extracting from the signs meanings which each time are inimitable. An act of soliciting which issues from people who would also belong to the process of the signification of what has meaning.... The very plurality as an unavoidable of the signification of meaning, and as in some way justified by the destiny of the inspired word, so that the infinite richness of what it does not say can be said or that the meaning of what it does say can be "renewed."... One may wonder whether the book, as a book, before becoming a document, is not the modality by which what is said lays itself open to exegesis, calls for it; and where meaning, immobilized in the characters, already tears the texture in which it is held. (BV 110–11)

Interpretation is not a constraint that derives from the difficulty to understand the meaning of the written text, but it is part of the text's essence and a partner in the generation of meaning. Multiple interpretations do not indicate the text's inability to be clearly construed; they attest to its richness and to the infinity that was "contracted" into the text. All commentators bring with them their uniqueness, their life experience, and their own perspective, and thus contribute to expanding the meaning of the text. The text's capacity to articulate for each person a voice that is construed specifically for the individual's own sake is its infinity.

If this is so, as one among many commentators, Levinas also contributes to expanding the texts he interprets, and in this way he becomes connected to their infinite meaning. He does not purport to expose the truth inherent in the texts or to understand them better than any other commentator; true to his theory, he offers his interpretive suggestions as options that enrich and expand understanding. Therefore, both the Talmud and

Levinas often propose various options for understanding the same issue without opting for a single interpretation. If the purpose of exegesis is to expand the text as much as possible, then the more meanings that are revealed the more it will be expanded. Indeed, in his commentary on the Talmud, Levinas makes use of the "another thing" (*davar aher*) form familiar from the *midrash* by offering several interpretations, albeit all his own and not originating from others, without deciding between them. In this way he connects with the Talmud's inspiration and infinity.

An example of this technique may be found in the talmudic lesson "Judaism and Revolution" (*NT* 94–119). The talmudic discussion in Tractate Bava Metzia 83b deals with the social benefits to which the daily laborer is entitled. Resh Lakish derives the proper duration of the workday by expounding a verse in Psalms: "Resh Lakish said: A labourer's entry [to town] is in his own time, and his going forth [to the fields] is in his employer's; as it is written, 'When the sun rises, they steal away and lie down in their dens. Man goes forth to his work and to his labor until the evening' (Ps. 104:22–23)." Levinas attempts to understand what Resh Lakish meant in his interpretation by deriving the laborer's employment terms from the verse in Psalms, and suggests: "Work belongs to the order of light and reason. The time of work, as Resh Lakish sees it, is not the time of frustration or alienation, is not cursed time. In a world in which work appeared as a mark of servitude reserved for the slave, Resh Lakish wants to see it as the perfection of creation. But in that case Resh Lakish would not have a sacred love for revolution. For in his beautiful reading of Psalm 104, he does not see how evil can enter the world through work" (104). Deriving the daily laborer's employment terms from a verse in a psalm describing the perfection of the world and the greatness of God's deeds indicates a naïve conception of work as part of the world's perfection. This is one way of understanding the interpretation offered by Resh Lakish. Its significance is in its defiance of the presumption that the laborer's very status, the very need to work, is a problem or even a calamity. Levinas is insinuating here that the Marxist approach, which perceives the proletariat as a repressed class by virtue of its very existence, is not the only possible conception. However he continues: "Maybe Resh Lakish is not at all blind to the imperfections of the creature; maybe the condition of the worker seems inhuman to him, but maybe he still thinks that the man who works is the only hope of the earth and that the tomorrows he prepares will be freed from the misery of a miserable condition" (104).

The added distinction here is between the existential state of work, the need to work in order to produce a better future, and the terms of employment, which can be either harsh or fair. The state of affairs in which one is forced to work on unfair terms must be corrected. But changing this state of affairs requires hard work. The only hope for change comes from human endeavors to promote change, and in this respect work is no calamity.

Levinas presents a third possibility for understanding Resh Lakish: "Resh Lakish, who seeks to base the length of the workday on a psalm verse, thus also finds himself grounding the rights of the worker on the very order of creation.... Or he at least thinks that the natural law attached to the person of the worker and consecrated by the Torah guarantees better than custom the rights of the person. Perhaps Resh Lakish is a revolutionary because he denounces custom" (*NT* 104–05). According to this interpretation, Resh Lakish bases workers' rights on this verse not because of the harmony in the world but because there is no better justification for defending workers' rights. For example, when the abuse of workers' rights is a common norm it is necessary to appeal to another normative system, one that is external to the abusive standard. The Bible offers such safe grounds. The laborer's rights are based on the portrayal of a proper, improved world.

Levinas proceeds to give the words of Resh Lakish a fourth meaning: perhaps he anticipated situations in which there is no accepted custom, such as modern industrial towns. In this case, there is no recourse but to ground the laborer's rights on his humanity and on the Torah, rather than on tradition, which does not exist: "Modern society depends neither on history nor on its sedimentation. It discovers its order in human dignity, in the human personality. It is established in regard to the person. Away with customs and myths ... all those instruments of enslavement" (*NT* 105–06). Every explanation given to the interpretation of Resh Lakish expands our appreciation of his words without invalidating previous understandings. In this way, the text gradually receives additional meanings, which Levinas wishes to reveal. There is no conflict between the different interpretations.

Thus, we learn that work is a natural part of the world, and that it does not detract from the world's wholeness. Although the laborer's employment terms are often a calamity, labor per se is the world's hope. And workers' rights can be grounded in an external law originating from the Torah, which is preferable over other options.

The talmudic passage that includes the *midrash* of Resh Lakish cites three different *midrashim* on these verses from Psalms, without giving preference to any one of them. Levinas subjects the words of Resh Lakish in the Talmud to the same treatment given by the Talmud to the verse from Psalms; although there the multiplicity stems from different speakers while in Levinas it stems from the creativity of a single commentator. In this way the text expands and draws closer to its infinity.[20]

This discussion by Levinas following the talmudic passage on the best way of grounding workers' rights can serve as an opening for contemporary *beit-midrashic* learning. Workers' rights and their abuse is a hot topic in Israel and all over the world in this era of globalization in which the wealthy make every effort to increase their profits at the expense of their workers. Fair labor laws are no guarantee when factories are transferred to locations where workers are willing to work for starvation-level wages and when migrant workers whose rights are not properly enforced compete against a labor force that is supposedly more protected. The talmudic passage and Levinas's interpretation make it possible to enter a real discussion of contemporary circumstances and of emerging questions. In the *beit midrash*, similar to the Talmud, additional interpretive options are proposed, supplementing those offered by Levinas to the Talmud. I have found fascinating differences between the analyses of these issues in groups mostly composed of employers versus groups of hired employees. In any case, this is a platform for a contemporary debate that is enhanced by the high normative level offered by the text.

In the lesson "Cities of Refuge," Levinas offers three different interpretations explaining the symbolic meaning of Jerusalem. He notes: "But it can be read in other ways. If the Talmud saying is so strange, it is not because it would take pleasure in stating in a complicated way what can be expressed in a simple way. On the contrary, it is because it leaves a multiplicity of meanings to its saying, because it calls for several readings of it,

Our role, precisely, consists in looking for them" (*BV* 37). By proposing many interpretive options without giving preference to one over the others, Levinas attempts to decipher as many meanings of the text as possible, to become closely connected to its infinite saying, to the inspiration embedded within it. Similar to the sages, he assumes that "the Torah has seventy faces," and multiple interpretations help reveal part of this infinity.

Nevertheless, as we have seen, Levinas also makes an assumption concerning the content of the inspiration, which is forever ethical. This content, this intent, is capable of assuming different forms within the written text; therefore, it is necessary to search and reveal as many ways of understanding as possible, providing they support this premise. As stated, this is an essential paradox in Levinas's conception, which indeed purports to be open and seeks to invite all people to come and take part in forming the text's meaning yet defines and limits the space of the interpretive act.

In the case of homiletical exegesis that upholds the ethical framework, Levinas demonstrates his creativity through many different interpretations. The summons extended to all readers or students to take part in producing additional interpretive readings is also a sincere invitation, one that is not intimidated by multiplicity but, rather, invites and seeks it. This is the aspect of infinity in the text, its inspiration, which connects with the infinity of every person.

Accordingly, exegesis is a way of taking part in the revelation, in formulating a saying that derives from a transcendent source and is located within the letters of the written text. Commentators open up to this otherness, and their actions are necessary in order to formulate the meaning of the text. They must constantly adapt it to any time and place, to any commentator that is a subject to whom the text's inspiration is aimed and for whom it is intended. One's willingness to open up to that which is outside of oneself, to the transcendence seen in the face of the other person or in the written text, is prophecy. On this basis, exegesis is not an explicatory technique but a necessary partnership of inspiration.

Both the sages and Levinas believe that by interpreting the biblical verses and the words of the Talmud they are taking part in revelation. Indeed, Levinas understands the story of Mt. Sinai and prophecy differently than the sages do, but they share the conjecture that no one (with the possible exception of Moses) ever went up to heaven and returned to report what is required of us humans; rather, we interpret the texts, and this is the true and best means of achieving the desired relationship with transcendence.

Levinas's suggestions for understanding the Revelation on Mt. Sinai and its holiness in a manner that does not require absolute faith in supernatural forces but focuses, rather, on the meaning of these ideas for the human world and for interpersonal relations, are important and interesting in the contemporary Jewish context. Many Jews are unable to accept the story of Mt. Sinai in its plain form, but they do not wish to relinquish their Jewish identity and their association with Jewish tradition. This seems to constitute a creative proposal that is not Torah from Sinai per se but nonetheless demonstrates a way of thought that relinquishes neither tradition nor its renewal in the spirit of humanistic, rational contemporary values.

The pluralistic *batei midrash* as well, similar to both the Talmud and to Levinas, invite a multiplicity of perspectives and readings with regard to the text, as "the Torah has seventy faces" and additional meanings are always waiting to be revealed. Resembling the Oral Law, these are not only many interpretations formed by a single commentator but also a multiplicity of voices, of different people who speak to each other and generate their interpretations by means of conversation and polemics.

Chapter 3

Levinas's Attitude to the Interpreted Text

The *midrash* is a way of approaching a text, an attitude with unique features. Are the rabbinic *midrash* and Levinas's interpretation of talmudic passages fundamentally similar in this respect? One of the most important features of the *midrash* is its frank attitude to the text, which involves quoting it, even when the *midrash* ultimately changes the plain meaning of the text. This feature is, of course, evident in Levinas's talmudic readings, which constitute an interpretation of talmudic passages delivered to the reader in translation, and he repeatedly quotes sections and clauses to which he refers in detail. Other aspects of this matter shall be examined below.

Torah Study

By choosing to teach Talmud to an uninitiated public at the colloquia of Jewish intellectuals in France, Levinas was making a statement. This was a practical manifestation of the value of Torah study. Levinas was skilled in manners of expression and instruction to which his audience was much more accustomed, and he could have lectured about his ideas based on sound reasoning and a variety of different sources. But he thought it preferable to deal with the most urgent Jewish existential issues of his time in the traditional Jewish manner, namely, by learning the ancient texts (Bible, Talmud, Midrash, Rashi's commentary, and others) and seeking their possible meaning for him and for his contemporaries—through *midrash*. Levinas writes:

> Jewish wisdom is inseparable from a knowledge of the biblical and rabbinical texts; the Hebrew language directs the reader's attention towards the true level of these texts, which is the most profound level of Being.... Judaism can survive only if it is recognized and propagated by lay people who, outside all Judaism, are the promoters of the common life of men.... The Judaism of the house of prayer has ceased to be transmittable. The old-fashioned Judaism is dying off, or is already dead. This is why we must return to Jewish wisdom; ... this is why Judaism of reason must take precedence over the Judaism of prayer; the Jew of the Talmud must take precedence over the Jew of the Psalms. (*DF* 250, 271)[1]

In his talmudic readings, articles, notes, and essays, Levinas frequently spoke and wrote about this method of interpretation, its goals and principles, and he always indicated the vital significance of studying and interpreting the Torah in a way that perceives it as a teaching rather than as only an object of historical or philological research. This may sound as if he devised his own unique method of interpretation, but in actual fact his interpretation consciously joined an ancient constitutive method of study, the *midrash*. One indication is the similarity between his comments on rabbinic interpretations of the biblical text and his methodological comments on his own interpretive work, but this is also evident from the definition of Torah study and its homiletical exegesis as a type of revelation, as seen in the previous chapter. Furthermore, it is

> a study which is not limited to the acquiring of knowledge. According to the Jewish tradition—and without being confused with another mystical practice—this study is the highest level of life where knowledge is no longer distinguished from imperatives and practical impulses, where science and conscience meet, where reality and justice no longer belong to two distinct orders. It is as if the human were to rise to it by attaining a new condition, a new mode of spirituality of the spirit.... The science and the culture of the Torah would thus be more important than the liturgy. (*BV* 47, 51)

The study of Torah is, therefore, learning that appeals to the whole person; it is a demand to realize that which is studied in practice. This is a special approach to the text, one that reaches beyond the learning, an attitude that is a shaping of man and of reality, and in this respect it is of a higher importance than the liturgy.

In the talmudic lesson "The Temptation of Temptation" (*NT* 30–50), Levinas discusses the passage in Tractate Shabbat (88a–b) on the giving of the Torah and speaks of the function of the Torah in real life: "Being receives a challenge from the Torah, which jeopardizes its pretention of keeping itself above or beyond good and evil. In challenging the absurd 'that's the way it is' claimed by the power of the powerful, the man of the Torah transforms being into human history. Meaningful movement jolts the Real" (39). The Torah teaches the concepts of good and evil, as well as the ability and responsibility of every person to make his or her own choices. It questions current reality based on the vision of an improved and better world, by both challenging the rule of power and acting to further a better existence for the weak. This conception runs through all of Levinas's works and is translated into philosophical language (which he calls "Greek") in his more general writing. In his talmudic readings he chose to study and teach the Torah itself, to receive the voice directly from the source or closer to the source (as he translated the passages studied and taught them in French) in order to fulfill this: "The world is here so the ethical order has the possibility of being fulfilled. The act by which the Israelites accept the Torah is the act which gives meaning to reality" (41).

The participants of the colloquia where the talmudic readings were taught — French Jewish intellectuals in the second half of the twentieth century — were mostly well-educated individuals from an assimilated background, most of whom had survived the Holocaust one way or another. Levinas was aware of the sense of alienation and the distance that separated most of them from their cultural origins, of their resistance to and prejudices against the ancient Jewish sources; however, in his view, it was not possible to rejuvenate Judaism in the context of contemporary challenges and problems without studying the Torah. He believed that a *midrash* of the ancient sources was the correct and primary way of renewing Judaism.

This belief emanated in his practice, as he showed how it is possible to give new meaning to passages from the Talmud, to take Judaism out of the dusty books and render it accessible to living people, and to extract from the old books answers or ways of thinking about new questions. "He asked whether Judaism has become a mere abstraction, so greatly does reality clash with the mythical model of the books.... Judaism will come out of the books which contain it and come out of the narrow circles which practice it" (*NT* 44–45). This is the vision Levinas wished to realize by teaching Torah to many who were not part of the narrow circles of Torah scholars, and by contending with their objections in his lessons, which attained great popularity. Similarly, the pluralistic *batei midrash* in Israel were founded by people who felt alienated from the origins of their culture and who seek the meaning of their Jewish identity. They too have chosen to study the Talmud and other sources in the hope and belief of finding a reply to their questions within the ancient texts and despite the many obstacles posed by studying these texts.

THE HOLINESS OF THE TORAH

The relationship between study and exegesis and the interpreted text is the focus of the talmudic lesson "Contempt for the Torah as Idolatry" (*ITN* 55–75):

> But I wish to speak of the Torah as desirous of being a force warding off idolatry by its essence as Book, that is, by its very writing, signifying precisely prescription, and by the permanent reading it calls for—permanent reading or interpretation and reinterpretation or study.... A book that is also by that very fact foreign to any blind commitment.... To base one's Jewishness on the teaching of a book is to see oneself above all as a reader, i.e., a student of the Torah, and to turn away from idolatry by true reading or study. The reading or study of a text that protects itself from eventual idolatry of this very text, by renewing, through continual exegesis—and exegesis of that exegesis—the immutable letters and hearing the breath of the living God in them. (58–59)

In the previous chapter, I discussed how the active role of the commentator in generating the meaning of the Torah constitutes participation in its revelation and involves a connection with its inspiration. Here another meaning of exegesis is stressed. It has to do with the distinction between two types of holiness, which Levinas characterizes by two similar French words to which he assigns different meanings. The word *sacrée* ("sacred") designates the quality of an object that is not dependent on any action, while *saint* ("holy") designates something whose holiness results from a human action. Levinas is extremely suspicious of anything that is sacred or which purports to be sacred, for in his opinion holiness is not a given quality and does not exist in and of itself. Man sanctifies, and this state of sanctification is subject to a certain relationship between one person and another. Objects or land cannot be considered holy if people are wronged in their name or as a result of this holiness. Thus, even the Torah is not itself a holy object; rather, it is or becomes sanctified through its interpretation and teaching to embodied people within the reality of their lives. Commentators sanctify the Torah and defend it from being treated as idolatry or empty liturgy. This is accomplished when the study and interpretation do not justify mistreatment of a person or group of people. The Torah becomes holy if its teaching is realized in acts of goodness that occur in real life.[2]

Levinas expounds on the concept of idolatry. He does not deny the plain meaning of the concept, but this meaning has little interest for him because the idolatry the biblical text objects to does not exist in his (or our) world. It is not what he is confronting; rather, he seeks a personally current and relevant meaning for the concept. This relevant meaning is intended to defend the Torah itself from idolatry, namely, from an attitude of alienated holiness that sanctifies the Torah as an inanimate object, as an essence closed in on itself. Exegesis makes it possible to hear the "breath of the living God" in the Torah by linking learners to the Torah in a way that is meaningful for them, thus revealing its living and regenerative essence. The study of Torah, which constantly renews the meaning of the letters as Levinas does here with the concept of idolatry, is the Torah's defense against its idolatry.

Why is it necessary to engage in constant interpretation? Why can the lesson not be understood once and for all and followed by appropriate action? Why is interpretation such an important part of how Levinas defines himself as a Jew? The holiness of the Torah as an inanimate object implies the danger that its message will be merely an intellectual matter, interesting, maybe even sacred, but with no practical implications. This is a constant risk. Study as an intellectual pleasure, as the acquisition of knowledge that increases power yet with no personal involvement or obligation to the text, is the most popular way of learning in our world. But being a student of the Torah means being personally involved in learning, being obligated to that which is learned, to ethics. Students of the Torah are required to implement their learning in practice. This demands an ongoing effort, a readiness to obey the commanding voice of the text. Because it is not a natural state but, rather, a reply to a summons that must be constantly renewed or else it becomes worn out and lost—this process is never exhausted. The meaning of the text for me, what I must learn from it, is not necessarily what you must learn from it, and what I must learn from it today is not necessarily what will be important for me to learn tomorrow. Thus, the study of Torah is a way of life rather than a body of knowledge. For this reason, all people and not only select individuals, are invited and even required to study the Torah.

Later in the same talmudic lesson Levinas says:

> But contempt for "the word of the Lord"—contempt for the Torah, the doubting of its heavenly origin—takes on a new meaning with the insistence on the extreme rigor by which another *baraita* affirms the transcendental origin of the scroll: Another *baraita*: "For having scorned the word of the Lord"—this refers to one who says: "The Torah is not from heaven." And even if he says: "The whole Torah is from heaven except this verse"...He has "scorned the word of the Lord" (Sanhedrin 99a). Obviously we may read here, on the first level, an absolute negation of all human intervention in the writing of the Torah, and hence a condemnation in advance of all critical exploration of the biblical text on grounds of idolatry. To the point of calling it a betrayal of Judaism to attribute to the human intellect the logical articulation of the teaching contained in the text, beyond the literal meaning! But are we not, in reading the text in this way, being too impatient? Everything depends on how we understand the unity of a spiritual work, and the spiritual unity of a people who are bearers of such a work, even if the human may have to intervene in the very formulation of the word of God. Is the human not the very modality of the manifestation and resonance of the Word? Is not humanity, in its multipersonal plurality, the very locus of interrogation, in which prophetic essence of the Revelation becomes a lived experience? "To be the Torah from heaven": is this its origin going back to a kind of transcendental dictation, or the affirmation of this life in the Torah? (*NT* 64–65)

Levinas understands the plain meaning of the text perfectly well. This meaning, however, is not compatible with his understanding of the text and the correct attitude toward it. It contradicts his premises. As he sees it, the holiness of the Torah and of the Talmud stems not from their origins or from the strict prohibition against human interference in their content. On the contrary, the Torah requires human intervention, intervention by commentators who mediate between the Torah and human reality, or else it remains a dead letter, an obscure text, alienated and remote from anything grasped by its readers. The verses call out: "Interpret me," and for this reason the conversation—the relationship between the text and the commentator's exegesis—is vital for the very existence and holiness of the text. The commentator does not ignore those parts of the passage that are not convenient and that appear to contradict one's premises, as in our example; rather, the commentator applies hermeneutical creativity. Here Levinas interprets the holiness of the text not as a transcendent dictation but as a process of study that becomes a life experience, an applied study.

Respect for the text and readiness to hear its voice and statements are basic premises, but they do not imply a demand to attribute excessive significance to the text. When that which is written contradicts what the *darshan* believes and perceives to be the objective of the text or part of its essence—the "spirit of the words" and the traces of infinity within it—the *darshan* expounds on it in order to uncover a meaning that is compatible with his or her views. This is how the *midrash* approaches the Torah, and this is how Levinas approaches the Talmud, the *midrash* that he interprets.[3]

I shall offer one example among many that illustrates such an approach to a text, which is from the *beit midrash* of "Nigun Nashim" at Hamidrasha. Women read the Torah and grapple with the plain meaning of major texts; they do not reject the holiness of the Torah; rather, they interpret it in a new spirit. In this way, Rivka Lubitch writes:

> Dina was like a mute, as it says: "Now Dina...went out to see" (Genesis 34:1). She went out to see, and not to hear. It also says: "He...lay with her and defiled her" (Gen. 34:2). And it does not say: "And Dina shouted." Can you possibly imagine that Dina did not shout? Nay, but she became like a mute, as her pain and her shame caused her to become silent and keep quiet...and Tanot would sit by the divine presence and cry for the most wretched daughters of Israel, and she said thus: Dina was very quiet and had

> no voice. Why was this? Because the people in her household did not listen to her and rarely spoke to her, as it is said: Do not prolong your discourse with women. This is why she went to see the daughters of the land.[4]

The writer is protesting the text's silence concerning Dina's feelings and the centuries-old tradition of silencing women, and she does this by filling in gaps in the text, a classic midrashic technique. Rabbinic *midrashim* hold the victim accountable for her rape, blaming Dina for leaving her home, which is an accusation still common in present times toward victims of rape. The writer is unwilling to relinquish the holiness of the text, but she also refuses to recognize Dina's venturing out as a guilty deed. Furthermore, she lends meaning to Dina's silence and says that, similar to many victims of rape, Dina also became mute as a result of her pain and shame and because she was taught to keep quiet. This approach resembles how the *midrash* treats the text and how Levinas treats the Talmud, insisting as they do on holding a discussion with the text even when it is vexing or when it contradicts the deep and true meaning of the text as perceived by the commentator or the *darshanit*. The exegesis bridges this gap.

THE MIDRASHIC METHODS EMPLOYED BY LEVINAS

Similar to all homiletical interpretations, Levinas's talmudic readings add new meanings to the plain reading of the text, meanings that are relevant for the *darshan* and for his or her audience. The point of departure of these lessons is always a passage from the Babylonian Talmud, which Levinas interprets consistently and methodically. It is usually possible to see how his interpretation distances the passage or parts of it from their plain meaning and gives them other, different meanings. A review of one of these talmudic readings shall provide a basis for exploring midrashic techniques and methods used by both the sages and Levinas.

The very choice of the talmudic passage on the Nazirate as a means of discussing "The Youth of Israel" (*NT* 120–35) illustrates the hermeneutical course of study. Levinas extracts the concept of the Nazirate from its plain meaning and gives it a new meaning in its new context. The colloquium at which the lesson was taught in 1970 was held about two years after the Student Revolt in France, and it aimed to discuss issues concerning contemporary Jewish teens. Levinas also chose to interpret the theme of the colloquium and extract it from its plain meaning. For this purpose, he referred to the term "youth" in its meaning as "adolescence" rather than "young people" (in French as in English the word *jeunesse* carries both meanings). In other words, he interprets it in relation to the relevance of Judaism for dealing with twentieth century issues that occupy the Western world. For this purpose he chose a passage from the Tractate Nazir (61a–b) and began by saying:

> The text which has been distributed to you has, on the surface of it, no connection to youth. More serious still is the little connection that the various parts seem to have to each other. But their most suggestive teaching may lie in the underlying unity which they invite one to discover. That was one of my reasons for choosing it.... Let us accept the givens of the text.... Let us suppose that the text is sincere, and let us ask what it wants to say. Let us suppose that there is thought in the terms it makes use of and, consequently, that its words and representations can be transposed into another language and into other concepts. It is in this transposition that interpretation probably occurs. It would be impossible without a prior presentation of things, according to the very words of the text. (*NT* 121–22)

Since the selected passage has no obvious connection to the topic under discussion (youth) nor does there seem to be any connection between its various parts, the interpretive effort shall be devoted to uncovering these connections; in this way its meaning shall be understood. This act of translation endeavors to interpret obscure symbols and translate them into contents and meanings that are relevant for the commentator. Then again, a necessary condition for such a process involves maintaining respect for the text, assuming its sincerity, and accepting its language and givens as meaningful. This text, like any oral or written text, is an expression, a said (*dit*), that contains traces of the infinite, of a saying (*dire*), obligation, or demand. The interpretive effort is intended, among other things, to hear the resonance of the saying within the said, saying, "Here I am" in response to its demand (*OB* 149–52). Therefore, the presumption is that there is nothing superfluous in the text, nothing irrelevant or obsolete. These are the premises of Levinas's exegesis, which has no interest in stating, for example, that a certain part of the text is a later addition or a scribal error. He refers to the text as it is, in an effort to not only understand it and hear in it an echo or traces of the infinite but also to translate it into philosophical language and to find within it new meanings that hold significance for his world and ideas.

The meaning of the Nazirate as portrayed in the Torah, the Mishna, and the Talmud, is unclear. They offer no discussion of questions such as the following: How is one affected by being a Nazirite? Why would someone choose to be a Nazirite? What does this achieve? What is the meaning or intention of being a Nazirite? The biblical text deals mainly with the Nazirite in Jewish law. According to Numbers 6:1–21, the Nazirite must not cut his hair, eat any product of the grapevine, or become ritually impure by contact with the dead. Typically of him, Levinas attributes an ethical meaning to the Nazirate, and he does so in reference to the laws of the Nazirite, which I discuss below.

On his attitude to the interpreted text he adds:

> I am now coming to the Gemara, where one would expect a commentary of the Mishna but where, to all appearances, something else is at issue. In fact, the entire Gemara of this last Mishna of the tractate *Nazir* seems to be made up of selected passages.... Would the Gemara be purely decorative here, ending a tractate of Halakha with a few aggadic words to leave us pensive or to inspire us with pious thoughts? *Such a way of reading should not be excluded, but it is not forbidden to be more demanding.* (*NT* 130–31; my emphasis)[5]

The reference here is to the simple meaning. Tractates of the Talmud usually end with an *aggadah* and the Tractate Nazir follows this format, so perhaps it is not necessary to seek any further meaning of this final passage. But Levinas insists on finding meaning in the redaction and in the association of this gemara with its mishna. This is the hermeneutical effort that values the text in its present form. He continues:

> Let us ask ourselves what themes are broached in our Gemara. They are two: The first, concerning the merit one acquires by saying grace—grace over wine, in our example—is compared to the merit of answering *Amen* when hearing the blessing. Which is greater? Just think how important this is!...As to the second theme evoked by the Gemara, it seems to be a pious thought and nothing more: the sages of the Talmud claim to make peace reign in the world.... Two problems arise: a) What does this Gemara mean? b) What is the intrinsic connection between the Gemara and our Mishna? There is even a third problem: the link between all this and youth. (131)

The subtle irony enhances the difficulties posed by the design of this passage. Any other approach to the text would have yielded, bringing claims of tendentious redaction, obsolete historical exigencies, and the like. Levinas does not forsake his loyalty to the text, the meaningful relationship between the text and his interpretation.

On the significance of saying grace and the hierarchy between the person saying grace and the person who answers "Amen," Levinas expounds:

> Saying grace would be an act of the greatest importance. To be able to eat and drink is a possibility as extraordinary, as miraculous, as the crossing of the Red Sea.... Nothing is as difficult as being able to feed oneself! So that the verse "You will eat and be full and you will bless" (Deut. 8:10) is not pious verbiage but a recognition of a daily miracle and of the gratitude it must produce in our souls.... The problem of a hungry world can be resolved only if the food of the owners of those who are provided for ceases to appear to them as their inalienable property, but is recognized as a gift they have received for which thanks must be given and to which others have a right. Scarcity is a social and moral problem and not exclusively an economic one. That is what our text reminds us of, through old wives' tales. And now we can understand that this internal and pacific war is to be waged not only by me, who in saying gives us possession, but also by those who answer *Amen*. A community must follow the individuals who take the initiative of renouncing their rights so that the hungry can eat. (*NT* 132–33)

According to Levinas, saying grace is not merely a religious act that is directed at God; rather, it is an act that has implications for human beings. Its purpose is to arouse the eaters' consciences and urge them to act. Saying grace is an acknowledgment of abundance and a reminder that this abundance is not the exclusive property of the person who attained it. Those individuals who say grace show the way to those who answer "Amen." Every person has a vital role in the rectification and redistribution of abundance. The blessing for the wine is directed not only at the source of abundance from whence the wine originated but also primarily at the person who says the blessing and those who hear him. Further, it is intended to create awareness or arousal toward assuming responsibility for the hungry and feeding them.

The end of the section refers to the surprising image portrayed in the gemara, comparing those who say grace over the wine and those who answer "Amen" to auxiliary forces who provide support to military heroes in times of war. How is war connected to the blessing for wine? This is the internal war against one's sense of ownership over food and drink. And since the Nazirate was also interpreted in terms of responsibility for the other person, the relationship between the mishna on the Nazirite and the gemara becomes clearer: "The linking apparently with so little basis, of our Gemara and our Mishna, is not due to some concern for piling up homiletic texts. Nor is it due to the fact that the protagonists of the Mishna are the same as the ones in the cited *baraita*. It teaches us that there must be a nazirate in the world—a source of disinterestedness—so that men can eat.... Here, then, is a good reason for linking the theme of the nazirate to the theme of saying grace and the *Amen*" (*NT* 133). The *midrash* formed by Levinas creates a logical link between those parts of the mishna and the gemara that at first glance seem completely unrelated. This meaning emerges as a result of his insistence on remaining loyal to the text and its structure, although interpreting it with an understanding that is far from its plain meaning. The Nazirate is a foreign concept to twentieth century readers in the Western world; it has almost no relevance for their reality. This homiletical interpretation gives the words a meaning that refers to current issues: the hunger of the lower class in plentiful Western society and hunger in the Third World or in developing countries. Linking seemingly unrelated but adjoining episodes, such as the Nazirite and the grace over wine in this case, is a classic midrashic procedure called *smichut parshiyot* (adjacent sections). This is a *midrash* that lends meaning to the proximity of two seemingly unrelated matters in the text.

Using the passage on the Nazirate as a basis for discussing the youth of Israel seems to have humorous undertones and, as Levinas himself said, an associative perspective. The link between these two topics is the long hair: at the time, long hair grown by young men and the loose hair of young women were considered a sign of protest against bourgeois conventions. The Nazirite, forbidden to cut his hair throughout the period of the Nazirate, must have grown long hair too. But Levinas does not stop at this and he proceeds to give the laws of the Nazirate current meaning. The emphasis on lucidity and contact with reality (the ban against grapes and their products), the disregard for one's external appearance (the ban against cutting one's hair), and keeping a distance from the dead which might lead to existential despair and relinquishing responsibility (despair might lead to nihilism, a danger of which Levinas frequently warns)— all of these are circumstances that encourage one to leave one's natural selfishness, the concern for sustaining one's existence and personal needs, and turn toward the other and the other's needs. The Nazirite seeks an open commitment to the other, with no personal stake.

Now, after this extensive review, the Nazirate appears more relevant to our world. The interpretation applied to the gemara refers to ethical problems that occupied people in the Western world of the 1970s — global poverty and hunger despite rampant affluence and prosperity. The Nazirite is a person who is committed to the Other, and in this he resembles one who says grace over wine. By now it is evident that Levinas is not speaking of the young people of Israel (with their long or short hair) but of the youth of Israel, of the relevance of those messages imparted by the Torah of Israel for his contemporaries and for ours.[6] Through the *midrash* we are called upon to deal with a problem in our own world, to open up to the other and the other's needs. This *midrash* acts upon its learners (us) as the customs of the Nazirate act upon the Nazirite, or as grace acts upon the person who recites it and upon the one who answers "Amen" — it awakens and arouses us to take responsibility and summons us to become involved.

This lesson also employs another one of the midrashic techniques devised by the sages: learning from one matter about another seemingly unrelated matter, based on the rule that the Torah does not follow any chronological order. This allows us to compare between prohibitions that apply to the Nazirite and those that apply to the priests when serving in the Temple, a comparison that produces another insight on the Nazirate. The next part of the talmudic lesson deals with a story taken from another part of the Tractate Nazir (4b), while the main passage taught in this lesson appears at the end of the tractate.

Other examples of applying the hermeneutical principle whereby the Torah, or in this case the Talmud, does not follow any chronological order can be found in the lesson "Cities of Refuge," where the seemingly questionable decision to discuss Jerusalem in the context of the cities of refuge makes it possible to understand the meaning of Jerusalem's holiness. Similarly, the lesson "Toward the Other" links a passage in the Tractate Yevamot and a passage in the Tractate Yoma (seemingly unrelated) in order to facilitate a complex discussion of the Jewish attitude to the Germans after the Holocaust.[7] The structure of this lesson strongly resembles the classic structure of the rabbinic *petihta* (a homiletic introduction). As in the *petihta,* its point of origin is remote and seemingly unrelated to the topic under discussion, thus generating interest among the audience. The lesson gradually leads to the main topic, and on the way it gathers insights that may not have arisen otherwise. In this case the theme of the colloquium was the attitude of French Jews to the Germans in the 1960s. The lesson opens with an interpretation of a passage on asking forgiveness and the Day of Atonement, and only further on does it reach a discussion of the main topic. The discussion on asking forgiveness is supplemented by the much more pointed teachings triggered by the passage in Tractate Yevamot, which inquires about the right to take revenge, about judgment, and about the compassion that keeps the world going despite the application of judgment.

Hence, midrashic methods are an important means used by Levinas in producing his interpretations. And what might seem an arbitrary process is easier to understand when one becomes aware that these are customary techniques based on strong and common premises, although in this case they are applied to the Talmud rather than the biblical text. Levinas truly did produce a *midrash* on the Talmud.

A Language of Symbols and Examples versus a Language of Concepts

One of the Talmud's typical strategies involves discussions held on all levels of reality, from the most concrete practical level to metaphysics and philosophical questions. Even when the Talmud refers to abstract and metaphysical issues, however, it does so through concrete symbols and examples. Levinas writes: "The Talmudic life and destiny of the Torah, which is also an endless return, in its interpretation of several degrees, to particular cases, to the concreteness of reality, to analyses that never lose themselves in generalities but return to the examples—resisting invariable conceptual entities. An analysis whose free discussion is ever current" (*ITN* 58).[8]

The association with the real world is direct, sometimes appearing trivial or even petty. It is necessary to recognize the exact proportion, precise boundary, or specific moment constituting the point of transition from one halakhic instance to another. Questions of essence, principle, and metaphysics are almost always discussed in the context of a concrete reality, of tangible objects, of operations that must be performed, or of questions with practical implications (for example, who is not entitled to a part in the world to come). In this the language of the Talmud is fundamentally unlike philosophical language with its focus on concepts. The concept is a generalization of many details to form a theoretical principle. It is an abstraction, a stripping of the symbol and of the figurative to reach the abstract; it is an abstraction of its objects from their concreteness and from their individuality.

Insisting on maintaining an association with the concrete world reflects a certain attitude to reality, one in which the individual does not become lost within the collective and does not disappear within the totality of the concept. Any person at any time, in any situation, has distinct meaning, and not merely as part of a historical process or as an incidental example of a general phenomenon. Thus, the hunger of the person standing before me is an immediate demand. Every individual has infinite value, reaching beyond totality, beyond concepts. This attitude to reality and to the details that compose it is typical of the *midrash,* and even the *darshan* mentioned by name does not become lost in the anonymity of redaction within the passage that cites his words. The conceptual soaring to generalizations might lead to blindness and to a lack of responsibility for their practical and moral implications. This is not true of a *midrash* on the Torah, which is a way of thought that insists on remaining loyal to concrete reality and to the shaping of an ethics.

Levinas is critical of conceptual philosophical language that is remote from the concrete world, offering a timeless ideology that generalizes diverse phenomena under one totality and often generates a theory disconnected from reality.[9] As Levinas sees it, the proper starting point of philosophy is not the mind's reflection on itself (Descartes) or the pure love of wisdom (Aristotle) but, rather, the concrete responsibility of an entirely personal self for another person who are both situated within their circumstances at a given moment. The transition from the concrete situation to the generalization, to abstract thought, follows from the appearance of a third person (*OB* 126–29). When a third person who also has infinite rights appears in a face-to-face encounter, this creates a need to limit the infinite rights of one to make room for the infinite rights of the other. In this way, a generalizing discourse is formed with a demand for justice, for equal rights. For Levinas, theory or abstract thought must follow from reality and refer to it; it must take responsibility for its moral consequences.

His approach to concrete reality may be said to resemble that of the Talmud more than it resembles common philosophical approaches. Even when he uses philosophical language he does not disengage from reality: his theoretical system does not dissolve or "swallow up" diverse phenomena, and people do not become mere anonymous illustrations. The attempt to think about the other, about that which is beyond, about the concrete encounter between two specific people with unique personalities—all this creates a philosophy that unsays its said, that consistently endeavors to leave a space of otherness within its definitions, and these in turn have no pretense of exhausting their subject matter. Similar to talmudic language, which is connected to concrete reality, symbols, the portrayal of uniquely named people, and to real acts—even when dealing with abstract questions—Levinas also tries to produce a philosophy and a language that does not lose sight of the individual as a more or less representative model of the concept of humanity. This is a language in which it is possible to grapple with the philosophical meaning of the hand holding the tool or of the conversation between two people. In his philosophical writing he makes an obvious effort to adapt form to content, to unsay his said, and to create a language that does not hold on to its objects. This language leaves room for doubt, for otherness, and for an other who is unique and does not adapt to a consistent, tight, systematic theoretical structure. Talmudic language easily fits such a manner of thinking. As a rule, the Talmud does not hold onto its objects of study and does not define them; rather, it remains loyal to concrete reality. In this respect, Levinas's choice of writing his talmudic commentary in a midrashic style is almost prescribed. This language is well suited to its contents, to the conceptual deconstruction also demanded of his philosophical writing. Of course, there are certain reservations. The benefits of philosophical language, as Levinas himself attests, are its universalism, its clarity, and its ability to explain and introduce order and rationalism in disorganized thoughts and ideas. Nonetheless, something about the unsaid, incohesive nature of talmudic language seems well suited to the content of Levinas's thought.

In his commentary, Levinas endeavors to explore the meaning or the world of contents borne by examples or symbols that appear in the Talmud. He does not exempt himself from this effort even when the situations or symbols seem completely foreign to modern sensibilities, such as punishing by whipping, ritual impurity by contact with the dead, impurity of the hands, as well as cities of refuge from blood avengers. In all of these, Levinas tries to find meaning that holds relevance for modern society, based on the assumption that the talmudic discussion deals with issues that have meaning for human life in all times. It is merely necessary to properly translate the old world of symbols to one familiar to the commentator.[10]

This approach forms a link between three dimensions: the reality to which the Talmud refers as a platform for its discussion; the concepts that arise from the discussion of this reality; and the world of the *darshan,* which differs from the often foreign talmudic world. The transition from the talmudic reality to the generalization, the concept, makes room for the metaphysical, philosophical discussion, and in this way becomes meaningful and important for the commentator as well. But aside from this, it establishes an attitude to contemporary reality, which does not cease to exist in the conceptual world. It remains present in its concrete form. Thus, a meaningful relationship is formed between the Talmud and the commentator's reality, and these illuminate each other, reflect each other, and facilitate new comprehensions of the text and of reality. The language of concepts, the rational, generalizing discussion, is at times the mediating element that facilitates this meaningful association.

This approach to the Talmud differs from the customary scientific approach to research of the Talmud, the philological approach. According to Levinas, as he states repeatedly, the Talmud's most important value is not as historical documentation, although many historical facts can be gleaned from it. Using the Talmud only for the purpose of comparing versions and learning about historical circumstances misses its essence and might even be misleading; it diverts one's attention from the main point—the capacity to learn from the Talmud teachings that are entirely relevant for modern life. Levinas wrote:

> The commentary on our excerpt from the Gemara raises many problems of erudition. We could inquire into the contingent circumstances to which it refers, the ways and customs of the past, the historical data it evinces. I shall avoid such questions as much as possible. A page from the Talmud, although it can be read as a document from a certain period reflecting a set of historical circumstances, is above all (even in the state of affairs and fact it sets forth) the expression of a teaching of Jewish culture and wisdom. Even if, for example, the account of the history of the translation of the Pentateuch into Greek in the second century B.C.E.—given in the central portion of the piece on which I am commenting—were but a legend...the miraculous history of this "guidebook blurb" is, in the Talmud, an apologue or, if you will, a *Midrash*. The very fact of its having been collected in the Gemara, the fact that the "redactors" of the Talmud considered it worthy of remembrance and transmission, and the concise form in which it is presented indicate that beyond its anecdotal value it contains a truth independent of its historical reality and is a teaching. It is this truth that interests us. Background knowledge and historical criticism are not, in my view, devalued thereby, and I shall have recourse to them on one point, as I conclude. But it is impossible to say everything everywhere at all times, and one must not miss seeing the forest for the trees, however interesting their genealogy may be! (*BV* 38)[11]

The historical aspect of the text is only one aspect, and in Levinas's opinion it is not the most important. He wishes to learn from the text that which it was designed to teach, the reason why the redactors of the Talmud see it as a matter worthy of remembering and transmitting to the next generations, assuming that this was their goal. Sometimes he says this outright: "Let us remind our listeners in all this we are not dealing with a problem of history. Were the Canaanites actually so mean? This is the hypothesis or the initial given within which we must place ourselves. Without it, everything we have just said is perfectly meaningless" (*NT* 68; cf. 72; *NTR* 83–84).

Even if the text contradicts recognized historical facts, its assumptions must still be accepted and treated on its own terms in order to reveal its meaning. In particular, not only is history not the focus of the exegesis, but sometimes it must be disregarded in order to generate that which should be learned from the text: "Scriptures are not history books: they are the *model* of the thinkable, opening onto the depths of *Midrash*. The scriptures confer a meaning upon events: they do not ask for a meaning from them" (*ITN* 19).[12] This is a fundamental distinction: unlike the study of history, which is an attempt to understand the meaning of events and facts, events related in the Scriptures, whether factual or fictitious, are a means of teaching content, and in this respect the Scriptures lend meaning to the events. Hence, this exegesis neither purports to seek the meaning of the text in its original context nor its precise plain meaning. The focus of the interpretation is the text's teaching for the *darshan*, in his or her own context and circumstances.

It seems to me that Levinas repeatedly clarified and stressed this principle, particularly in light of the common approach to the Talmud in university departments. He saw himself as part of the academic world, where he taught for many years, but he was fundamentally opposed to the customary methods of study, methods that explore the Talmud as an object of scientific research.[13] Can scientific value be attributed to his hermeneutical method? Can focusing on the contents of a text and its interpretation be considered science? Perhaps this approach blurs the boundaries of different disciplines—literature, hermeneutics, and Talmud. I tend to think that when discussing Levinas's exegesis these are not the most important questions. I wonder whether and to what degree they occupied him. They seem to have mainly occupied his critics.[14]

The interpretive method employed by Levinas is also essentially different from what is customary at most yeshivas, which is known as the "Brisker method" and was initiated by R. Chaim Soloveitchik. This positivist method uses analytical tools. Its two basic premises are that the Talmud is first and foremost a halakhic text and the significance of its aggadic parts is secondary; and second that halakhic thought, similar to mathematics, has rules of its own, which once understood, reveal the one real meaning of halakhic discussions.[15] Levinas rejected both of these premises. In his opinion the essence of the Talmud is its organic integration of *halakha* and *aggadah* and therefore, when interpreting a passage, he emphasizes all its components, both halakhic and aggadic (see *NT* 194–95). He admitted to mostly dealing with *aggadah,* although he did not refrain from interpreting halakhic discussions. He also completely rejected the presumption that the text has a single correct meaning, which can and should be revealed, and contends that the Talmud is intended for all people in all times. On the contrary, the force of the Talmud is in the multiple interpretations that it invites.[16]

In this matter, there is a similarity and affinity between the interpretive method employed by Levinas, reflecting the rabbinic approach to the text interpreted, and the approach of the pluralistic *batei midrash* to the texts taught therein. The learning at these *batei midrash* always begins with a text presented to the learners. They do not occupy themselves with the history of the text or the historical circumstances that led to its composition and do not assume that it has only one truth. Learners are invited to delve into the text in order to learn from it something that is relevant for their own world. Their attitude to the text is not that of scholars but, rather, of students listening to the teaching voice of the text, each according to his or her ability and comprehension. This is also the reason for the interpretive effort to avoid dismissing any part of the text as unrelated or irrelevant.

By referring to symbols and examples within the texts he interprets, Levinas not only expresses his attitude to the Scriptures as texts whose holiness stems from their complete relevance for every person, and for modern people in particular, but he also expresses a certain attitude to time:

> Faced with the "historical meaning" which dominates modernity, the meaning of becoming which, for the Westerner, certainly carries the real to its conclusion, but a conclusion which is unceasingly deferred in the false Messianisms of modern times...faced with the "historical meaning" which thus calls into question, relativizes and devalues every moment or which, foreseeing a supra-temporal eternity of ideal, yet, in reality, incomparable relations, is capable of a mathematically perfect science in a badly made or un-made world;[17] faced with all this historicism, does not Israel attach itself to an "always"—in other words, to a permanence in time, to a time held by moments of holiness by the way in which they have a meaning or are "so close to the goal"—and where not one of these moments is lost, or to be lost, but they are all to be deepened, that is to say, sublimated?...do not this predilection and this signification of the always call for whole structuring

of concrete human reality and a whole orientation of social and intellectual life—perhaps justice itself—which would render only such a signification possible and significant?

But before entering into such a serious debate, I still owe an explanation to the critical minds present in this room, who might precisely be surprised that such serious and topical problems are being treated in the context of bread and tables (the fantasies of rabbis), which have long since disappeared![18]

I would like, in fact, to recall what, according to Rabbinic tradition, the significance is, notably of the ritual of the Shewbread and the table on which it remains exposed.... The crown of the table is thus the royal crown. The king is he who keeps open house, he who feeds men. The table on which the bread is exposed before the Lord symbolizes the permanent thought that political power—that is to say, the king, that is David, that is his descendant, that is the Messiah—is vowed to men's hunger.... Not to the end of times, to the hunger of hungry men;[19] kingship in Israel is always Joseph feeding the people.[20] To think of men's hunger is the first function of politics. (*BV* 17–18)

The given moment, any moment, is important in and of itself; it is an opportunity for holiness, that is, for immediate ethical attention. It is not a point of transition on the way to eternity, to the Messiah. It is a distinct moment, a moment in which it is possible to feed a hungry person. The historical perspective loses its significance when one turns to see the hunger of the individual in the here and now. Levinas recognizes the role of the Torah and of the Scriptures as responsible for directing our view at the person whom we encounter; therefore, he does not deal with the scientific aspects of the text but with the human, ethical aspects.

Time is a major theme in the philosophy of Levinas.[21] He approaches it from many different angles, including identity, language, death, and epistemology. But the basis of his approach on this topic is that time is not a separate entity but is, rather, always "time for"—time for encountering another person, time for talking, time for giving birth. The past is the time from which the ethical demand is derived, a time that cannot be re-created because it precedes all memory (*HO* 49–52). The future is the self who sacrifices herself for the other by giving birth and by devotion to a child (who is in a certain respect myself, but also completely other), and it is eschatology, the future of peace that is beyond all war (*TI* 22–23). Time does not underlie one's identity and entity; it is the potential and the obligation to act in the world, to influence and improve it. This is also the basis of Levinas's reserved attitude to history, as seen above: it is not history that constitutes a standard for judging man; on the contrary, it is man who is called upon to judge history and to affect its course. A person who feeds the hungry individual that he or she encounters is one who shapes reality, and thus, resists the predetermined course of history.

Does this concept of time have anything to do with Levinas's rejection of the talmudic method of study as a reconstruction of the past? Since in his view history does not have much significance for its own sake, as there is no way to operate within past history, there is also no reason to treat it as an object of interpretation. Talmudic interpretation is intended to invite people to learn about themselves and about the world here and now; it strives to voice the ethical demand of caring for the other person. All this occurs in the present and future, not in the past.

The Context of the Verses

Another aspect of reference to the text is the assumption, which is consistently applied by Levinas in his interpretations, that every verse cited in the talmudic passage brings its original biblical context with it to the discussion, thus adding another level of meaning to its new context, even if at first glance the connection seems merely technical.[22] Hence, it is necessary to return to the original context of the verses and try to understand what meaning they add to the matter under discussion.

> While the sages of the Talmud seem to be doing battle with each other by means of biblical verses, and to be splitting hairs, they are far from such scholastic exercises. The reference to a biblical verse does not aim at appealing to authority—as some thinkers drawn to rapid conclusions might imagine. Rather, the aim is to refer to a context which allows the level of the discussion to be raised and to make one notice the true import of the data from which the discussion derives its meaning. The transfer of an idea to another climate—which is its original climate—wrests new possibilities from it. (*NT* 21)

Exploring the context of the verse adds an entirely new level of meaning to the discussion. This principle is often illustrated in Levinas's talmudic readings. Such links sometimes require considerable creativity. For example, in the lesson on Tractate Sanhedrin 36b–37a, "As Old as the World?" (*NT*

70–88), the structure of the Sanhedrin is learned by expounding a verse from the Song of Songs. Levinas says:

> Chapter 7, 3 of the Song of Songs would then be proclaiming the Sanhedrin.... Perhaps justice is founded on the mastery of passion. The justice through which the world subsists is founded on the most equivocal order, but on the domination exerted at every moment over this order, or this disorder. This order, equivocal *par excellence,* is precisely the order of the erotic, the realm of the sexual.... The danger preying upon justice is not the temptation of injustice.... The danger which lurks it is vice. (76)

Levinas is trying to understand the association between the structure of the Sanhedrin, a legal body responsible for justice, and the verses from the Song of Songs, an erotic book of love. Aside from the midrashic technique, which he explains, he uses the midrashic link between the verse from the Song of Songs and the structure of the Sanhedrin in order to say something about the essence of justice. The choice of verse from which a *midrash* is generated, in a completely different context, is no technical or incidental matter. Levinas is entirely consistent in implementing this interpretive principle, even when the verse cited and its *midrash* lack any visible association or connection. It is also used to interpret the appearance and meaning of verses mentioned in the Talmud with no *midrash* or interpretation.

Levinas appears to utilize this principle in his choice of passages for interpretation as well. Sometimes there is no apparent association between the passages and the topic to be discussed—that of the colloquium at which his lesson was taught. The link between the passage and the topic adds meaning to the discussion, particularly when this link seems puzzling or enigmatic. Nonetheless, Levinas almost always dissociates the selected passage from its context in the talmudic tractate. The circumstances—the theme of the colloquium, the type of audience, the time allocated—may have ruled out a more extensive exploration of the passage's context in the original tractate. Unlike quoted verses, whose context might be the chapter in which they appear or even the entire book, as in the example from the Song of Songs, Levinas does not go beyond the limits of the passage interpreted or discuss its context and place in the tractate. Sometimes he comments on this explicitly: "To excerpt from a Talmudic treatise a passage that lends itself to a study on the problems addressed in these meetings or colloquia is a hazardous enterprise. The very idea of excerpting from the Talmud is a difficult one. The limits of the excerpt always remain uncertain. It is uncertain whether the different sequences of each treatise, apparently connected to one another in many cases by the accidents of compilation, may not have a deeper coherence not visible at first" (*ITN* 93; cf. *NTR* 50).

Interpreting the Whole Passage

Many of the passages in the Babylonian Talmud seem, at first glance, an incidental collection of unrelated segments. The current assumption in research, however, is that this is a redacted text and that the compilation is meaningful, at least with regard to the single passage.[23] This assumption proves most helpful when studying talmudic passages. Exploring issues of redaction, context, and sequence often provides additional levels of comprehension and meaning.

Levinas anticipated or foresaw most of this research. He accepts the presumption of meaningful redaction, and in his interpretations he remains loyal to the current sequence of the interpreted text. We saw this in the lesson "The Youth of Israel": "I will comment on the text I have chosen from the beginning to the end and not only the least difficult passages, which can give rise to moments of brilliance" (*NT* 72).[24] In many cases the textual sequence does not cause any comprehension problems. But in others, when the passage appears to be a fairly incidental collection of unrelated segments, adhering to the given sequence of the text allows one to discover meanings that may not have otherwise come to light. Levinas's interpretation stresses his insistence on revealing the organizing principle, the hidden logic underlying the structure of the passage in its current form, and he says so repeatedly, speaking of "the little connection that the various parts seem to have to each other. But their most suggesting teaching may lie in the underlying unity which they invite one to discover" (*NT* 121; cf. *BV* 15; *ITN* 14, 93).

Adhering to the given sequence of the text, connecting its different parts even when they sometimes seem unrelated, and filling in its gaps—all these show respect for the text, its presentation, and a readiness to open up to it. The commentators do not assume a position of supremacy over their text, permitting its critique. On the contrary, they make an effort to understand what at first glance seems incomprehensible. This effort is rewarded by the discovery of additional meanings within the text. As stated, this rule should also be expanded to the context of the passage and to its place in the talmudic treatise; although as we have seen, Levinas did not do so in his talmudic readings, albeit indicating the desired methodological principle.

THE BIBLE AND THE TALMUD

How did Levinas grasp the relationship between the Bible and the Talmud? What characterizes this relationship and how does it affect his exegesis? He writes:

> Clearly, the oral teaching of the Talmud remains inseparable from the Old Testament. It orients its interpretation.... It is the Talmud that allows the Jewish reading of the Bible to be distinguished from the Christian reading or the "scientific" reading of the historians and philologists. Judaism is definitely the Old Testament, but through the Talmud. The spirit guiding this reading, which is said to be naively "literal", perhaps consists, in actual fact, in maintaining each "specific" text in the context of the Whole.... The freedom of exegesis is upheld at this Talmudic school. Tradition, running through history, does not impose its conclusions, but the contact with what it sweeps along. (*BV* 136–37)[25]

Talmud study is a necessary condition for Jewish reading and interpretation of the Bible; this is not in order to dictate the contents of the interpretation but, rather, as a point of reference both for questions that should be raised and for previous discussions of these questions—in order to agree or disagree and to create a new interpretive alternative. Jewish readings[26] of the biblical text are not formed in a void. They are part of an interpretive tradition that began with the Talmud. This is the takeoff point. Starting from this point, from continuous study of the Talmud, an intricate conversation is formed between the biblical text, the Talmud, and the commentator, who does not submit to the talmudic interpretation but, rather, converses with it.[27]

Another characterization is the "context of the Whole," that is, the reference to the text's system of values or general intent. Levinas assumed that the Bible deals with ethics, that its thought is beyond being, a thought that directs my responsibility for the other person. He believed that the Talmud uncovers this dimension of the biblical text. This principle of content joins the methodological principles underlying the biblical interpretation. He did not prove this premise. As stated above, according to his conception this is the content of revelation, the context of the whole.

An essential difference can be discerned between the degree of freedom that Levinas allows when engaged in biblical interpretation and that which he requires when interpreting the Talmud: "I venture to propose an interpretation of this text that is less special. If we must be extremely shy when interpreting biblical texts because the Talmud has already said something about them, audacity is allowed with the Talmudic texts, which immediately address themselves to our intelligence, soliciting interpretation and always saying *Darshenou*" (*DF* 89). The Bible can be interpreted in different ways. Talmudic interpretation guides the commentator to the right context, the spirit of the words, the ethics. Therefore, biblical exegesis requires attention to and study of talmudic and midrashic exegesis. As to the Talmud itself, Levinas thinks that greater interpretive license can be taken, as it is in the right context to begin with:

> But the Talmud, despite its antiquity and precisely because of the continuity of Talmudic study, belongs, as paradoxical as this might seem, to the modern history of Judaism. A dialogue between the two establishes itself directly. Herein, no doubt, lies the originality of Judaism: the existence of a tradition, uninterrupted through the very transmission and commentary of the Talmudic texts, commentaries overlapping commentaries.
>
> The Talmud is not a mere extension of the Bible. It sees itself as a second layer of meaning; critical and fully conscious, it goes back to the meanings of Scripture in a rational spirit. The sages of the Talmud, the Rabbis, are called *Hachamim*. They claim a different authority from that of the prophets, neither inferior nor superior. (*NT* 6–7)

The continuous interpretive tradition has an important role in connecting between the ancient text and the present, as it holds relevance for modern people through its mediation between the text and people along the dimension of time. Throughout the generations, commentators have approached the Talmud and occupied themselves with it, further transmitting tradition. In this way, a continuous bridge was formed between people and the Talmud.

The publications issuing forth from the pluralistic *batei midrash* reflect different attitudes toward the text. This is clearly a topic that occupies learners, and it is reflected in the multiple genres and graphic designs that attempt to give substance to the live conversation between the learners and the text. The question of textual hierarchy is reflected in the design of the pages. For example, the treatise "Exposure and Coverage in Language" by Yariv Ben-Aharon and Eli Alon focuses on the essay of this name by Chaim Nachman Bialik as the interpreted canonic text. They link this text to its origins in the Jewish bookcase and add their own interpretations. The pages are designed to resemble the Mikraot Gedolot edition of the Bible. As they say in the introduction: "The basic discourse between the different sources, and between them and their learners, develops on the page itself,"[28] and they intentionally chose a traditional design. In this way they are making a statement about the canon and about the intergenerational cultural discourse that continue to emerge and are studied in the *beit midrash*.[29]

Conclusion

The talmudic commentary of Emmanuel Levinas is characterized by a strong relationship with the interpreted text. First of all, the text is physically present in the commentary (although translated into French). The reference to the text is multi-dimensional. On a fundamental level, this reference is present through the very engagement in the interpretation of the text and its holiness as a saying. It is also present in the interpretation of most of the text's components—finding meaning in the various symbols within the text, understanding the context of the verses cited with regard to the topic under discussion, and the sequence of the passage. All this widens the meaning given to the text.

Levinas is familiar with the methods of the classic *midrash* and he often uses them among his tools of interpretation, without losing contact with the text. One of the midrashic methods extensively used by Levinas in his writing on other topics is almost completely absent from his talmudic readings—that is, deconstructing words or utilizing double meanings. The reason may very well be that these lessons were created and taught in French, and perhaps he did not feel confident enough of his version to introduce changes. Another reason may be that his commentary is on the Talmud rather than on the biblical text, and not all means used for biblical interpretation are appropriate for interpretation of the Talmud, even when acting on the basic assumption that the Talmud is a holy text. In contrast, Levinas makes much use of midrashic methods involving the structure of the text, its redaction, and its relationship to other passages.

I am not saying that Levinas's talmudic interpretation is a type of *midrash* because it uses midrashic techniques. Nonetheless, this topic joins features that seem to me no less fundamental and express something of the essence of this interpretation. The use of midrashic methods is only one aspect of drawing on tradition, of casting new contents in an old form. And maybe this is also another manifestation of a position toward the text, one that assumes that the text was born of the inspiration of many generations and that it can serve as a way of learning that which heaven desires of human beings. In any case, maintaining close contact with the text, including all its components and aspects, is essential for the content and form of this interpretation. This is a hermeneutical attitude.

Chapter 4

THE RELATIONSHIP BETWEEN EXEGESIS AND REALITY

The first chapter defined the *midrash* as a balanced relationship between commentator and text, one intended to impact reality. *Midrash* and Torah study are not the ultimate goal, their great value notwithstanding. The purpose of study and exegesis is to outline a way of life, to form new understandings with regard to reality. The truth that the *midrash* seeks in the text is always associated with its implementation. The *midrash* asks the text questions that derive from and deal with the commentator's reality. It is not a purely intellectual pastime. Indeed: "R. Tarfon and the Elders were once reclining in the upper story of Nithza's house in Lydda, when this question was raised before them: Is study greater or practice? R. Tarfon answered, saying: Practice is greater. R. Akiva answered, saying: Study is greater. They all answered and said: Study is greater, for it leads to practice."[1]

Study is meant to influence students' actions and their world, including that which is extrinsic to learning. The large number of sources occupied with the affiliation between study and practice clearly show that this was and still is a troubling issue. Different views exist on this matter; however, the responses provided in most of the sources indicate, as does the segment cited above, that the significance of study derives from its ability to affect practice. Normally, an essential dialectical relationship is maintained between study and its realization in practice. A majority of the sages, however, contend that "study is greater" because, or provided that, it "leads to practice."

The *midrash,* with its occasional dissociation from the plain meaning of the text, has an intention and purpose that are associated with life. The *midrash* is a "partisan" exegesis. Levinas writes of the relationship between Torah study and reality: "The text which follows indicates, in its fashion, the true way to study the Torah. A study which is not limited to the acquiring of knowledge. According to the Jewish tradition—and without being confused with another mystical practice—this study is the highest level of life where knowledge is no longer distinguished from imperatives and practical impulses, where science and conscience meet, where reality and justice no longer belong to two distinct orders" (*BV* 47).

Both the *midrash* and Levinas's commentaries on the Talmud assume a constitutive relationship between the text and reality. The talmudic readings make perfectly clear that no study can be undertaken only for its own sake. The readings' point of departure, that is, the themes of the colloquia at which they were taught, are realistic questions that address the text. Learning the passages, however, also leads to conclusions pertaining to reality, although these were not self-evident at the outset. I have chosen to focus this discussion on two main issues: how questions that address the text are derived from the current circumstances of the commentator and the implicit idea within each of the lessons. The latter is usually a current issue, one occupying the *darshan* Levinas and his contemporaries and a matter arising from the study, even if not intentionally so. Other aspects of the association with reality in this exegesis shall be discussed in chapter 6 on the uniqueness of Levinas's *midrash,* as it indeed has distinct characteristics.

CURRENT ISSUES

The *midrash* assumes that the text holds relevant meaning for any period in time. Can it indeed be presumed that a text written many centuries ago has meaning for the present? What is at the basis of this presumption?

In the following quotation, not taken from one of his talmudic readings, Levinas responds to Spinoza's criticism of traditional Jewish biblical exegesis as it appears in the Talmud. His words offer the beginning of an answer to these questions:

> What is sought after, and often achieved, is the incessant return to verses by the Talmudic scholars...is a reading where the passage commented upon clarifies for the reader its present preoccupation (which may be either out of the ordinary or common to its generation). And where the verse, in its turn, is renewed in the light of this clarification.... This intimate relation with the text, this renewal and constant updating of meaning..."the very decoding of life in the mirror of the text"—is, in its fashion, practiced and even instituted here.... Exegesis would be the possibility for one epoch to have a meaning for another epoch. (BV 170)[2]

This is Levinas's statement about talmudic commentaries on the Bible. Exegesis forms a living relationship between the text and the commentator by illuminating an aspect of his reality that was unclear to him, and at the same time it uncovers a new meaning within the text that was not previously known. Hence, the renewal is mutual, of both the commentator and the text. This is a hermeneutic assumption, forming the setting for both the rabbinic *midrash* and for Levinas's commentary on talmudic passages.

To illustrate this idea, the following is an example: "If fire breaks out and catches in thorns so that the stacked grain or the standing grain or the field is consumed, he who started the fire shall make full restitution" (Exod. 22:5). This biblical verse is easily understood. The Mishna (Bava Kamma 6:4) takes this verse as the basis of the law: "If someone brings on a fire which consumes wood, stones, or earth, he would be liable." However, in the Gemara (Babylonian Talmud, Bava Kamma 60a) the verse receives additional meaning. First it is interpreted through a *midrash halakha* to determine the specific situations in which one who sets a fire is responsible and liable for the damages, even if the fire was out of his control. In other words, his responsibility is extended. However the Gemara does not stop at this but continues:

> Rabbi Samuel Bar Nahmani in the name of Rabbi Jonatan: Calamity comes upon the world only because there are wicked persons in the world, but it always begins with the righteous, for it is said: "If fire breaks out and

catches in thorns." When does fire break out? When it finds thorns; but it begins by consuming only the just, for it is said: "so that the stacked grain is consumed"; it does not say: "*ve'akhal gadish*" (so that it consumes the stack) but: "*vene'ekhal gadish*" (so that the stack is consumed), which means that it is already consumed.

This *midrash,* alluding to the same verse, addresses the question of suffering and asserts that morally upright behavior is no defense against calamity. The *darshan* was most probably preoccupied by calamity and its infliction on the just due to the circumstances of his times. By interpreting the verse he claims that there is indeed a relationship between moral behavior and calamity, but it is an inverse relationship. In contrast to what might have been expected, the righteous are the first to suffer (and this will of course be immediately followed by the question: why?). What appears to be disorder is a different order, a reverse order, which requires an explanation. In this way the commentator learns about his world. The verse, which deals with fire, receives a completely new meaning in addition to its plain meaning and teaches about suffering in the world. In this way, the encounter between the commentator and the verse facilitates a mutual process of renewal.

Levinas interpreted this *midrash* in his lesson "Damages Due to Fire" (*NT* 178–97) at a colloquium on the topic of war held in 1975, after Israel's 1973 Yom Kippur War. Hence, his point of departure involved current circumstances and the question of suffering inflicted on people who are not wicked was not a theoretical question. His commentary translates the words "wicked" and "righteous" to the context of his reality. The wicked, according to his first interpretation, are sharp-tongued intellectuals who spread violence through their ideas. Levinas maintained that totalitarian regimes are predicated on lofty but violent ideas, ideas formed by resourceful people who disregard human faces and individual human suffering. His second interpretation is more relevant for people in general: "Social evil already contains within itself the uncontainable force of war" (186). And who does not bear some degree of responsibility for social evil? The wicked includes all people. Indeed, his initial interpretation of the second part of the *midrash,* whereby the righteous are the first to be afflicted in times of calamity, is that the righteous are responsible for the evil and they are afflicted because they did not prevent it. Responsibility for social evil and for not preventing it justify punishment. This might explain the reverse logic of calamity.

But Levinas does not engage in theodicy (justification of God) and does not attempt to justify wartime suffering by human wickedness. On the contrary, he intensifies the absurdity and chaos arising from the *midrash* by offering additional interpretations: the righteous are afflicted first so that they will not be able to stop the calamity, or in order to atone for the others through their own suffering. "The *reason* of war consists in the very *turning upside down* of Reason" (*NT* 186), the work of the devil. And as if the absurdity arising from these possibilities is not enough, his final suggestion is that in times of trouble the righteous and the wicked are afflicted together. The calamity cancels all distinction between them. In this way Levinas arrives at a point where any attempt to explain suffering is morally difficult: a theodicy that clashes with one's life experience and basic sense of justice at the affliction of the innocent, or nihilism—existential despair that wears away all moral responsibility.

Interpreting the *midrash,* Levinas sees before him World War II and the Holocaust, as well as the unnecessary suffering caused by all wars, including the Yom Kippur War. He avoids dealing with the question of who set the fire and whether it was justified. In his usual manner, he chooses to face the real people afflicted by the war. Through his interpretation he speaks about the dangers of totalitarianism, theodicy, existential despair, and social evil. In this way, by means of the commentary, the *midrash* addresses each of us, listeners and learners, and relates to our lives and our sufferings.

Consequently, the *midrash* is a conversation between people and the text regarding reality. No conversation can take place without an interlocutor, without an Other who is completely separate from me. I find a structural similarity between Levinas's conception of language as a relationship between people and his conception of exegesis as a relationship between humans and the text. He assumes that conversation is not a symmetrical relationship, for in the encounter with the other my responsibility for him is greater than my responsibility for myself. I shall always have additional responsibility for his responsibility as well.[3] I reply and respond to the other who speaks to me. Speech links two separate people who cannot be generalized. The word "I" can be an answer to an entreaty (Do not murder!) or to a question (Who?). It has no separate existence. The relationship with the other is a necessary condition for one's ability to relate to that which is outside of the self, and even to think.[4] In a conversation, despite the lack of symmetry, both sides go through a process of renewal when they come into contact with that which is different from themselves, with that which is not an object of their consciousness, and when they hear the words of the other.

This is also true of the text: the commentator is prepared to hear, to be commanded by the holy text, and to comply with its demand. The relationship is not an equal one—the verse is a demand and the commentator complies or obeys. Even if the verse poses no outright demand, even if it tells a story, it ultimately encompasses a message of responsibility for the other person. The verse is also an Other. It does not originate from the commentator, and it has never previously come into contact with this person by whom it is about to be interpreted. This encounter, similar to any dialogue and despite its asymmetry, allows its participants to meet that which is outside them, and in this way become renewed.

As stated, Levinas subjects the Talmud to the same treatment as the Talmud's treatment of the biblical text, as he sees it. The point of departure of his talmudic readings is always a current issue occupying his generation, chosen as that year's theme for the colloquium of Jewish intellectuals in France. For many years Levinas was part of the colloquia's organizing team; thus, he also had a hand in selecting the topics. Some examples include "Forgiveness" in the context of the Jewish attitude to the Germans in the 1960s and "Judaism and Revolution" following the 1968 Student Revolt, as well as topics on the attitude to the State of Israel, to Jerusalem, to community in modern industrialized societies, to the contemporary meaning of the Bible, to idolatry, and so on. Sometimes his choice of text is easy to understand and relates directly to the topic of discussion, but this is not always the case. When the association between the talmudic passage and the selected theme is unclear, it is clarified during the study session and adds a meaningful dimension to both the theme and the passage.

Sometimes the main effect of the encounter between text and reality, achieved by means of the colloquium's theme, is a renewal of the text's meaning, as in the lesson "The Temptation of Temptation" (*NT* 30–50),[5] which deals with a passage from Tractate Shabbat and lends it philosophical meaning. Other times this encounter illuminates a new and surprising aspect of the issue under discussion thanks to the exegesis, as in the lesson "Cities of Refuge" (*BV* 34–52) taught at the colloquium on "Jerusalem the Single and the Universal." Choosing a text on the cities of refuge for a discussion of Jerusalem is incomprehensible and even enigmatic, as Levinas himself speaks of "the unusual idea, or the unusual audacity, to present Jerusalem in the context of these cities of refuge, or in contrast with these cities" (40). But before we attempt to solve the riddle of this association, let us hand over the reins to the talmudic lesson, which demonstrates how Levinas expects the Talmud to teach him meaningful things about his own reality:

> I would like to mention what topical significance the institution of these cities and the recognition of the "avenger of blood" might have for us, beyond the reminder of picturesque and outdated customs.
>
> Do not these murders, committed without the murderers' volition, occur in other ways than by the axe-head leaving the handle and coming to strike the passer-by? In Western society—free and civilized, but without social equality and a rigorous social justice—is it absurd to wonder whether the advantages available to the rich in relation to the poor—and everyone is rich in relation to someone in the West—whether these advantages, one thing leading to another, are not the cause, somewhere, of someone's agony? Are there not, somewhere in the world, wars and carnage which result from these advantages? Without us others, inhabitant of our capitals—capitals certainly without equality, but protected and plentiful—without us others having wanted to harm anyone? Does the avenger or the redeemer of blood "with heated heart" lurk around us, in the form of people's anger, of the spirit of revolt or even of delinquency in our suburbs, the result of the social imbalance in which we are placed? (40).

Cities of refuge were the solution to a problem typical of societies in which blood avenging was an accepted custom. They provided protection from vengeance for those who had committed involuntary manslaughter. What meaning can this possibly have for residents of France in the latter half of the twentieth century, where blood vengeance is forbidden by law and is considered merely another type of murder? What meaning can the city of refuge have for those for whom blood vengeance is an absolutely barbaric custom? What can we learn from a text dealing with a matter so foreign and alien from all that appears to us as relevant and civilized?

Levinas sees an opportunity to expose his listeners to a current socio-economic problem. Any contemporary Western city may be perceived as a city of refuge, since the economic method in which we, their inhabitants, are complicit and active (I use the present tense as the relevance of these matters has only grown) is predicated on the emergence of both local and global social and economic disparities. Levinas, in the 1970s, was already aware of that which has by now grown to calamitous dimensions, that is, globalization. Entire urban populations—migrants and foreign laborers but also entire societies, particularly in third world countries—have become enslaved to the unquenchable pursuit of corporate profits. By being part of this system, whether actively or passively, we are committing involuntary manslaughter of people dying of hunger and AIDS in third world countries, involuntary manslaughter in defense against the violence resulting from growing poverty among the margins of society in major cities. This reality, so easy to disregard in the process of modern daily life, is exposed here in all its brutality. It is not only a matter of interpreting an outdated symbol by lending it relevant meaning, but also a jarring of our consciousness—of both the readers and learners—a shaking of our self-satisfaction, by providing an acute and critical view of our reality.[6]

The lesson, which goes on to mention other current problems, also decodes the plain meaning of the passage, describing those places worthy of being a city of refuge. Levinas summarizes these criteria: "Life can thus mean only life worthy of the name; life in the full sense of the term: exile, of course, but no prison, no hard labor, and no concentration camp. Life which is life. The humanism or humanitarianism of the cities of refuge!" (*NT* 42). Countless labor camps and concentration camps, which abounded during the twentieth century, are present in Levinas's consciousness when writing these words. The city of refuge, a penalty imposed on those who were not vigilant enough to avoid committing involuntary manslaughter, does not detract from the essence of life, from the ability to support oneself, or even from study; rather, it only limits one's freedom of movement. All of life's components must be retained in the city of refuge, and this is what he terms its "humanitarianism." The Talmud teaches that it is possible to punish someone without denying him his humanity.[7] The commentary manages to extract a current lesson from the ancient text.

The next part of the commentary follows the ethical spirit typical of Levinas—opening up to the other and responding to his or her summons and needs—and discusses the role of the Torah in this opening up:

> The hermeneutic of the *Gemara* wants the Torah of Moses to be a city of refuge. But if the Torah is a refuge, how is it that the person who practices it and has committed manslaughter must be exiled? Has he not taken refuge in the Torah itself?...Is the Torah being treated in the cities of refuge as answering only to cultural needs, like the sun and water necessary to our physical condition? Is it not also eternal life itself, a pure act of the intellect and consequently indifference to death, and thus a Torah that is stronger than death? A complete awakening of the soul!...And, subsequently, perhaps beyond the protection against the avenger, a life which is already the origin of all "incapacity" to murder?...One is protected, one is above death and murder, during the lesson, or when asking questions and listening to replies. But there are interruptions. (*BV* 44)

Beyond the plain meaning of the Talmud, here Torah study is an awakening of one's consciousness, an opening up to that which is beyond being (*au-delà de l'Être*) and to the Same (*Même*). In this respect, Torah study is also a defense against death, or to be exact, a defense against the fear of death. When the self opens up to the Other, I fear the death of the other rather than my own death. Torah study, which leads to such opening up, defends me against my fear of death. But Torah study is also alertness, attention to the other, a defense against the distraction that might become involuntary manslaughter. Nonetheless, the studying can be interrupted. The alertness disappears and the fear of death returns. No one can trust him or herself to unceasingly maintain the necessary level of vigilance and openness that constitutes full protection against committing manslaughter—hence the need for cities of refuge. The Torah, which as stated is a defense against death, is no substitute for the city of refuge, because it can always be only a partial defense, due to the interruptions. Reality challenges that which is acquired through study.

The force of this commentary is in its reference to itself as well, to the here and now in which the lesson is being taught. While we are learning

Torah, the contents in which we are engaged at this moment arouse our consciousness, and we may become more aware of the other's needs, of our own fear of death, and of the vigilance that is necessary in order to avoid committing involuntary manslaughter. But once the lesson ends, when we have finished learning, we shall close the book and return to daily matters, to persevering our being.

Through the text and its interpretation, Levinas observes reality and responds to it, addresses us directly, and perhaps manages to awaken our consciousness for a moment. But he has few illusions. This is a moment of openness. This interpretation stems from the reality of the *darshan,* is associated with it and attempts to influence it, to influence life itself—his life and that of his listeners and readers, and our life.

Further on, following the talmudic passage, Levinas develops the topic of Torah study, and with the passage he takes a leap to Jerusalem:

> "What is the meaning of the (Psalmist's) words, *Our feet stood within thy gates, O Jerusalem!* (Psalm 122:2)? [It is this.] What helped us to maintain our firm foothold in war? The gates of Jerusalem—the place where students engaged in the study of the Torah!" [Babylonian Talmud, Makot 10a]
>
> The Torah, which elsewhere does not even permit the protection against the avenger of blood, has it that here, in Jerusalem, we "maintain our firm foothold in war." Is it a war where the Torah would permit victory? Justice will undoubtedly conquer, and the science of justice, in Jerusalem, includes the justice of acts. But in the context of the cities of refuge, this can also be read differently. There are cities of refuge because we have enough conscience to have good intentions, but not enough not to betray them by our acts. Hence the manslaughters.... In Jerusalem, the city of authentic Torah, it is a more conscious consciousness, completely brought down to earth. It is the great awakening. We have a footing. (*BV* 50)

We have returned to the question of why Levinas selected this passage, one that seems unrelated to the topic under discussion, the theme of the colloquium. Why deal with the issue of Jerusalem's holiness in the context of cities of refuge? The journey we took was lengthy but vital. Only now that we have learned the meaning of the cities of refuge can we understand the meaning of Jerusalem in this context. The meaning is one of greater, more constant vigilance, than that which can be achieved through Torah study. Is Levinas contemplating a certain Jerusalem reality? The psalm from which the verse was taken speaks of an ideal Jerusalem, a sanctuary of law, tranquility, and peace. It is a "single and universal" Jerusalem, which is also the title of the colloquium at which this lesson was taught. In the psalm, and consequently in this talmudic passage and commentary, Jerusalem is a model of the perfect city. Nonetheless, in this instance a mixture of the real and the ideal is evident.[8] At the beginning of the lesson Levinas makes an effort to stress how "there is no spiritual plenitude for Israel without the return to the earthly Jerusalem" (37) and speaks of "Jerusalem, an exceptional, unique city, twinned with the city of God, a city of all religions, a city twinned with its ideal, a city twinned with its model" (37–38). And he also considers "the impossibility for Israel—or according to Israel—of religious salvation without justice in the earthly city. No vertical dimension without a horizontal dimension" (38). Namely, even when dealing with the perfect model, with a utopia, it is necessary to maintain the demand and desire that this model have a practical impact on an existing city, Jerusalem as a real city, which is very far from its ideal. Is this a realistic expectation? The crux of the matter is that there is a model, one that contrasts with the reality of all existing cities, which are all cities of refuge, cities in which one's consciousness becomes oblivious and therefore manslaughter is committed unintentionally or inadvertently. This model is supposed to effect a change in the reality of all cities, but first and foremost of Jerusalem as a real city. The distance between Levinas's conception of Jerusalem, its optimal state, and the actual state of affairs remains disturbing, and perhaps this was his intention.

If the study of Torah is not enough to defend us from committing manslaughter or from those who seek revenge for such acts, then Torah study in Jerusalem as an ideal city, a sanctuary of justice where people maintain constant awareness of the other person, is even more powerful. In what way? Is this not a return to customary religious conceptions of the charm and power of Jerusalem? Levinas appears to be aiming higher:

> It is precisely in contrast to the cities of refuge that this claim of the Torah through which Jerusalem is defined can be understood. The city of refuge is the city of a civilization or of a humanity which protects subjective innocence and forgives objective guilt and all the denials that acts inflict on intentions.... A civilization of the law, admittedly, but a political civilization whose justice is hypocritical and where, with an undeniable right, the avenger of blood prowls.

> What is promised in Jerusalem, on the other hand, is a humanity of the Torah. It will have been able to surmount the deep contradictions of the cities of refuge.... The longing for Zion, Zionism, is not one more nationalism or particularism; nor is it a simple search for a place of refuge. It is the hope of a science of society, and of a society, which are wholly human. And this hope is to be found in Jerusalem, in the earthly Jerusalem, and not outside all places, in pious thoughts. (*BV* 52)

The Torah taught in Jerusalem is an alternative to the realistic model. This is no realistic description of a current state of affairs; it is, rather, the challenge of a different way of thought, a desired state, a hope. But Levinas emphasizes that it is not merely a theoretical model, a pleasant thought with no implications for real life. As he understands Zionism[9] and the unique meaning of Jerusalem within it, this is an opportunity to try and shape a reality on which the desirable has more of an effect, a reality that questions the given unchangeable status of the current state of affairs.

This is an attempt to judge reality and to influence it through a challenging horizon of thought.[10] Levinas occasionally speaks of the conflict between ethics and politics. Politics is a structure that equalizes all citizens, a system of law and justice before which everyone is allegedly equal. But sometimes it is precisely such justice that inflicts injustice on individuals, and sometimes the interests of one country, whether economic or political, have immoral implications for another country or for a subgroup of its citizens. Ethics should play a part within politics, as a subversive critical underpinning, specifically for such cases. Ethical thought, which sees each person as an infinity, needs the state in order to ensure shared human life, but it also works against politics in cases of contradiction. Levinas perceives the role of the State of Israel as devising a political model that has more room than usual for the ethical influence. The State of Israel offers an opportunity to construct a society that not only provides physical protection of Jewish life, a worthy cause in and of itself, but also introduces an ethical perspective in politics. The desirable model is not an ideal that is separate from reality. Its role is to try and influence reality. Torah study, the *midrash,* is committed to reality and strives to change it, to improve it. This is the ideological horizon of the current talmudic lesson, which observes reality from a critical standpoint while also striving to influence and change it.

But the design of the talmudic passage itself is puzzling. It proceeds from a discussion of cities of refuge to Torah study and its meaning. As early as the time of the Amoraim who created the passage, cities of refuge were a remote theme, distanced from contemporary reality. In contrast, Torah study occupied the center of these sages' lives. If so, by attempting to link the cities of refuge to Torah study, they are endeavoring to link theoretical study to the realities of their time. Thus, for example, a connection is formed between Moses' yearning to observe the precept of cities of refuge and the correct way of teaching Torah by means of a *midrash aggadah* on the two parts of a verse, forming a parallel. In this context, it is now easier to understand the need to take a leap to Jerusalem, where it is possible to think and to generate a perfect model of study and of observing the commandments, and perhaps even to realize this model. Considering that the topic discussed herein is a certain manner of Torah study intended to influence reality and the behavior of its learners, perceiving Jerusalem as the location of that which is worthy makes it possible to judge reality and to proceed toward this model, from the current state in any location. The dimension Levinas adds to the passage by his *midrash* is a universal role given to Jerusalem by presenting an ideal of the proper combination of politics that does not completely contradict ethics and that notices the individual and his or her needs. It is a politics influenced by criticism, by that which is beyond politics.

Levinas is aware of the intricate design of the talmudic passage and he adds another level of interpretation. Torah study and observance of the commandments are probably not among the highest priorities of many of his listeners; rather, the issue occupying them is Jerusalem's holiness and the violent conflict over its dominance. The passage indicates a link between observing the commandments and Torah study; similarly, Levinas points to the link between the uniqueness and holiness of Jerusalem and observing the commandments and Torah study. Holiness is not a given quality; it is a challenge, the challenge of shaping reality in the spirit of that which is learned from the Torah and the commandments based on an awareness and vigilance that preclude manslaughter and shirking one's responsibility to the other person. Manslaughter is only a prototype of regular behavior, of normal life conducted according to regular standards of persevering one's being, of concentrating on the needs of the Same. The city of refuge is a mechanism that facilitates the regularization of shared life in this state of lack of awareness that culminates in acts of manslaughter. Jerusalem signifies a horizon of shared life, a life of much greater alertness to the Other and responsibility for the other's life, a responsibility from which there is no refuge. And this horizon can effect a reshaping of reality, at least to a certain degree.

In the context in which Levinas is speaking—with the issue of dominance over Jerusalem at the heart of a bloody struggle between Jews and Arabs precisely because of the city's holiness—these words are cause for thought. The idea that holiness is not a quality but, rather, a work plan changes the frame of reference with regard to the situation in Jerusalem and how it should be treated. At stake is a current, burning issue, and the interpretation of the text facilitates a new point of view and attempts to change our approach to this matter. This is the *midrash*. It is mutually enriching: the text receives a new meaning in addition to previous meanings, and the issue under discussion is illuminated from a different perspective.

Viewing this *midrash* from a completely contemporary perspective, we can see that reducing the footing of non-Jewish residents of Jerusalem and trampling their basic rights in the name of an ideal of Jewish dominance, in the name of the city's holiness, contradicts its very holiness. The *midrash* demands that Jerusalem set an example of tolerance, multiculturalism, and an ethics of the Other and concern for the other's needs as a basic element acting in resistance to political and national interests. Tools are provided here for both ethical and religious criticism of injustices committed in the name of the Jewish faith.

But although the *midrash* faces reality and addresses it, this does not ensure its power to influence the real world. On the one hand, Torah study seems to facilitate a critical discussion of reality from an original and productive point of view, but on the other hand, there is always the question of its power to affect reality in practice. This is a troubling question. It troubled the sages and has troubled many leaders over the generations; it also troubled Levinas who dealt with it, among others, in the lesson "Damages Due to Fire" mentioned above, while focusing on the failure of intellectuals to influence reality and to prevent its injustices. In the same way, it also troubles current-day pluralistic *batei midrash,* occupied as they are with the question of their ability to influence Israeli reality.

These *batei midrash* were established and continue to be established in response to problems in the real world, and they offer study that consists both of a statement about reality and of proposals for a solution. People who seek a link to their cultural roots—observant and nonobservant, Jews and Arabs, women exploring their status within the Jewish culture and faith—study Torah with great commitment and address their questions to it. Worthy *midrashim* and important ideas are generated at these *batei midrash.* But their voice is only barely heard, on the margins of society. They do not have much influence on the shaping of reality. Nevertheless, would it be right to relinquish this type of Torah study and the existence of these *batei midrash?* Perhaps it would be preferable to ask how these *batei midrash* can increase their influence.

Without knowing the context of the cities of refuge and its interpretation by Levinas, it would be hard to understand his words about Jerusalem. The journey on which the readers are taken, through the understanding that they themselves may be committing involuntary manslaughter, allows them to grasp Jerusalem as meaningful for all people, as a horizon of judgment and resistance to their reality, an essence that awakens their consciousness. The hermeneutic process becomes an inseparable part of the saying. And all this directs a critical gaze at that which is taking place in Jerusalem, supposedly in the name of its holiness.

The Implicit Theme

Outlining the format of the *midrash,* prominent *aggadah* researcher Jonah Frankel discerns four concurrent levels: the plain meaning (*pshat*) of the verse, the *midrash* on the verse, the new (explicit) idea, and the hidden general idea.[11] While learning a *midrash* it is necessary to relate to all of these levels in order to understand it due to the complex relationship between the text, the *darshan,* and the reality that is being considered in the *darshan*'s commentary.

Many of Levinas's talmudic readings follow this pattern: the reference to the *pshat* is evident in the structure of the lessons, which follow the interpreted passage while quoting sections of it (in translation) and interpreting them. The midrashic techniques he uses are discussed throughout the current volume. The new explicit idea is usually the theme of the colloquium at which the lesson was taught. Interpretation of the passage follows this idea, and Levinas's attitude toward it is revealed by studying the commentary. The general hidden idea is associated with Levinas's world, and it usually includes an additional dimension of association between the commentary and reality.

Many of the talmudic readings include segments that seem like digressions, with no integral link to the passage or to the topic under discussion. After wandering down these side alleys, he then returns to the main road, to the major topic. A review of these segments shows that they focus on another issue, another topic, which is somehow related to the major topic. This is the implicit theme, or the hidden general idea, and it reflects another way of relating to reality — whether directly or by engaging in philosophical questions.

I shall demonstrate this by returning to the lesson "The Youth of Israel," which I discussed in the previous chapter. In my previous treatment I skipped some parts of the mishna's interpretation and I disregarded some of the lesson's conclusions. This is the mishna: "Samuel was a Nazirite, according to the words of Rabbi Nehorai, for it is said: 'And the razor [*morah*] will not touch his head' (1 Sam. 1:11). For Samson the word *morah* was said (Judg. 13:5) and for Samuel the word *morah* was said. Just as the word *morah* in the case of Samson indicates the Nazirate so it also indicates the Nazirate in the case of Samuel" (Mishna, Tractate Nazir, 9:5). The two examples brought by this mishna for Nazirites are people who did not choose to become Nazirites: they were predestined for this way of life even before they were born, Samuel by his mother and Samson by an angel. On this Levinas writes:

> What an odd nazirate! In the biblical text it is Samuel's mother who makes the vow: "The razor will not touch his head." Samuel himself has not yet been conceived when the promise is made.... But everything happens as though the vow made by the mother counted, as if personal engagement, freely undertaken — the guarantee of spirituality in our philosophical West — was not the supreme investiture of a vocation. As though beyond the cult of youth, of newness, of the personal engagement which

this liberalism contains, a high density of obligation could begin before our beginning, in the internal value of the tradition. That is at least what is at stake here. (*NT* 128)

Levinas is commenting on two related topics, two central themes in his philosophy—freedom and time. Freedom, in his opinion, cannot be derived from itself. "Is one already responsible when one chooses responsibility?... This is a vicious circle.... Freedom begins in what has all the appearance of a constraint due to threat" (37, 40). Responsibility precedes freedom, both temporally and categorically. Human beings are given responsibility by virtue of their being. Freedom is the choice of how to conduct oneself responsibly, as one is obliged to do when encountering the other person. This responsibility precedes any freedom; it is always anachronistic, coming from a past time that cannot be remembered. Consciousness is not free and therefore cannot choose to be responsible. Responsibility is already present and freedom is a given within this state. Always, before all else, is responsibility, and only then is there the choice of whether to adhere to it or not. People do not have the autonomy to choose their own obligations (in contrast to Kant). Responsibility is imposed on them heteronomously, by virtue of their being, and from a past time that cannot be remembered. Levinas writes, "The responsibility for the other cannot have begun in my commitment, in my decision. The unlimited responsibility in which I find myself comes from the hither side of my freedom, from a 'prior to every memory' an 'ulterior to every accomplishment,' from the non-present par excellence, the non-original, the anarchical, prior to or beyond essence" (*OB* 10).[12]

Thus, also in the two examples brought by the mishna, Samuel did not choose to become a Nazirite; rather, he was born into this state as a result of his mother's vow. Samson also did not choose to be a Nazirite; his mother obeyed the command of the angel who revealed himself to her when she first became pregnant and demanded that she dedicate the child to the Nazirate. "An angel of God utters the vows for you and, there you are, committed! Nothing is more scandalous to a consciousness for which everything must begin in a free act and for which self-consciousness, completing consciousness, is supreme freedom" (*NT* 128). Levinas defines the point of contention between his own outlook, based as it is on an interpretation of the Bible, and common philosophical views in general, and the existential approaches in particular.

But what does all this have to do with the youth of Israel? "But Samson is a youth. His whole tragedy is a tragedy of youth, made of the mistakes and loves of youth.... The Nazirite would be defined, according to Rabbi Jose, as the one who fears no one, or, more precisely, as the one who does not fear power. Definition of the nazirate or definition of youth? They overlap in the person of Samson" (*NT* 129). Hence, Samson is the prototype of a Nazirite who is also young, a man who was committed even prior to his birth to a lifestyle of devotion to the other person (this is true of every person but of the Nazirite even more so, as the precepts of the Nazirite are interpreted in this talmudic lesson), with no fear (*mora*) of conventions or of authoritative figures. His responsibility exceeds all of these. The theme of the colloquium, "The Youth of Israel," thus receives new meaning. This is not a biological age but a certain cultural attitude to time; it is an attitude that preserves the fundamental essence of youth. Israel is a people always preceded by its commitment to goodness, always young with regard to this commitment: "The absolute nazirite is older than his life. Extraordinary old age! But also the absolute nazirite bears, throughout all his life, the mark of an unimaginable youth, of a youth before youth, a youth which precedes all aging. The children of Israel are quite an anachronism! The nazirate is not the youth of beginnings; it is preteroriginal youth, before the entry into historical time" (135).

The explicit theme of this lesson—the ethical meaning of the Nazirate and its role in promoting the commitment to feed the hungry—is based on Levinas's conception of time and freedom, his implicit themes. As stated, these are two major elements in his philosophical thought, but here they do not seem to be at the center of attention, and he does not think it necessary to explain them at length. Nevertheless, they are the very ideas underlying the hermeneutic interpretation of the Nazirate and its social role. This implicit theme originates from the philosophical world of Levinas, from his cultural reality. The implicit themes of many of the talmudic readings are revealed only when one insists on reading each lesson in its entirety, in an attempt to understand those segments that seem unrelated to the topic under discussion, and they are often the ideological underpinnings of the readings.[13]

Another example of an implicit theme may be found in the lesson "Toward the Other." The statement that each person and each situation merits special attention is manifested throughout this lesson. There is no general accounting, no universal course of development, no constant rules of behavior, and no absolute formulas. Each person is an entire world, and responsibility toward that person necessitates recourse to the individual's personality, circumstances, and special conditions. As Levinas says: "There is no heart without reason and no reason without heart" (*NT* 27).

This is a major element in the philosophy of Levinas, and particularly in *Totality and Infinity*. In the context of this talmudic lesson, which deals with mechanisms of atonement and with the Jewish attitude to the Germans in the 1960s, it adds a meaningful dimension both to the theme of the colloquium and to the discussion of totality and infinity. Perceiving man as an infinity, rather than as part of a totality, is perhaps the most important means of resisting the murderous violence of ideologies such as Nazism. But this is not stated explicitly, and the concepts of totality and infinity do not appear in the text. These ideological underpinnings are only revealed by attending to the course of the lesson and to the association between its different parts.

In the lesson "Damages Due to Fire" (*NT* 178–97) mentioned above, the implicit theme is the relationship between the spiritual world and reality. This theme is evident in two seemingly unrelated sets of contrasts: the dialectical relationship between *aggadah* and *halakha* and the relationship between intellectuals and reality, regarding their ability and obligation to influence it (e.g., the righteous who are the first to be punished).

The passage chosen by Levinas for interpretation in this lesson, a passage that moves freely between *aggadah* and *halakha,* is an attempt to form a proper balance between them, to seek a way of reaching mutual enrichment of *halakha* and *aggadah,* law and philosophy, traditionalism and innovation. From a wider perspective, by effecting a philosophical interpretation of talmudic passages, Levinas is responding to the need to establish a revised consideration of Judaism, of its tradition, and to let the text influence reality.

This topic, however—the relationship between study and reality, between the intellectual and the world, and between philosophy and its implementation—which is interwoven throughout the entire lesson, becomes the focus of the discussion toward its conclusion. It is evident in questions inquiring whether the righteous can or wish to prevent war, and what their function is once it has erupted. Who are the righteous—those who take responsibility for the state of society? Intellectuals? Political leaders? Religious leaders? Or perhaps any person who assumes the functions of the righteous? All these answers seem correct, and in this way Levinas appeals to himself and to his audience and alludes to their role in shaping their own reality.[14] The question of the correct relationship between the spiritual and reality is encompassed within the sequence of Baraitas that assumedly provide instruction on how to conduct oneself in times of calamity. The passage and Levinas do not answer this question. Reality is always complex; it requires a concrete *aggadah* in order to apply it to *halakha*, to translate it into practical terms. Interweaving a discussion on the relationship between *halakha* and *aggadah* within a lesson on war may imply that even in a state of war philosophy and thought should not be relinquished. *Aggadah* has a role in every reality, even the most extreme and the most violent.

In contrast to common conceptions in present-day Israel, to the convention that security exigencies and radical states of war or military operations are above moral criticism—as though they themselves are essentially moral in their function as defenders of Israeli citizens—the idea proposed herein is that the spiritual, the *aggadah,* has a role in any situation. Further, it is incumbent on adequate leadership, on intellectuals and religious leaders, to remain critical and to examine reality in light of moral principles. *Aggadah,* which is free in its very essence, cannot be subordinate to *halakha.* It must challenge *halakha.*

"The Temptation of Temptation" (*NT* 30–50) is one of the most philosophical of the talmudic readings. Prior to his discussion of this passage Levinas provides a relatively lengthy introduction describing a type of knowledge called the "temptation of temptation"—namely, the need to know and understand before taking action, which are processes of thought and philosophy that contradict innocence. He portrays Western culture as based on rationalism and resistance to any deed that cannot be justified and explained—on the "temptation of temptation." In this value system mere rationalism is more important than its practical implications. He lectures on this idea very clearly, and it seems that this would have been enough. However, in his interpretation of the talmudic passage that constitutes a *midrash* on the Revelation on Mt. Sinai he presents an alternative to the temptation of temptation, centering on a discussion of freedom and responsibility as types of nonchildish innocence, that is, a value system whereby human reality is more important than rationalism. Under the surface, however, Levinas converses with an existential anxiety, which he terms *il y a*. This is a central concept in the early philosophy of Levinas, which may be imperfectly translated as "there is," the entire nonpersonal existence that is oppressive and makes one sick. This is an existential experience in which being threatens to swallow the individual within its totality due to the lack of boundaries and distinctions. Generalizing rationalism intensifies this existential oppression, while the face-to-face encounter with the other person entails a departure from it.

In the talmudic lesson "The Temptation of Temptation," the anxiety of the *il y a* experience is evident in the threatening "mountain like a barrel" image, in the image of the world possibly resuming a state of chaos, and also in the concern for the very existence of Judaism. The point of origin of existence, before receiving the Torah, is one of sweeping existential anxiety. What does the lesson say about this? Not much, but it concludes thus: "The impossibility of escaping from God—which in this at least is not a value among others—is the 'mystery of angels,' the 'We will do and we will hear.' It lies in the depths of the ego as ego, which is not only for a being the possibility of death, 'the possibility of impossibility,' but already the possibility of sacrifice, birth of a meaning in the obtuseness of being, of a subordination of a 'being able to die' to a 'knowing how to sacrifice oneself'" (*NT* 50).

I was charged with safeguarding the existence of the Creation, although not my own creation, even before I came into being, "to work it and take care of it" (Gen. 2:15). This responsibility may be one possible answer to the existential anxiety—a consciousness of meaning based on a role with which I am charged by virtue of my very being. Existential anxiety, among other things, is widely present in twentieth century Western thought due to contemporary events. Levinas is implicitly conversing with this anxiety, and he offers a philosophy that observes the world from a different, meaningful point of view. Innocence as he portrays it, the willingness to obey and to assume responsibility, is, perhaps, an alternative not only to the temptation of temptation but also to existential anxiety.

At the beginning of this chapter we saw how, in the lesson "Cities of Refuge" Levinas discussed the cities of refuge, what can be defined as reasonable living terms in a city, the holiness of Jerusalem, and the association between all of these and Torah study. The implicit theme of this lesson may be summarized in one sentence: "As if the scandal of murder, even if it is committed in innocence, were stronger than the power of death itself" (*BV* 45). The major cause of concern is the death of the other person, any harm to him, even before my concern about my own death. The holiness of Jerusalem, the cities of refuge, and Torah study, all have in common the call for vigilance and the expectation to prevent manslaughter. Constant vigilance is necessary in order to avoid liability for human death so that we should not find ourselves responsible (even if not guilty for) manslaughter.

The lesson "And God Created Woman" (*NT* 161–77) deals with femininity and with the relationship between femininity and masculinity. Before beginning its discussion of this topic, however, the first third of the lesson is devoted to the creation of human beings as reasoning creatures with free choice, who are capable of obeying and responsible for the Other by virtue of their very creation. In this, Levinas follows the structure of the talmudic passage he is interpreting, where the discussion on the creation of woman is preceded by a short section on the duality of humanity.[15] Indeed, the lesson focuses on femininity and Levinas presents his complex attitude to the topic at length.[16] But in my opinion the structure of the lesson adds an additional level of meaning. First of all, it refers to femininity as secondary to humanity. Women, like men, are first of all people, and in this respect their obligations and rights are equal to those of men. The significance of the difference between the sexes is secondary. But his extensive comments on a humanity that is not defined by freedom, on the heteronomous source of the obligation to obey as defining humanity no less than freedom, and on the tension inherent in human beings between law and existence — all imply that women who fight for equal rights, an issue targeted by the theme of the colloquium, should not be fighting first and foremost for freedom (particularly in the case of women's sexual freedom, one of the contemporary foci of the feminist movement). There is certainly good cause to stand up for the equal rights and obligations of women in their primary status as people, even before they are women. Rightful status, rather than freedom, is the main issue—the equal rights and obligations of every person, whether man or woman. Freedom is the result of one's rightful and equal status, and not the reverse.

The lesson "Promised Land or Permitted Land" (*NT* 51–69) presents a complicated picture. The explicit message and the implicit message are intermingled to such a degree that the message is no longer obvious. Interpreting a passage on the affair of the explorers (*parashat hameraglim*), Levinas intensifies their moral concerns about conquering the country from its inhabitants. He identifies contemporary explorers with leftist intellectuals who severely criticize the State of Israel for its attitude to the Palestinians, and he appears to justify this criticism. But he is also cynical and disapproving of the purism and self-righteousness demonstrated by both the explorers and the intellectuals who criticize the State of Israel. The sin of the explorers is the sin of contemporary leftist intellectuals, and it is a double sin, consisting of both excessive purism and doubts as to whether the utopian vision will indeed materialize. But his alleged justification of the explorers' concerns is also a criticism of the State of Israel, exposing the moral dangers involved in the state's existence. As Levinas sees it, the land is permitted, but not unconditionally so; there are serious moral problems and there is a danger of corruption. The attitude gradually exposed here is complex. He does not show unreserved support of the State of Israel and of Israel's right to the land, but neither does he uphold the outlook that renounces Israel's moral right to exist. This tension is maintained throughout the entire talmudic lesson, with its constant movement between moral criticism and justification of Israel's existence despite these concerns. The message here is both explicit and implicit; in any case, it is a complex message that clearly addresses contemporary reality.[17]

The lesson entitled "The Pact" (*BV* 68–85) has as its theme the significance of the community in a world not designed to fit community structures. The explicit statement is that communities are based on a network of responsibilities in which I myself am always responsible for every single other in the community and even for their responsibility. However, the lesson consists of a fabric in which several other implicit themes are interwoven. These include the relationship between the Written Law and the Oral Law, which is forged by a human community attempting to implement the Written Law; the relationship between the vertical and horizontal dimensions when establishing a community, which is manifested in multiple commandments dealing with community relations and originating from the divine; and the tension between the particular and the universal, where the goal is a pact (covenant) among all humanity but is implemented within a more limited covenant community in which every person sees every other person. Another implicit theme that appears throughout the entire lesson is the infinity of the single person, the individual, versus the total structures of Western society and thought. These topics are affiliated with the central topic, community, and they add important dimensions for understanding the nature of the covenant, which is the foundation of a worthy community.

The lesson "Model of the West" (*BV* 13–33) is dedicated to criticism of Western culture, that from which the philosophy of Levinas takes its context and language, while presenting the possibilities inherent in the Torah. Levinas focuses his criticism on the question of time. He places persistence—a concept which the passage attempts to clarify—against what he terms the "historicism" of the Western world and theories that perceive time as merely a means of attaining fulfillment.

The *tamid* (persistence) is interpreted as a constant element at the heart of change, a collaboration between people that ensures continuity over time, and commitment to the same mission, which even without linear temporal continuity facilitates succession and progress. This persistence in the constant fulfillment of a mission (in this case Torah study), entails constant vigilance in reading and exercising with no interruptions, a limited action whose influence on life exceeds its own boundaries, and an obligation that can never be conclusively met and left behind.

All these types of persistence have in common the separation of time into moments that call for action. Time is a means of fulfilling missions of holiness, which join to form persistence—whether due to the collaboration between people, personal persistence, a common element, or a single cause. The issue of time or persistence is not disconnected from other issues. But if time is a means, what cause is served by all the moments that call for action? The answer given is on several levels: the Mishna and the first part of the talmudic passage reply that persistence is necessary in order to carry out the rituals of the Temple. Further on, the talmudic passage projects this on Torah study. Levinas, in his usual manner, transposes both to "shaping human reality"; every moment is a time for responding to the responsibility of encountering another person, for "the infinity of duty—which is perhaps the very modality of the relation to the infinite" (*BV* 30). This is the locus of holiness at which both the Temple rituals and Torah study are directed.

When studying the passage, other foci of Western culture criticized by Levinas are uncovered: rhetoric, "pure humanism," as well as a form of completely rational thought that has no room for the personal that is beyond the logical. That which originates from the human cannot establish itself as a value. For example, freedom cannot be grounded in itself without falling victim to infinite regression. In these criticized foci, similar to time, no space remains, no reference to the infinite; they themselves represent totality or serve totality. People who use rhetoric do not respect the otherness of the other person; rather, they try to eliminate this otherness. They try to redirect the other from his or her opinions to those of the speaker, through manipulation, while eliminating the space between them, the infinity of the other. Humanism and rational thought, which have nothing beyond themselves, are total as well, in the respect that they leave no space for infinity, for otherness not included in the structure considered, in the object of thought or reference. All these contradict the Torah and its teachings—the attitude to infinity, to the Other. In this way, Levinas criticizes *totality* in order to propose an approach to *infinity;* he criticizes essence as a concept capable of exhausting reality in order to propose an approach to that which is beyond essence. He criticizes the perseverance of being in order to suggest an "otherwise than being"—bringing to mind the names of his major books. His criticism examines these concepts, indicates their limitations, and suggests supplementary ideas, which are points for further thought.

Choosing a passage that portrays an ancient ceremony and including details of concrete actions as the point of origin for a discussion about the concept of time is, as Levinas states at the beginning of his lesson, a statement and an attempt to match the content of the criticism to its form. How can we say that every moment is important and an opportunity to generate holiness through a certain approach without falling victim to the totality of the very language used to express this statement? Focusing on the tables and shewbread in the Temple and on setting aside time for Torah study appears to provide a type of concrete discourse, one that is attentive to detail and thus portrays itself as an essentially different manner of expression, as a possible supplement to the Western model. All components of the description are interpreted symbolically; for example, the transition from the marble table to the gold table becomes representative of a manner of evolvement. But the symbol is not left behind; the lesson remains loyal to its concrete language, and thus, it is possible to understand the significance of how a certain priest collaborates with another priest in properly switching the shewbread on the holy table in the temple. And when they indeed manage to complete the mission and see each other, that is where persistence is formed and that is the model for human relations: seeing each other, being aware of each other and ready to respond accordingly. This movement between symbolic interpretation of every detail in the text and not relinquishing its details is a model of discourse and teaching that differs from the Western model.

Underneath all of these—interpretation of the passage, criticism of the Western model, and dealing with the question of time—this lesson is also based on the idea of the significance of the individual, the personal, which exceeds rational thought and historical time. No one model or definition is always appropriate. Time is not an abstract concept. It is a collection of moments, in which people meet and relate to each other (or ignore each other), look at the world, collaborate in fulfilling missions, study Torah, or provide the other with bread.

The lesson "On Religious Language and the Fear of God" (*BV* 86–98) centers on Torah study as a religious language, no less so than prayer, and on the limits of religious language, which if exceeded, causes the transcendental otherness to become an identity closed within itself—ontology, the opposite of fear of God. Another implicit theme, the question of divine justice, remains under the surface. The passage itself states that God should be thanked not only for the good and that the commandments should not be justified by God's compassion. Levinas includes in his lesson a passage from elsewhere in Tractate Berachot on the blessing for both the good and the bad. The issue of divine justice is a piercing question in times of suffering and calamity, as in Levinas's generation with its firsthand experience of the horrors of the Holocaust. The implicit answer provided both in the talmudic passage and by Levinas is that this question has nothing to do with religious language or with fear of God. These do not and cannot involve the justification of God, whose justice is incomprehensible to us, as explained to Job. Religious language turns us toward each other; fear of God is manifested in caring for the other. Beyond this we have no information and no way of understanding how the world operates and how evil and good are reckoned.

This implicit theme converses with a certain type of religiosity, but also with a fundamental human need to understand human fate and justify it, to find in divine justice a reason for adversity. This need, which is derived from historical reality and from learners' life experiences, should not be met by justifying God. Levinas consistently rejects such a theodicy (*NT* 187). Such a solution is an affront to the victims of this adversity, and it is not a religious answer as it revokes the absolute otherness of transcendence.

As stated, the implicit themes underlying many of the talmudic readings are major issues in the philosophy of Levinas and address his reality. Another aspect of the association between Levinas's talmudic commentary and reality is the distinctly ethical emphasis of the former. This topic will be discussed in chapter 6, which considers the uniqueness of Levinas's *midrash*, as it is not typical of all *midrashim*. The focus on the ethical aspects of the texts and the ethical interpretation of texts that are seemingly unrelated to human relationships stems from an interest in the association between Torah study and its implications for human reality. This study is intended to affect the reality of the learners, including their relationships with other people. Levinas's talmudic commentary addresses reality and is oriented toward it with the aim of influencing this reality, as do all *midrashim*. By studying the Talmud it is possible to observe reality and to appraise it from an atypical point of view.

Chapter 5

INTERPRETIVE PLURALISM

~∞~

MULTIPLE COMMENTATORS AND INTERPRETATIONS

The sages acted on the premise that "the Torah has seventy faces"; the Written Law can be grasped in many ways and it has the tools needed to relate to any human problem. The *midrashim* they produced were a major method of uncovering and revealing these meanings and relationships. The study of Torah and its exegesis are conducive and even necessary in order to connect with its source of inspiration. Since the Torah is inexhaustible, having an infinite capacity to be meaningful for different people in different eras and contexts, it invites and requires infinite expositions, infinite pluralism. As we have seen, the inspiration is revealed in the association between the text and the commentator. Since every person is unique, every person has a different perspective on the world in general and on a specific text in particular. In this way, anyone can offer an original interpretation of any verse, an interpretation that derives from one's unique personality and life circumstances. Nonetheless, in rabbinic literature this pluralism is restricted to the sages—those who engage in Torah study and who are immersed in the study environment of the *beit midrash,* with a teacher and study colleagues, are allowed to engage in interpretive creativity. These people alone have the privilege and the obligation to study and to interpret the Torah.

Levinas accepts the premise that the holy text is designed to address all people in a manner compatible with their personality. It has relevant meaning for their individual experience of being, which differs from that of other people, thus resulting in the invitation extended to all people to try and discover these meanings. The interpretation of one person cannot exhaust the text's appeal to another due to each individual's diversity and uniqueness. Therefore, any additional interpretation is essential in the ongoing endeavor to expose the text's infinite meanings. This forms a process of accumulating interpretations that is never exhausted, a process in which constantly more meanings of the Torah are revealed. Hence, this is the connection to the holy text's source of inspiration:

> When exegesis goes beyond the letter, it is also going beyond the psychological intention of the writer. A pluralism is thus accepted for the interpretation of the same verse, the same biblical character, the same "history-making event," in the acknowledgement of the various levels, or various depths of meaning. In this polysemy of meaning the word is like "the hammer striking the rock and causing countless sparks to fly."[1] The various epochs and the various personalities of the exegesis are the very modality in which this polysemy exists. Something would remain unrevealed in the Revelation if a single soul in its singularity were to be missing from the exegesis. (*BV* 171; see 110–11, 144; *NTR* 76)

This multiplicity is not a compromise with an existing but undesirable reality. On the contrary, building on diverse interpretations is an essential part of the Torah. Every voice is necessary, coming from its own special perspective and specific place and time. Only in this way can the text's rich and varied significances be revealed, with its full abundance and additional meanings always awaiting discovery.

The *darshan* is invited to address that which is of interest in the text; the *darshan* is asked what is being said for this moment, how it touches upon his or her world, thoughts, feelings, and sensations. The *darshan* learns about the self and the world through the object of this exegesis.[2] All this is part of the text, a component of the revelation embodied in it.

There is no pretense of or search for an objective or exhaustive exegesis. Different interpretations are not necessarily right or wrong. They illuminate different aspects of the interpreted, and therefore many different interpretations are correct concurrently.

Levinas understands the process of interpretation being produced ad inifinitum with every additional commentator who addresses the text, not only as a way of revealing the meanings of the holy text but also as a way of expressing an attitude toward that which is human. "I have spoken of the importance which seems to be preserved, in the Torah—of the person of the author in relation to the statement. It is not only to stress the eventually subjective character of all truth but also to avoid losing, in the universal, the marvel and the light of the personal, to avoid transforming the domain of truth into the realm of anonymity" (*ITN* 17; cf. *BV* 84). Here Levinas is referring to the common talmudic custom of giving credit to the author of a statement cited. He attributes this inclination to the need to maintain the text's multiple voices and the distinct identity of different commentators, who are not swallowed up by the totality and uniformity of the Talmud. It is not "the Talmud says," but, rather, a certain sage, cited by name, who states his opinion and disagrees with that of another sage. This manner of bringing a statement and crediting its author establishes an attitude to biblical exegesis and exegesis of the Talmud itself as an ongoing process throughout the generations until the present.

"The realm of anonymity" ignores the individual and the personal in order to encompass all people within a single cognitive structure. According to Levinas, any generalizing system of thought, which he designates as totality, where one's individual personality is eliminated, constitutes a violent system.[3] This is a major component of his philosophy and I shall try to clarify it in this context:

> The visage of being that shows itself in war is fixed in the concept of totality, which dominates Western philosophy. Individuals are reduced to being bearers of forces that command them unbeknown to themselves. The meaning of individuals (invisible outside of this totality) is derived from the totality. The unicity of each present is incessantly sacrificed to a future appealed to bring forth its objective meaning. For the ultimate meaning alone counts: the last act alone changes beings into themselves. They are what they will appear to be in the already plastic forms of the epic. (*TI* 22)

Totality as a concept dominates Western philosophy. Generalizing concepts and historical processes are considered proper objects of thought and they grant the individual value and meaning as part of the generalization. This meaning cannot be grasped outside the totality. In other words, only that part of the individual subject to generalizing concepts or confirming the course of history is addressed, and even then only as part of the whole and not as a distinct entity. The essence is the generalization, and the details are only anonymous incidental components of this essence.

Indeed, examining the major philosophical theories throughout the ages, it is evident that attempts to understand being through generalizing concepts are indifferent toward personal existents, which merely serve as illustrations of the concept (Platonic "Ideas" with all their influences) or as a cog in the machine of history (Hegel and Marx, for instance).[4] Notably, Levinas was neither the first nor the only one to voice this criticism of Western philosophy. Franz Rosenzweig, for example, begins his book *The Star of Redemption* with a similar criticism.[5] Levinas offers an alternative to totality:

> This "beyond" the totality and objective experience is, however, not to be described in a purely negative fashion. It is reflected *within* the totality and history, *within* experience. The eschatological, as the "beyond" history, draws being out of the jurisdiction of history and the future; it arouses them in and calls them forth to their full responsibility. Submitting history as a whole to judgment, exterior to the very war that mark its end, it restores to each instant its full signification in that very instant: all the causes are ready to be heard. It is not the last judgment that is decisive, but the judgment of all instants in time, when the living are judged. (*TI* 23)

Here the terms "beyond the totality" and "the eschatological," as well as "infinity" elsewhere, are presented as alternatives to totality. These terms signify the horizon of moral thought, ethics, as distinct from the thought of existence or of being, ontology. By departing from totality they make room to facilitate the meaning of every detail and every moment. Every person is an infinity, is beyond totality. This is the significance of those who are present, who are created human beings—not as the designation of a species but, rather, as specific individuals whose value is in their uniqueness, who have no substitute, who are each one and only. When looking at living people, at values of peace and morals, every person and every moment can

Interpretive Pluralism 119

be evaluated separately, not only as part of a whole. And each individual, for example, myself, can and must be accountable for my deeds, not in the general historical sense but here and now in my attitude to other people who suffer from my actions or in how I find in them a demand to respond to their needs. Levinas further explains this:

> The eschatological notion of judgment (contrary to the judgment of history in which Hegel wrongly saw its rationalization) implies that beings have an identity "before" eternity, before the accomplishment of history, before the fullness of time, while there is still time; implies that beings exist in relationship, to be sure, but on the basis of themselves and not on the basis of the totality. The idea of being overflowing history makes possible *existents* [*étants*] both involved in being and personal, called upon to answer at their trial and consequently already adult—but, for that very reason, *existents* that can speak rather than lending their lips to an anonymous utterance of history. Peace is produced as this aptitude for speech. (*TI* 23)

Every person has an individual identity, is personally responsible for their own actions and can express themselves through personal speech. This identity is infinite and the command, "Do not murder" addresses it unconditionally. Every person has special, unique meaning. The present time of each individual, including every decision, act, and speech, has meaning and is subject to judgment and appraisal, and in this respect their significance is infinite. The horizon of thought is eschatological, a vision of peace between people; in contrast ontology is the thought of that which exists. Instead of the human deriving meaning from being, the human gives it meaning through individual efforts to promote peace. And in an attempt to avoid totality, the formulations offered by Levinas do not generalize; instead, he describes a certain encounter between one specific person and another specific person as a formative event.

If every person has a distinct, unique, and infinite identity, in both the individual's right to live and responsibility, then there is no room for "the domain of truth in the realm of anonymity." People have their own opinions and views of the world, and they have the capacity to articulate this in speech. Thus, there are many different standpoints concerning the truth.

The attitude taken by Levinas with regard to the truth and to the infinite value of the individual is reflected in his approach to exegesis. The individual is not swallowed up within the unity of truth. The commentator's individual voice is maintained as a personal voice, with all its charm and light, and this maintaining withstands the violence of its inclusion within a total system. This is the ethical meaning of Levinas's interpretive approach.[6]

Commentators who maintain the uniqueness of their voice require "freedom, invention, and boldness" (*NT* 5). All people are called upon to apply their freedom, invention, and boldness to the text in order to hear its meaning for them, a meaning that is relevant and true for them in their place and time. Exegesis is not a passive process, a hearing of the voice; rather, it is an active creative process in which the interpreting self, with all of one's intricacies, connects with the text in a very special, personal, and unique attachment. How is this process generated? Levinas writes:

> Everything depends on how we understand the unity of a spiritual work, and the spiritual unity of a people who are the bearers of such a work, even if the human may have to intervene in the very formulation of the word of God. Is the human not the very modality of the manifestation and resonance of the Word? Is not humanity, in its multipersonal plurality, the very locus of interrogation and response, the essential dimension of interpretation, in which the prophetic essence of the Revelation becomes lived experience of a life? "To be Torah from heaven": is this its origin going back to a kind of transcendental dictation, or the affirmation of this life in the Torah? (*ITN* 64–65)

According to Levinas, the word of God has no meaning in the absence of a strong relationship with the human world. Revelation is expressed in language, both written and spoken, in a human manner of expression. Furthermore, revelation was intended for humans in order to affect their life and behavior; therefore, "the human may have to intervene in the very formulation of the word of God." Without the human voice revelation has no meaning; it remains a disconnected essence, closed within itself, and unintelligible in any real context. However, the human voice is not a single voice, but multiple voices, stemming from the invention, freedom, and boldness of different people who cannot be generalized. The position occupied by Levinas in his role as commentator is that of someone offering an interpretation or an array of interpretations with no pretense of exhausting all options or of exclusivity.

The many faces of the truth, "these and these are the living words of God," its varying significance for different people—is a basic concept of rabbinic literature, one accepted by Levinas. He does not limit this invitation to rabbinic scholars. It is open to any person who approaches the text with an honest desire to study it and to learn from it, to learn about the self through it. Are there no restrictions? Are all people free to interpret the text at will? This question shall be discussed below in the section entitled "Study-Oriented Conversation and the Bounds of Freedom," but not until additional pluralistic domains are portrayed.[7]

INTERPRETIVE FREEDOM

A prominent feature of the *midrash* is the liberties it takes with the interpreted text, which are considered legitimate so long as the commentary refers to the text. At times, words may be taken out of context or split into their separate components, generating a different meaning from the plain meaning, all in the service of the reading reached by the *darshan*. As stated, there are some limitations, mainly with regard to the purpose of the commentary and its reference to the "context of the Whole" (*BV* 137). This, however, does not detract from the statement that interpretive freedom is one of the conspicuous qualities of the *midrash*.

> It is as if the words of the verse signified for the *midrash* both through their usual or main meanings, which are confirmed by their insertion into the context, but also by their secondary or even occasional meaning—which they take on, for example, by their proximity, or association, elsewhere in the vast expanse of the Bible's pages, with another verse, and other circumstances.... This is a remarkable freedom of interpretation, a freedom of the spirit that is willfully misunderstood when called "prisoner to the letter." It is as if the reverberation of each term from Scripture, the resonance of the divine word gathered up in these twenty-two signs of the holy Jewish language, were progressively more completely understood as the reading continued—with its repetitions—keeping the soul awake. (*ITN* 104 05)

These words refer to a *midrash* on the biblical text, and we have already seen that Levinas's talmudic commentary employs considerable freedom as well. What is the source of this freedom and what purpose does it serve? Once again, I shall use an example from one of the talmudic lessons to answer these questions. In Levinas's interpretation of the end of the passage in Tractate Berachot 61a in his lesson "And God Created Woman"

(NT 161–77), he describes the choice between two paths, which are both occupied. An order of priorities is proposed for choosing between problematic options: "Rabbi Johanan said: Behind a lion and not behind a woman, behind a woman and not behind an idol worshipper, behind an idol worshipper and not behind a synagogue (on the side opposite the entrance) when the community is praying" (175). This is a puzzling statement that does not seem particularly connected to anything in our current reality. How does one interpret something so foreign and irrelevant? Levinas, in his usual manner, neither ignores nor flinches from this challenge. After explaining the simple meaning of the text he adds: "To walk behind the lion: to live life, struggle, and ambition. To experience all the cruelties of life, always in contact with lions or, at least, with human guides who can suddenly turn around and show you their lion face. To walk behind a woman, to choose the sweetness of intimacy, perhaps dove coos removed from the great upheavals and the great shocks which scan the real? What peace there is in the intimacy of love! The text of the Gemara prefers the danger of the lions to this intimacy" (175). Levinas expounds on the lion and the woman as symbols representing two spheres of human life: the public and the intimate. Although lions are not commonly found on our streets, they signify public life due to their cruelty and volatility. Difficulties involving earning a living and managing a career, turbulent and even intimidating leaderships, coping with the world—all these are often experienced as threatening and even dangerous, as out of one's control. On the symbolic level, hunting, life in the wild, and the unrestrainable natural world have given way to the need to earn a living and to public life.

The statement that it is preferable to walk behind a lion than behind a woman, on the level of the *pshat,* seems to belong to a world of superstitions, of apprehension aroused by the female other, of magic. All this seems outdated and irrelevant in a society where women are involved in all spheres of life, side by side with men. But if, as a metaphor, women signify the realm of the intimate, the complete opposite of the public realm, then the dilemma portrayed in the Talmud becomes relevant for modern life as well, with regard to both men and women. To what degree should one focus on one's safe and protected intimate life, and to what degree should one leave this shielded space for the "jungle of life"? In the Talmud, the identification of women with the intimate realm is common and almost taken for granted (the word *beyteh* is used for both one's wife and one's home, indiscriminately). Levinas's attitude to women and to the feminine is an extensive, intricate topic[8] and it shall not be explored here. In this talmudic lesson, Levinas suggests that women's femininity is secondary to their humanity, a humanity common to all human beings. If we reduce the term "femininity" to this meaning, it may be what one misses when at the center of public action.

According to this interpretation, the position taken by R. Johanan sides with leaving the safe protected intimacy of the home for public life, for coping with the cruel world outside the home. Levinas further interprets another symbol that may seem meaningless to modern people:

> But our text still prefers the sentimental road to that of idolatry. Idolatry, that is no doubt the State, the prototype of idolatry, since the State adores being an idol, idolatry, that is also the cult of the Greek gods and hence all the appeal of Hellenism. It is probably because it evokes Greece that idolatry can still be preferred to something else! But idolatry encompasses all the intellectual temptations of the relative, of exoticism and fads, all that comes to us from India or China, all that comes to us from the alleged "experiences" of humanity which we would not be permitted to reject. (NT 176)

Idolatry in its plain meaning has little significance for secular people living in a society of monotheistic faiths, but the state with its inclination to self-worship—and the state is always inclined to self-worship—has a presence in their lives and constitutes a problem for them. The violent mechanisms wielded by the authorities against the individual are familiar to all citizens everywhere. But this comment seems to be addressed mainly at those who believe that all human problems can be solved by changing the system of government (communism, for example). The state is always a type of idolatry, serving itself before it serves the individual, and for this reason Levinas is suspicious of it. The relationship between Western culture with its roots in ancient Greek thought, to which most of Levinas's audience belongs, and Judaism, is a current issue as well. Who should we walk behind if we are to adopt the figurative language of the interpreted segment? Should one become assimilated in Western culture or be a Jew and only then a member of Western culture? And perhaps, are there also intermediate courses of action, as illustrated by Levinas in his entire enterprise?

The false charms of New Age culture have not disappeared. On the contrary, their power is increasing, and Levinas objects to them as well and calls them idolatry. He permits himself a great deal of interpretive freedom, allowing himself to link the text to his audience, and in this he seems to be acting as a *darshan* rather than as a philosopher. Everything identified here as idolatry has values in common that seem to attract contemporary people but reflect a misguided world of values.[9]

Is walking behind the lion, meaning leaving the sphere of intimacy, not the equivalent of politics? What is the distinction between public life and politics, between the lion and idolatry? It may touch upon the boundary between ethics and politics. Involvement in public life might become idolatry when one loses one's judgmental-critical attitude toward the state, once the individual fully identifies with its way. The state is essential for the existence of justice, and this is the purpose of its legal and judging mechanisms; but it is also aggressive and blind to individuals and their unique needs. The individual is responsible for confronting the state from a critical standpoint and for seeing that those whose needs are disregarded by the state and whose rights it tramples are protected. In this respect, "walking behind idolatry" means identifying with the state instead of identifying with and acting on behalf of those who are repressed by the state and whose rights it tramples. Hence, walking behind the lion, which means acting in the world, is not the same as walking behind idolatry, which means identification with the state.

Levinas's complex attitude to Hellenism is evident in his comment that recognizing idolatry as Hellenism makes it possible to prefer it to that which appeared subsequently. Hellenistic culture has many reprehensible elements, and his philosophy deals with them; however, this culture also represents universalism and a rational language that is a common basis of thought and conversation.[10] If we return to the language of the text, which this interpretation treats as a parable, then walking behind the lion as leaving the realm of the individual, leaving the home for public life, a life in which one is responsible for one's colleagues, is indeed preferable to remaining in the intimacy of the home.[11] All this precedes and predicates political and cultural life, which run the risk of idolatry. And finally: "The fourth thing is the worst; worse than the enthusiasm for idolatry. Isolation within Judaism, a *no* uttered to the community. To be outside a synagogue filled with people, that is the extreme apostasy; to say: that does not concern me, that concerns the Iranians and not the Israelis, that concerns immigrant Jews and not French Jews" (*NT* 176).

Here too, that which on the level of the *pshat* might seem a superstitious act—walking behind the synagogue when prayers are in progress—receives meaning that is entirely relevant for the audience. Beyond the statement that walking behind the synagogue is an intentional choice to exclude oneself from the community, this seems to allude to contemporary events (what did those Israelis have to do with the Iranians, and the French Jews with the immigrants?) and to the position taken by some of those present with regard to these events. Renouncing the public—renouncing one's collective affiliation and the responsibility that is derived from it—is even worse than idolatry, than complete identification with the authorities or with a foreign culture. This interpretation is an implicit but direct criticism of some of those in the audience.

Levinas provides a commentary on a segment that seems puzzling and irrelevant for contemporary readers, and he gives it meaning that not only is comprehensible but also arouses fundamental questions associated with the reality of most of his listeners. He makes a double effort: on one hand, he does not consider any part of the text unnecessary, outdated, or uninteresting. If it was written, it must be important. On the other hand, he does not let go of the premise that these words must be understood and meaningful for all readers in all eras, and in particular for Levinas and his audience. This is the strict and restrictive framework that keeps the mechanism of interpretive freedom and creativity in motion. Any commentary that allows one to keep all parts of the text and give them meaning and significance for the readers is admissible and desirable. This is the tension that exists between tradition and innovation, and it is an essential part of the *midrash* as a major tool in the development of Jewish culture. Addressing and connecting to a constantly shifting reality demands and facilitates interpretive freedom.[12]

Interpretive freedom, while a means of linking the text and the reader, is also intended to turn us toward each other and to teach responsibility for the other person. This responsibility is imposed on human beings as members of the human race, originating as it does from transcendence, from the commanding God. This is the meaning of the inspiration embedded in these texts, and this is the purpose of studying and learning them. Torah study itself, unlike intellectual preoccupations, invites the commentator to open up to a voice of otherness that addresses him or her through the text, that invites the commentator to interpret it and be turned toward the other person. This premise requires interpretive freedom, because the text does not always appear to be dealing with human relationships. In many cases, that is not the plain meaning. Let us consider, for example, the lesson "For a Place in the Bible" (*ITN* 11–32), which interprets a passage in Tractate Megillah 7a. Its second part deals with the question of whether the Scroll of Esther defiles the hands, which is the halakhic way of asking whether the scroll is considered holy.[13] The affirmative answers given are based on various verses showing that the scroll was written "in the holy spirit"; it consists of things that humans cannot know. These proofs are all refuted by Rabba, who finds a human, rational explanation for each. The argument he accepts as proving the scroll's holy status is the *midrash* by Shmuel: "Shmuel said: If I had been there, I would have said a stronger word than all those: It is written therein: 'The Jews fulfilled and accepted…' (Esther 9:27). It was recognized on high what the Jews had accepted down below. Rabba has said: 'In the remark of each one there is difficulty, except in the remark of Shmuel'" (*ITN* 27).

Shmuel says that the scroll's holiness is proven by its acceptance and by the Jewish holiday commemorating its events. All this was recognized, he says, "on high" as well. How does Shmuel know what happened in heaven? That is the very point of his *midrash:* that which is accepted and recognized by the people exists inherently in heaven as well and thus receives the status of a religious precept. Levinas explains this: "What guarantee is there that the acceptance of the law of Purim and of the Megillah and their entry into the liturgy and the Bible belongs to the order of the absolute? It is the very fact that the acceptance took place in the History of Israel. Shmuel teaches that it is the historical Israel that continues Holy History and

Interpretive Pluralism 127

ensures the inspired meaning of the texts" (*ITN* 29). The historical factor, that is, continuous observance of the precept for generations, attests to its holiness. The inspiration of the Scriptures owes its existence to the fact that there are those who occupy themselves with the Scriptures and there are those who live their life accordingly. This is the interpretation of Shmuel's approach. The talmudic discussion ends here, with no manifest discussion of the scroll's contents. It limits itself to a discussion of the scroll's holiness and its acceptance in practice. This is emphasized by the two final statements: "Rav Yosef deduces [the inspired nature of Esther] from this: 'These days of Purim will never disappear from among the Jews' [Esth. 9:28]. Rav Nachman deduces it from this: 'Their memory will not disappear from among their descendants'" (30).

But for Levinas this is not enough: "There remains for me, however, an important question, perhaps the most important one of all. 'They fulfilled and they accepted.' Does this give no indication, then, with respect to the content that this Holy Story—the history of Israel—is called upon to bring forth? Does Esther's right to a place in the Bible remain purely formal?" (*ITN* 31). On the *pshat* level of the Gemara the answer to this question is in the affirmative, but Levinas presumes that it must be related to the contents of the scroll, capable of teaching and enhancing what he perceives as the purpose and content of the Scriptures. Therefore, he adds his own *midrash*: "I think that fundamental ethical event narrated in that book is already of itself the confirmation by the Heavenly Tribunal of the welcome the Jews gave the feast that commemorates it and the Book that relates it" (31). This event is Esther's choice to approach the king in an attempt to save the Jews from his decrees, even at risk of her life: "And then I will go to the king, though it is against the law, and if I perish, I perish" (Esth. 4:16). On this Levinas writes: "The death of the other takes precedence in my concern over my own, 'They fulfilled and they accepted.' This is not simply a midrashic interpretation arising from an unexpected order of terms in a text, to affirm the privilege of a history without regard for what it contains. It is rather the saintliness that a book consecrates that allows it to enter into the Holy Scriptures" (31–32).

These ideas were added by the commentator and are not implied in the talmudic text. This is a very free *midrash,* free even from the text. But it is still part of the text's interpretation due to its deep affiliation with the spirit of the words or with what the *darshan* grasps as the essence of these texts.[14] Levinas's boldness resembles the boldness of the sages who allowed themselves to expound the text in a way that contrasted with its plain meaning, based on their confidence that this is the real aim of the text.[15] Both the sages and Levinas presume that the Torah can't possibly contradict ethics, and they allow themselves maximal interpretive freedom in order to confirm this assumption. Levinas goes even further by finding ethical meaning where the text appears to be discussing something else.

Interpretive freedom is typical of Israeli pluralistic *batei midrash* as well. For instance, people who do not adhere to halakhic authority seek in the text cultural and social meaning that is relevant for their world, and they take a great deal of liberty when interpreting the distinctly religious aspects of the text. This is also true of feminist commentaries that interpret the text in a way that supports the values of women's equality and the visibility and articulation of feminine perspectives, which are almost completely absent from the texts and give voice to female characters who are silenced in the text. All of this is grounded on the same premises as the *midrash* of the sages and of Levinas. The premises entail a deep respect for the text as the basis of a culture, as its origin and source, yet without relinquishing value systems formed outside the text and influenced by the commentator's time and place. This course of action reflects not a bowing down to the text but, rather, a creative conversation with it, possibly culminating in a transformation of its meaning but not in its rejection.

STUDY-ORIENTED CONVERSATION AND THE BOUNDS OF FREEDOM

This multiplicity of diverse voices and interpretive freedom raise the question of limits. Is all commentary legitimate? Does this freedom have no bounds? As stated above, Levinas claims that interpretations that contradict what he defines as "the context of the Whole" (*BV* 137), which directs the Self toward the Other, are not legitimate interpretations. He also often speaks of the correct approach to interpretation: he objects to intellectual engagement in the text, to exegesis that disregards the practical implications of studying. In his opinion the Torah should not be treated as an object of research but, rather, as a teaching (Torah) aimed at life.

This is the basis for the principles that guide his commentary. But this is not enough. The exegesis must be informed by discourse between people, in a process of study-oriented conversation. The process of interpersonal learning connects students to the text's study tradition, provides them with tools to understand and compose commentary, and allows them, by way of questions and exploration with others, to form their own unique interpretation. Commentators do not generate their commentary in a void. They require a study-oriented environment, including a teacher and colleagues, with whom they can form a study dialogue. Why is this so?

> Does human intelligence allow itself to be thought as the excellence of a particular? General reason must start with a human assembly and must be able to connect with others and with universality. It participates in the glory of the genus. Intelligence is by essence teaching and is nourished by its very communication. Students' questions are indispensable to the teacher's answer. Such at least is the way of the Torah, always studied in a group, and between men bent over the text who do not spare themselves objections, refutations, attacks, defense—"wars of the Torah"—in which father and son mercilessly confront, repulse and collide with one another. Here, contra all dogmatism, are the dialogues, vehement as they must be, necessary to the spiritual unity of a dispersed Judaism. (*NTR* 98; cf. *ITN* 58–59; *OB* 26–27)

The idea that each personal voice is crucial in order to expose the meanings of the revelation makes it difficult to maintain "the spiritual unity of a dispersed Judaism." Levinas is well aware of the danger of dispersal and dissolution that is inherent in the call to give voice and significance to each personal unique voice. But in his opinion, study-oriented conversation is that which makes it possible to maintain the diversity without reaching a state of complete dispersal. Exchanging opinions, attempting to understand the opinion of the other, and arguing with the other form a unity despite the diversity. This should not be construed as agreement or as one uniform voice but, rather, as dialogue—an encounter between different people, the discourse formed between them, and their need to relate to each other's words. Study-oriented conversation takes the holy text as its point of origin. Individuals, whether students or teachers, are free to express their opinions and to explain them. But they are not completely free: the people learning with them constitute the framework of this freedom and scrutinize that said. Indeed, rabbinic literature includes clear traces of study-oriented conversation. The talmudic study methods developed and maintained over the ages are dialogue-oriented as well. The figure of the teacher and of the *havruta*—the colleague with whom one studies—who explore the meaning of the text and argue have a prominent place in the *beit midrash* and the *yeshiva*. The study process is an ongoing conversation, a relationship between the written text and the people who address each other. Unlike libraries, the *beit midrash* is a noisy place where people talk and even argue with each other.

When the truth is composed of multiple truths or different perspectives, study-oriented conversation ensures a certain unity. But it also has a role in the process of forming an individual interpretive voice involved in the process of learning the text within a specific context and has the aim of expanding this context:

> That study is not the activity of a lone individual and that essentially truth must be communicated, that the "I think" is sociality, and that communication of truth is not an addendum to truth but belongs to the reading itself and is part of the reader's concern. But, if it is necessary to teach the Torah in order to perpetuate it, it is probably also necessary that the student should ask questions. The student, being both other and, generally speaking, younger, must come with questions, in the name of the future, and bodily, despite the respect due to the master. The student will ask questions based on what the Torah will mean tomorrow. The Torah not only reproduces what was taught yesterday, it is read according to tomorrow; it does not stop at the representation of what yesterday and today goes by the name of the present. (*ITN* 66; cf. *BV* 47–50)

Study-oriented conversations occur in a shifting reality; therefore, the gradually emerging exegesis changes as well. The Torah, or the revelation, is a continuous process of interpretation formed by different people, arising from study-oriented conversations that take place within time and are transformed by time. Students studying under their teacher accept the teacher's suggestions and thus connect to the previously formed interpretive tradition; their role, however, is to renew it and to adapt it to their perspective, which stems from changes in reality. In this way the process continues over time. The commentator must be familiar with the text's interpretive tradition and must refer to it when developing the commentary, even if he or she objects to previous proposals. Through knowledge of tradition and by reference to it, a certain unity is maintained, resulting in a common reading of the text within the pluralistic diversity. Hence, the interpersonal study process facilitates a delicate balance between tradition and innovation. This approach is not innovative, but it is the customary Jewish approach. Classical editions of the Pentateuch, Mikraot Gedolot, and the Vilna Edition of the Babylonian Talmud reflect this approach by placing the interpreted text at the center of the page, surrounded by many levels of interpretation that argue about the text. This intergenerational conversation is still ongoing.

Levinas studied Talmud under Mr. Chouchani, whom he frequently mentions both explicitly and implicitly, and with his study colleagues, whom he mentions from time to time. His talmudic lessons were delivered orally before appearing in written form, and in this respect he remains loyal to his principle that the Torah should be learned in a process of conversation. What is the meaning of this principle? The study-oriented *havruta* (partnership) facilitates a deep and vital study process: the individual's comprehension is limited. Exchanging opinions with other people reveals new points of view and other understandings of the text that are inaccessible to the independent learner. Moreover, the consideration of different interpretations, whether in consent or in disagreement, allows learners to refine, expand, and intensify their own opinions and to further understand their significance. Through the process of learning and conversation, questions and responses, learners are able to clarify their own position and the implications of the text for their world. In other words, study-oriented conversation is a way of connecting with the lives and various points of view of different people on the same matter, both within the text and in reality. Assuming that the texts studied are aimed at shaping the face and lifestyle of society, studying in a society, albeit a small one, is a type of laboratory for the material studied. This study experience is inseparable from the contents that are taught. This is the power of the Torah study tradition, developed and preserved as a dialogic tradition.

The group aspect of study and its value for shaping social norms outside the *beit midrash* were developed and refined at the *beit midrash* of Hamidrasha at Oranim and others like it. This pedagogy combines awareness of the group process with the studying of the content. The basic conception is that Torah study in a group, while maintaining awareness of the relationship between the learners and the changing dynamics of this relationship, is an inseparable part of the study process. It is a form of training destined to eventually influence participants as well as their interpersonal relationships outside the study setting and the walls of the *beit midrash*. Moreover, the multiple voices and the exchange of opinions are enriching and are considered to have a great deal of value for understanding the many facets of the text. The option of disagreeing with the interpretation proposed by a colleague, without undermining its legitimacy, is an exercise in pluralism. In this way studying in a group, in conversation between learners and inviting multiple interpretations, is strongly related to the study goals.

As Levinas says, "In itself, this Talmudic text is intellectual struggle and courageous opening unto even the most irritating questions. The commentator must carve out a path toward them without letting himself be deceived by what appears to be Byzantine discussions. In fact, these discussions conceal an extreme attention to the Real. The pages of the Talmud... register an oral tradition and a teaching which came to be written down accidentally. It is important to bring them back to their life of dialogue or polemic in which multiple, though not arbitrary meanings arise and buzz in each saying" (*NT* 4). And here Levinas adds a note about his own exegetical writing: "Dialogue is not easily brought to life again in its written remains. We have, at any rate, kept our commentary in the form of oral delivery it had at the colloquia, not even eliminating from it the addresses to this or that friend or interlocutor present in the conference room" (10n4). All publications designated "talmudic readings" (*lectures talmudiques*) are a subsequent transcribing of lessons originally taught by Levinas orally. He chose to leave traces of the original oral form with the intention of reflecting talmudic writing:

> We have retained the rhythm of their original oral version in their current written form and have included as well few reminders of the circumstances in which they were spoken.... This form seems suited to the presentation of passages from the Talmud, which is an oral teaching. Even in its transformation into tractates, the Talmud preserved the openness and the challenge of living speech. It cannot be summarized by the term "dialogue" which is so abused today. This discourse does not resemble any other literary genre: talmudic speech is no doubt its model and its proper, privileged place. (91; see *DF* 59)

In what way do Levinas's talmudic readings differ from the rest of his works? *Beyond the Verse,* which includes five talmudic lessons, also encompasses two other essays based on talmudic interpretation: "The Name of God according to a Few Talmudic Texts" and "Revelation in the Jewish Tradition" (*BV* 116–28, 129–50); however, these are presented within a section entitled "Theologies." What is the distinction? Levinas writes about this: "'Theologies' includes studies which certainly also refer to Talmudic particulars, but concern, more especially, exegetic methodology, points of doctrine and religious philosophy" (xiv). The treatise on the names of God studies a selection of segments from the Talmud and was first published in a collection of essays following a conference held in Rome in 1969. Perhaps it was not included in the category of talmudic lessons due to its selective and inconsistent structure or because it is a thematic study focusing on a specific topic, unlike his continuous interpretive readings of entire talmudic passages.

This point is further clarified by comparing his essay on Jewish exegesis—a more consistent although not entirely continuous reading of a page in Tractate Makot 13b—with his interpretation of the same page in a slightly different adaptation but with similar contents, which appeared as a talmudic lesson in *New Talmudic Readings* (*NTR* 47–77). What does this comparison teach us? The talmudic lesson was taught in 1974 but only published in writing in 1996, while the essay was first published in 1979. There are many differences between the two, but I shall only point out several that are relevant for us. The written version of the talmudic lesson appears to have been carefully edited by the author, leading to the conclusion that traces of its oral origins were retained intentionally and with much thought. The most fundamental difference between these two texts, however, which subsequently generated others, has to do with the attitude to the talmudic text. The essay focuses on its topic, the role of exegesis, its features, and its connection to the inspiration of the text. Indeed, an entire paragraph on this topic is absent from the talmudic lesson. Then again, the essay skips the commentary on several sections of the passage that are irrelevant for the topic discussed in the essay. "The Will of God and the Power of Humanity" (*NTR* 47–78) is closely aligned with the continuous form of the passage, delves into all its parts, and deals with the connection between heaven and earth, between transcendence and the commentator's hermeneutical interpretation of the verses. The different context is important here since a foundation of the talmudic lesson, as of the *midrash,* is that the specific context of the exegesis affects its contents. Levinas listens to what the text wishes to say to him as a specific commentator, in a specific time and place, and in a specific context; therefore, different meanings are heard. However when he teaches Talmud he is committed to the text and its continuity more than to the topic on which he chooses to focus. The essay is a thematic study of the passage while the talmudic lesson is a continuous and attentive study of it, Torah study.

All this leads to the conclusion that "talmudic reading" is not merely a title. It is the name of a genre, whose features include the continuous reading and interpretation of a talmudic passage, making connections between its parts, and taking care to clarify that this is a written post hoc version of an oral lesson. Does this inform and affect the contents?

Loyalty to the course and order of the interpreted text may be a good way of allowing it to teach and give voice to that which the self finds difficult to extract from within, that is, openness to the Other, which in this case is the written text. Learning the text while responding and listening to its structure, to the order that may sometimes appear incongruous and illogical, may itself be an exercise in opening up to otherness. Unlike an essay that collects quotes in order to construct a well-built argument, an essay whose author arranges his or her knowledge to form a logical structure, loyalty to the text summons a different type of consciousness. It is no longer a matter of having knowledge, of conceptualization but, rather, of listening and opening up. It is an attempt to understand that which is written, to question, explore. It is an attitude of respect toward the text.

What characterizes Levinas's talmudic readings, which were taught orally and subsequently written down? Each talmudic lesson has an introduction. In these introductions he regularly apologizes for pursuing talmudic exegesis, for the quality of the translation provided, and for the lack of time. He explains his choice of passage, which at first glance might seem puzzling or incomprehensible, and refers to the current issues that motivated his discussion of the topic. Once the talmudic readings were gathered in a book, these introductions tended to repeat themselves. Levinas was probably aware of this and seems to be inviting the reader of the talmudic lesson to enter it as a student hearing a lesson and not as a scholar reading an article. He is also connecting the reader to the concrete circumstances of the original lesson. This commentary was intended for a certain audience—Jewish intellectuals in France in the second half of the twentieth century—that was preoccupied, as was Levinas, with topics arising from their reality. At times, the commentary has a universal meaning or a meaning that goes beyond the circumstances that prompted it; however, it was not produced in isolation from them and it is one of many routes that could possibly be summoned or facilitated by other circumstances and other *darshanim*.

In his lessons, Levinas often alludes to members of the audience whom he mentions, as well as people with whom he argues, quoting their words. For example: "I want to acknowledge those who have allowed me to penetrate into my text more deeply, in the study sessions and classes in which we 'turned in every which way,' and I want to cite not only my friend Dr. Nerson, for the whole interpretation, but also on this particular point my friend Theo Dreyfus" (NT 59).[16] He often mentions his Talmud teacher, Mr. Chouchani, mainly in connection with the exegetical method and not necessarily as a source of interpretations. In the lesson "Toward the Other" the *darshan* relates that he consulted with Mrs. Atlan in order to figure out the meaning of Rav's dream and he thanks her (24–25). One lesson ends with quotations from the book *Vie et destin* (*Life and Fate*) by Vassily Grossman (ITN 89–91).[17] He often refers to the words of other commentators, mainly Rashi and the Maharsha, and sometimes even bases his words on their commentaries.

However these references only serve to underscore the fact that, unlike the rabbinic *midrash*, these talmudic readings were generated by a single person. They constitute transcripts of open lectures, and not of symposiums in which different people took part in the creative process and offered their interpretations. The talmudic readings lack the horizontal dimension of discourse between teacher and students or among colleagues, at least in generating the commentary. Levinas, who often stresses and wonderfully interprets the meaning of the sages' different opinions in the talmudic passages and the way in which each opinion and debate illuminates other sides of the truth, other outlooks, or the complexity of the topic under discussion, does not demonstrate this aspect in his lessons. When he refers to something said by a member of the audience, he usually does not use an exact quotation but only refers to the contents of their words. And when referring to a specific person present in the audience, or whose words were heard or read by those present, these words are not quoted in full or in a way that would allow the reader to relate to them directly; rather, they are adapted by Levinas through his opinion and response to them. This may be attributed not only to the difficulties involved in converting study-oriented conversation to written form but also to the fact that Levinas belongs, in a deep and essential sense as he says of himself, to Western culture and to the academic world where people convey their ideas to others in the form of an article or lecture. In this world, the creative location of discoveries is the scientist's study or the library where the scholar sits quietly, and not the study hall of a yeshiva where many people study concurrently, speaking to each other, arguing, and exploring issues. Thus, although he attributes a great deal of significance to study-oriented conversation, the talmudic readings are not a distinct outcome of such a conversation. His commentary, however, is a real conversation with the text, with its structure and what might appear to be its oddities, and it is an attempt to involve his audience and the live circumstances of the study process.

In this context it should be noted, once again, that Levinas has no pretensions of offering the one true interpretation of the passage that occupies him. He states repeatedly that his efforts are only his own attempt at understanding and decoding the text, among one of many previous and future attempts. He gives this serious statement a humorous twist: "Will you again allow me to guess at one of the 2,400,000 meanings that the prohibitions I have just summarized comprise?" (*NT* 123). The truth embedded in the Scriptures is an endless collection of these unique voices, of which his, with all its significance and uniqueness, is only one. This is the position and the point of origin to which Levinas adheres, despite his arguments with different interpretive approaches. Hence, the author's apologies in the introduction to each of the talmudic readings seem to express an approach to the text, to the interpretive act in general, and to his own commentary.

This talmudic commentary, with its many midrashic features, was generated by a single man and not in conversation with others, and in this respect it differs from the classical *midrash*. It carries within it the echoes of past voices, quotations of talmudic commentaries, citations of his teacher and colleagues, and traces of that which took place among those listening to the lessons when they were delivered orally. The multiple voices are also evident in the multiple interpretations offered by Levinas himself and in his arguments with other interpretive methods. The close link between the commentary and the circumstances in which it was formed, its approach of not purporting to have produced an exhaustive commentary but only one of many possible options, and its adherence to the continuity of the text all represent the pluralism of the *midrash*.

The clarification that the text was written in retrospect, following oral study, is an invitation to open up to the otherness of the text. It consists of neither judgment nor research but, rather, entering into a dialogue with the text and an involved reading that summons other interpretations. This design has an effect on the contents. And just as the Talmud invites studying that consists of conversation—not only between the learner and the text but also among the learners themselves—Levinas's talmudic lessons do so as well. These lessons should be learned in conversation with other people—a *hevruta,* a teacher, or a group of colleagues.

Torah study of the type proposed here establishes a society. It requires a community of men and women with different opinions and perspectives who creatively and fearlessly study together, converse, and exchange opinions. This study group is a type of laboratory or a model of a proper society, with room for multiplicity and diversity, in which the individual is empowered by the group and the force of conversation and listening are acknowledged. In this respect, Levinas's talmudic readings offer formative principles for pluralistic *batei midrash* as well as suitable study materials to be used therein.

Chapter 6

Unique Features of Levinas's Midrash

The current volume builds on the basic assumption that the *midrash* has served as a major method of Jewish biblical exegesis, one that significantly contributed to its development over generations. Although the *midrash* has many common features, *midrashim* of various types, periods, and sources are discernable. The relationship between certain commentators and the text is evident in the orientation of their exegesis. It is indeed possible to distinguish between different midrashic orientations of the sages, such as the school of R. Ishmael and the school of R. Akiva in the case of tannaitic *midrashim,* or Hillel and Shamai and other well-known scholarly opponents. Essential differences are also evident between the rabbinic *midrash* and that of the Zohar literature, between an Orthodox rabbi's lesson on the section of the week, and a feminist *midrash*. The mere idea of the *midrash,* with the major place it accords the commentator's outlook, world, and personality, invites different types of *midrashim*. Therefore, questions regarding the focus of a certain *midrash,* its emphases, and what it chooses to disregard, among other things, can facilitate its comprehension. All this is also true of the *midrash* devised by Levinas, and in this chapter I shall discuss its unique features.

The Purpose of Exegesis Is to Expose the Ethical Meaning of the Text

According to Levinas, the holiness of the Torah is derived from its contents, as it redirects people from a concern for persevering their own being and toward the other person and assuming responsibility for the other's needs. The Torah seeks to influence the conduct of those who study it, and first and foremost their relationship with the other. The Scriptures direct those studying them to the face of the other person: "The direct relation with the true... that is, the reception of Revelation—can only be the relation with a person, with another. The Torah is given in the light of a face. The epiphany of the other person is *ipso facto* my responsibility toward him.... Integral knowledge or Revelation (the receiving of the Torah) is ethical behavior" (*NT* 47). In other words, the basic assumption of Levinas's exegesis is that there is a strong, inseverable connection between the holy text and one's attitude to the other person, and that the *darshan* must uncover the text's call for action on behalf of the other person. This is the gist of his exegetical consciousness: exegesis as he sees it is not merely a proper understanding of the text. It is, first and foremost, a decoding of the call for action, for ethical behavior. In this respect, it is a revelation. The creative consistency employed by Levinas in transposing all religious concepts into something that is also aimed at one's ethical behavior, even if indirectly, has to do with the association between the vertical and the horizontal dimensions—that is to say, with the association between commandments dealing with human relationships (*ben adam lahavero*) and those dealing with the relationship between human beings and God (*ben adam lamakom*).

The word "religion" (*dat*) in modern usage is usually used to designate the relationship between humans and God, a sphere perceived as unrelated to socioeconomic relationships, which are considered secular. In biblical and rabbinic literature, however, these spheres are not so distinctive; on the contrary, they are interrelated. For example, two major sages, Hillel the

Elder and Rabbi Akiva, perceive human relationships as the Torah's focal point: "Hillel said: What is hateful to you do not do to your friend, that is the whole Torah, while the rest is the commentary thereof, go and learn it" (Babylonian Talmud, Tractate Shabat 31a). "'You shall love your friend as yourself' (Lev. 19:18). R. Akiva said: This is a great principle of the Torah" (Jerusalem Talmud, Tractate Nedarim 9:4). The relationship between religion and ethics has occupied many throughout the generations, and it is a major issue in current-day Jewish thought as well.

The question of the relationship between ethics and metaphysics in the philosophy of Levinas has attracted considerable research attention.[1] In our context it can help to explain his systematic hermeneutical interpretation of every religious and theological concept in the text as having an ethical meaning.

In his essay "Demanding Judaism" Levinas describes Judaism as a "demand for justice which is its actual religious message" (BV 3), but is this indeed true of Judaism? Is it merely a demand for social justice? If so, how can we understand ritual commandments such as *kashrut*, the types of work forbidden on the Sabbath, and prayer? How can we explain concepts such as "sanctity," "God," "sacrifices and worship of God," and "fear of God"? The course represented by Levinas is not a reduction of religion to ethics. It reflects a more intricate, complex relationship of integral interdependence between the vertical and horizontal dimensions.[2] They are indeed distinct and not identical, but it is not possible to single out the one dimension and disregard the other.

The lesson "Toward the Other" was taught in 1963 at the colloquium of French-speaking Jewish intellectuals entitled "Le Pardon," meaning both forgiveness and repentance. In the lesson, Levinas links the two meanings. This lesson centers on the other person and one's responsibility toward the other, not only as the essence of human existence but also as the contents of religious experience. Both the worship of God and repentance are distinctly human processes that occur between people even when their meaning is religious. Let's consider several segments of this lesson that focus on this topic:

> Those present for the first time at this session of Talmudic commentary should not stop at the theological language of these lines. These are sages'

thoughts, not prophetic visions. My effort always consists in extricating from the theological language meanings addressing themselves to reason. The rationalism of the method does not, thank God, lie in replacing God by Supreme Being or Nature or, as some young men do in Israel, the Jewish People or the Working Class. It consists, first of all, in a mistrust of everything in the texts studied that could pass for a piece of information about God's life, for a theosophy, it consists in being preoccupied, in the face of each of these apparent news items about beyond, with what this information can mean in and for man's life. (*NT* 14)

The basic assumption of this statement and of Levinas's talmudic commentary in general is that theological language, what might seem like theosophy, has meaning in and for human life. Theology does not precede ethics and cannot be separated from ethics. One must guard against any pretense of knowing God. Theology that is unrelated to ethics is ontology. It transforms God into an object of consciousness, which takes hold of its objects and generalizes them within its totality as part of the Same (*le même*). This is an aggressive and violent course, to which Levinas strongly objects in his writings, and particularly in *Totality and Infinity* (*TI* 33–52, 187–201, 254–86). God is transcendent, beyond the comprehension of human consciousness; God interferes with the persistence of the same as the Other that is completely other and therefore unknowable and unperceivable. Theology considered separately from ethics is easily separated from reality and ignores the practical implications of its ideas in a world where people live together.[3]

Hence, in the introduction to the lesson "Toward the Other," Levinas asserts that God must not be perceived in isolation from reality and social life and from the human meanings of this concept. In fact, he chooses to deal with this aspect only, as he declares in the introduction to *Of God Who Comes to Mind*: "The various texts assembled in this volume represent an investigation into the possibility—or even the fact—of understanding the word 'God' as a significant word. This investigation was carried out independently of the problem of the existence or nonexistence of God" (*GCM* xi).[4] This is a radical course—disregarding the question of God's existence and the possibility of understanding the concept of God in isolation from the horizontal dimension, and instead, focusing on "what this information can mean in and for man's life" (*NT* 14). If so, the way to infinity, to God, is irrevocably tied to human relationships: "Through my relation to the Other, I am in touch with God. The moral relation therefore reunites both self-consciousness and consciousness of God. Ethics is not the corollary of the vision of God, it is that very vision.... The knowledge of God comes to us like a commandment; like a *Mitzvah*. To know God is to know what must be done" (*DF* 17). It is indeed possible to distinguish between self-consciousness and consciousness of God, and between my relationship with the other person and my relationship with God, but they are strongly linked. The revelation is of the human other and of the Divine concurrently. The encounter with the face of the other person is the revelation, an encounter in which the self is transcendentally commanded to take responsibility for this other person. This is an event that cannot be divided into components. It happens all at once and its full significance is both religious and moral.

My relationship with God consists of obeying commandments that direct me to the other person. "God revealed in his Names is given a meaning from out of the human situations" (*BV* 123). The revelation is embodied in the face of the other person, in the responsibility he imposes upon me, which brings God to mind. God is the source that commands a type of relationship between people, a community of responsibility and obedience. This is Levinas's metaphysical ethics, or ethical metaphysics, and his interpretation of the Scriptures and location of ritual, prayer, and Torah study follow from this outlook. The ritual commandments are predicated on obedience and teach awareness of the other person. The course is clear and consistent, and it keeps away from customary concepts and from the plain meaning of many parts of the text (86–99, 116–28).

The organizing element, the most dominant value, is a certain attitude toward the other person, one of responsibility and commitment. Thus, it is not possible to think of or to perform a religious act while ignoring its social implications. There can be no *mitzvah* that results in harm to another person or that even ignores its offensive consequences.[5] Then again, one's attitude to the other person does not exist independently; rather, it is related to one's attitude to God. Consider another section of the lesson "Toward the Other":

> We know since Maimonides that all that is said of God in Judaism *signifies* through human *Praxis*. Judging that the very name "God," the most familiar

to men, also remains the most obscure and subject to every abuse, I am trying to shine a light on it that derives from the very place it has in the texts, from its context, which is understandable to us to the degree that it speaks of the moral experience of human beings. God—whatever his ultimate and, in some sense, naked meaning—appears to human consciousness (and especially in Jewish experience) "clothed" in values, and this clothing is not foreign to his nature or to his supra-nature. The ideal, the rational, the universal, the eternal, the very high, the trans-subjective, etc., notions accessible to the intellect are his moral clothing. I therefore think that whatever the ultimate experience of the Divine and its ultimate religious and philosophical meaning might be, these cannot be separated from penultimate experiences and meanings. They cannot but include the values through which the Divine shines forth. Religious experience, at least for the Talmud, can only be primarily a moral experience. (*NT* 14–15)

Levinas is referring to Maimonides' rejection of any positive statement about God, because God's essence is unknown to us. All we can say about God is necessarily in a negative form: God is not anything we can imagine. For example, we cannot say that God is wise, because God's wisdom vastly exceeds that which we are capable of understanding as wisdom, and therefore, this statement has no real content. This is explained at length and in detail in his doctrine of the divine attributes, where Maimonides barely "allows" the use of words that designate actions rather than their actor: "He performs acts similar to those which when performed by us, originate in certain psychical dispositions…and not a result of any emotion.… The same is the case with all divine acts: though resembling those acts which emanate from our passion and psychical dispositions, they are not due to anything superadded to His essence.… To show that all attributes ascribed to God are attributes of His acts, and do not imply that God has any qualities."[6] Levinas bases his own conception on that of Maimonides, though remaining distinctive: "Everything I know of God and everything I can hear of His word and reasonably say to Him must find an ethical expression" (*DF* 17).

Maimonides says that through the actions of human beings it is possible to understand something of God's actions, while Levinas claims that any reference to God "must find an ethical expression." Speaking of God's actions in isolation from a relationship of responsibility between people has no meaning, and no other discourse on God or obedience to his words can have meaning if it lacks such an orientation (*BV* 126–28). Speaking of

God outside of any ethical context is meaningless. The vertical dimension always guides the horizontal dimension, always redirects us to the other person.

Let's return to the Talmudic lesson: "Above all, my concern will be to keep this moral plane" (*NT* 15). Levinas reveals his hermeneutical premises: "We can thus boldly approach this religious text, which lends itself in a wonderfully natural manner to philosophical language. It is not dogmatic, it lives off discussions and debates. The theological here receives a moral meaning of remarkable universality, in which reason recognizes itself. Decidedly, with Judaism, we are dealing with a religion of adults" (15). "A moral meaning of remarkable universality" asserts that the Jewish texts have universal messages. This is an example of how Levinas transposes religious concepts, such as "*am segulah*," that is, a people "chosen from among all the nations" and gives them moral meaning. A concept that appears to belong to the religious sphere, to the relationship between God and the people of God, is translated into one bearing universal social meaning with practical implications in the world. He rejects a meaning that seems obvious due to its possible ramifications and, in contrast, offers an interpretation that addresses the moral face of all humanity. "A religion for adults" is a religion that holds people fully responsible for their actions and for the consequences of these actions.

Further on in this Talmudic lesson, Levinas interprets the Mishna in Tractate Yoma:

> "The transgressions of man toward God are forgiven him by the Day of Atonement; the transgressions against other people are not forgiven him by the Day of Atonement if he has not first appeased the other person" [Yoma 8:9].
>
> A few quasi-terminological explanations are in order: The Day of Atonement permits the obtaining of forgiveness for faults committed toward God. But there is nothing magical about this. It is not sufficient that dawn break on *Yom Kippur* for these faults to be forgiven. The Day of Atonement is certainly a fixed date in the calendar, and forgiveness, that is, the freeing of the guilty soul, requires a set date in the calendar. For the work of repentance requires a set date: to enable this work to take place every day, there must also be a day reserved especially for repentance. At least such is Jewish wisdom. (*NT* 15–16)[7]

According to Levinas, the commandments—the concrete practical form of ideas—are intended to encourage and perhaps even to demand the practical realization of values. "Jewish wisdom" knows that it is not enough to determine a system of values in order to ensure that people will abide by this system. The commandments, the set dates, and the practical framework of Jewish law are intended to help one realize the values that the Torah wishes to promote. It is not enough to ascertain that it is important to rectify misguided deeds, and it is not enough to show remorse internally. Jewish law states that processes that take place within a person's inner regions are not enough to change a situation or to change behavior. The date and the rituals involved in this day are intended to ensure, or at least to facilitate, the realization of repentance in the life of a person committed to this value system. The Day of Atonement is not merely a date; it encompasses an entire legal framework:

> But the Day of Atonement does not bring about forgiveness by its own virtue. Indeed, forgiveness cannot be separated either from contrition or from repentance, or from abstinence, fasts, or commitments made for the Better. These inner commitments can become collective or ritual prayer. The interiority of the engagement does not remain in this interior stage. It gives itself objective forms, such as the sacrifices themselves were in the time of the Temple. This interdependence of inside and outside is also part of Jewish wisdom. When the Mishna teaches us that the faults of a man toward God are erased by the Day of Atonement, it wants to say that the celebration of *Yom Kippur* and the spiritual state it brings about or expresses lead us to the state of forgiven beings. But this method holds only for faults committed toward the Eternal. (16)

It is easy to express remorse. It is harder to make a commitment to real change in one's behavior. That is the purpose of the commandments one is required to observe on the Day of Atonement—prayer, fasting, and asceticism. Levinas stresses the association between the idea and its translation into a certain series of actions. But all of this is only true of transgressions against the Eternal, transgressions that do not involve an offense against another person but only against God. Hence, transgressions against other people are not identical to religious transgressions: an injustice committed toward another person cannot be fully rectified in the religious sphere. This is a statement of the Mishna, and Levinas only underscores it here. If the sin committed is a moral sin, religion is not an easy solution for reaching a clean conscience. It is not enough. He continues:

> Let us evaluate the tremendous portent of what we have just learned. My faults toward God are forgiven without my depending on his good will! God is, in a sense, the *other, par excellence,* the other as other, the absolutely other—and nonetheless my standing with this God depends only on myself. The instrument of forgiveness is in my hands. On the other hand, my neighbor, my brother, man, infinitely less other than the absolutely other, is in a certain way more other than God: to obtain his forgiveness on the Day of Atonement I must first succeed in appeasing him. What if he refuses? As soon as two are involved, everything is in danger. The other can refuse forgiveness and leave me forever unpardoned. This must hide some interesting teachings on the essence of the Divine! (16)

Is it not surprising that, according to Levinas the process of interpersonal forgiveness, though dependent on the good will of the offended, exemplifies the essence of the Divine and not, as we would expect, the essence of interpersonal relations? Of the other as reflecting the divine essence Levinas writes elsewhere: "In the access to the face [of the other] there is certainly also an access to the idea of God" (*EI* 92). The relationship with the other person has religious significance; it is a divine commandment and also the only way of drawing closer to the Divine. The ethical relationship is a relationship with God; therefore, it is capable of illuminating the Divine.

At the same time, the statement that "as soon as two are involved, everything is in danger" emphasizes that although the ethical relationship has religious significance it is not fully encompassed by religion. It is necessary to directly approach the other person. And here, each person is a separate, unique infinity that cannot be generalized within any type of totality. There is no formula for rectifying an offense committed against human beings. In the relationship between a person and God a general, perpetually appropriate mechanism of atonement can be ascertained, but the infinite uniqueness of each person precludes such a possibility among human beings. Asking the other for forgiveness requires a special act, that of appeasement. This idea shall be explained below, but first I shall clarify the difference between commandments dealing with human relationships and those dealing with the relationship between human beings and God.

Levinas may appear, at times, to intentionally blur the distinction between these realms, but he does not present them as indistinguishable:

> How are the transgressions against God and the transgressions against man distinguished? On the face of it, nothing is simpler than this distinction: anything that can harm my neighbor either materially or morally, as well as any verbal offence committed against him, constitutes a transgression against man. Transgressions of prohibitions and ritual commandments, idolatry and despair, belong to the realm of wrongs done to the Eternal. Not to honor the Sabbath and the laws concerning food, not to believe in the triumph of the good, not to place anything above money or even art, would be considered offences against God. These are the faults wiped out by the Day of Atonement as a result of a simple contrition and penitential rites. It is well understood that faults toward one's neighbor are *ipso facto* offences toward God. (*NT* 16)

Human transgressions against God belong to two categories: transgressions of ritual commandments and transgressions related to one's inner self. The latter consist of beliefs, inclinations, and mental states that hamper one's ability to function in a moral setting, such as despair, lack of faith in the triumph of the good, and not placing anything above money. But according to Levinas, ritual commandments also have a role that exceeds their mere existence:

> For there to be justice, there must be judges resisting temptation. There must be a community which carries out the *mitzvot* right here and now.... That is because the power of these *mitzvot* is presupposed—their power to penetrate the soul. Also presupposed is the history that has made Israel submit to them, and, above all, the force of will which at Mont Sinai could decide for the *mitzvot*—which are stronger than all the forces of evil and vulgarity that Jews and the rest of mankind undoubtedly have in common as long as one keeps to the "purely natural" plane. (83–84)

This passage does not distinguish between different types of commandments. All the commandments are intended to subdue the natural evil and vulgarity common to all humankind.[8] The entire system of religious commandments was intended to mold and educate people, to restrict their natural tendency to persevere their being, with the aim of arousing them to awareness of their responsibility for the other. Hence, it is not possible to understand the system of human transgressions against God outside of an interpersonal or moral context, as these commandments are also associated with human relationships. Levinas does not leave room in his philosophy for a theology detached from human relationships; he objects to the mere concept of theology, and thus, his commentary is to a large degree an attempt to translate theological concepts.

The distinction between the two types of commandments is determined by their different perspectives: is it a commandment that deals directly with the other person or one that predicates and facilitates the observance of these commandments by restricting natural human inclinations? This could lead to the conclusion that Judaism as perceived by Levinas is nothing more than an improved and developed ethics. He is aware of this possibility and responds by saying something else: every transgression among people is also a human transgression against God. Namely, this is not an ethical reduction. This idea is elucidated further on:

> One could no doubt stop here. It could be concluded a bit hastily that Judaism values social morality above ritual practices. But the order could also be reversed. The fact that forgiveness for ritual offences depends only on penitence—and consequently only on us—may project a new light on the meaning of ritual practices. Not to depend on the other to be forgiven is certainly, in one sense, to be sure of the outcome of one's case. But does calling these ritual transgressions "transgressions against God" diminish the gravity of the illness that the Soul has contracted as a result of these transgressions? Perhaps the ills that must heal inside the Soul without the help of others are precisely the most profound ills, and that even where our social faults are concerned, once our neighbor has been appeased, the most difficult part remains to be done. In doing wrong toward God, have we not undermined the moral conscience as moral conscience? The ritual transgressions that I want to erase without the help of others would be precisely the one that demands all my personality; it is the work of *Teshuvah,* of Return, for which no one can take my place. (*NT* 16–17)

Transgressions against God "undermine the moral conscience." Levinas is concerned by a solution characterized by a clear hierarchic order whereby "Judaism values social morality above ritual practices." He appears to be contending here with two different value systems and, incidentally, also with the following question: if the attitude to other people is the heart of the matter, what is the purpose of religion? Morality exists independently of religion. He takes a dim view of Western humanism, which, despite its wonderful values with regard to human relationships, failed to prevent the injustices of the twentieth century, including the mass murders committed in the name of Nazism as well as those of the communists—based as they were on these very values. In his opinion, the advantage of Judaism is in its practical orientation, which relates both to the obligation to realize its values in practice and to the implanting of obedience, thus instilling and forging a spirit that more effectively links the world of values and the practical world. Western humanism has failed, and Levinas appears to be searching for a solution to this failure, presuming to have found it in the Jewish faith, to which people are committed beyond themselves and despite themselves. Defending the weak is not only a matter of conscience; it is also a religious demand supported by a halakhic system that trains people to obey and to be aware of the needs of the other.

Levinas is also implicitly taking issue here with classic Reform Judaism, which enthusiastically embraced the commandments that concern human relationships while ignoring those that concern relations between people and God.[9] In his opinion, this type of Judaism is afflicted by the same ailments as Western humanism and is condemning itself to a fate of assimilation. Studying the Jewish texts and observing the ritual commandments are essential in order to shape and nurture that which is good in humankind and to preserve the unique Jewish message for the world. This is why he repeatedly stresses the significance of the ritual commandments, although he perceives them as directing and facilitating the ethical life, and observance of the commandments that concern human relationships.[10]

With regard to his argumentative technique, as in his talmudic readings, Levinas offers suggestions rather than lecturing. When he says, "It could be concluded a bit hastily that Judaism values social morality above ritual practices. But the order could also be reversed," he is offering two interpretive options. The style here requires interpretation and enables more than one reading, but it also accepts a complex message, whereby the moral commandments are indeed the crux of the matter but are inseparably tied to the ritual commandments. If he had chosen to convey this sentence in the form of a plain statement, he would have lost an important part of his message. The mutual relations between the realm of human relationships and the relationship between people and God, where neither of these two components can be relinquished, is the meaning conveyed here in a language that does not force itself on the listener or the reader. Levinas was speaking to an audience comprised mainly of people not committed to the ritual commandments, a situation that may have aroused his urge to emphasize this component. By taking the form of an interpretive suggestion his words enable a true consideration of the argument without letting anyone feel under assault. If he had said outright that the ritual commandments are indispensable, this might have aroused the strong objection of those who do not observe them. Thus, his style here makes it possible to relate to his arguments in a more matter-of-fact way, with the listener capable of choosing how to understand them and which conclusions to reach.

Levinas continues:

> To be before God would be equivalent then to this total mobilization of oneself. Ritual transgression—and that which is an offence against God in the offence against the neighbor—would destroy me more utterly than the offence against others. But taken by itself and separated from the impiety it contains, the ritual transgression is the source of my cruelty, my harmfulness, my self-indulgences. That an evil requires a healing of the self by the self measures the depth of the injury. The effort the moral conscience makes to reestablish itself as moral conscience, *Teshuvah,* or Return, is simultaneously the relation with God and an absolutely internal event. (NT 17)

"My cruelty, my harmfulness, my self-indulgences" are corruptions that prevent me from conducting myself morally, and that is why the offense is so deep and so difficult to rectify. This is the "absolutely internal" component of repentance. By emphasizing the severity of transgressions against God—the significance of the vertical dimension for the horizontal dimension of proper human relations—Levinas distances himself from the humanistic option. Both spheres and dimensions are vital and interdependent. On the one hand, any perception of the religious dimension in isolation from its significance for human relationships is meaningless; on the other hand, the social-moral dimension, that is, human relationships, cannot be contained in an exclusively human sphere. Levinas continues:

> There would thus not be a deeper interiorization of the notion of God than that found in the Mishna stating that my faults toward the Eternal are forgiven me by the Day of Atonement. In my most severe isolation, I obtain forgiveness. But now we can understand why *Yom Kippur* is needed in order to obtain this forgiveness. How do you expect a conscience affected to its marrow to find in itself the necessary support to begin this progress

Unique Features of Levinas's Midrash 151

> toward its own interiority and toward solitude? One must rely on the objective order of the community to obtain this intimacy of deliverance. A set day in the calendar and all the ceremonial of solemnity of *Yom Kippur* are needed for the "damaged" moral conscience to reach its intimacy and reconquer the integrity that no one can reconquer for it. This is the work that is equivalent to God's pardon. This dialectic of the collective and the intimate seems very important to us. The Gemara even preserves an extreme opinion, that of Rabbi Judah Hanassi, who attributes to the day of *Yom Kippur itself*—without *Teshuvah*—the power to purify guilty souls, so important within Jewish thought is the communal basis of inner rebirth. Perhaps this gives us a general clue as to the meaning of the Jewish ritual and of the ritual aspect of social morality itself. Originating communally, in collective law and commandments, ritual is not at all external to conscience. It conditions it and permits it to enter into itself and to stay awake. It preserves it, prepares its healing. Are we to think that the sense of justice dwelling in the conscience, that wonder of wonders—is due to the fact that for centuries Jews fasted on *Yom Kippur,* observed the Sabbath and the food prohibitions, waited for the Messiah, and understood the love of one's neighbor as a duty of piety? (*NT* 17)

In this section, Levinas repeatedly clarifies the vital role of the ritual commandments in shaping a spirit and a state of consciousness that enable repentance. But he adds the communal component of the religious ritual, resulting in the dialectic of public and private, of the external and internal. People do not live in a bubble; they need a community to provide them with support and to maintain their "Jewish sense of justice." The community provides a supportive partnership. Rectifying one's interiority is a difficult operation, and the mere proximity of people who are going through a similar process can be helpful. Moreover, human society is important in order to achieve the final goal of repentance, that is, improved moral behavior. The ethical approach dictates relations within the community. The presence of other people beside me emphasizes, by simply existing, the severity of my deeds and the need for internal rectification. From this respect, the community is both the reason and the purpose of repentance.

Further on in the talmudic passage interpreted by Levinas (Tractate Yoma 87a), Rabbi Joseph bar Helbe takes issue with the Mishna's opinion and quotes a verse in which Eli the Priest says to his sons: "If a man offends another man, Elohim will reconcile. If it is God himself that he offends, who will intercede for him?" (1 Sam. 2:25). According to the plain reading of the verse, God grants atonement for a person's transgressions against other people but not for a person's transgressions against God. It is as though transgressions against other people are merely religious, and therefore, their process of rectification is religious, and that is sufficient. R. Abbahu, his opponent who represents the opinion of the Mishna, rejects the opinion of Rabbi Joseph bar Helbe, which seems to be the plain meaning of the verse, by using a bold hermeneutical interpretation that involves supplementing the words of the biblical verse. And since the opinion represented by R. Abbahu concludes the discussion, the redactor of this passage wishes to reinforce this opinion, and that of the Mishna, and to remove any doubt as to whether atonement for transgressions against other people can be achieved without asking the other person for forgiveness. The text completely rejects any attempt to separate religion from morality. But for Levinas this is not enough, and here is his interpretation of the opinion of Rabbi Joseph bar Helbe:

> But does Rabbi Joseph bar Helbe, who is so expert in exegesis, uphold the literal meaning of the verses? Doesn't he also have an idea in the back of his head? "If a man offends another man, Elohim forgives or Elohim straightens out or Elohim reconciles...." Is it possible that Rabbi Joseph bar Helbe thinks that incidents between individuals do not shake the equilibrium of creation? Will you interrupt the session if someone leaves the room offended? What is it all in the face of Eternity? On the superior plane, the plane of Elohim, within the absolute, on the level of universal history, everything will work itself out. In a hundred years, no one will think about our sorrows, our little worries and offences!...
>
> The tears and the laughters of mortals do not count for much, what matters is the order of things in the absolute. You must see Rabbi Joseph bar Helbe's exegesis to the end: The irreparable offence is that done to God. What is serious is the attack of a principle. Rabbi Joseph bar Helbe is skeptical regarding the individual. He believes in the universal. An individual against an individual has no importance at all, but when a principle is undermined, there you have catastrophe. If man offends God, who could set the disorder straight?...
>
> The text of the Gemara rises against this virile, overly virile, proposition,[11] in which we can anachronistically perceive a few echoes of Hegel; it is against this proposition, which puts the universal order above the interindividual order, that the text of the Gemara rises. No, the offended individual must always be appeased, approached and consoled individually. God's

> forgiveness—or the forgiveness of history—cannot be given if the individual has not been honored. God is perhaps nothing but this permanent refusal of a history which would come to terms with our private tears. Peace does not dwell in a world without consolations. On the other hand, the harmony with God, with the Universal, with the Principle, can only take place in the privacy of my interiority, and in a certain sense, it is in my power. (*NT* 19, 20)

The *midrash* offered by Levinas on the opinion of Rabbi Joseph bar Helbe is anachronistic, and in it he gives voice to Hegel's historicism as well as to the great ideologies of the twentieth century. He translates the danger of separating the vertical from the horizontal dimension—the danger of placing supreme, absolute values above the individual and his or her tears—into current-day language and a context that is not necessarily religious. But even when speaking of God or of religion, or when speaking of some ideology, I cannot justify in the name of absolute values ignoring a certain person whom I encounter and who needs me. On the contrary, the proper order is always to meet the needs of the other person and only then to fulfill any other type of duty. This is also the attitude of the *midrash* elsewhere: when Abraham saw three people walking in the desert (not knowing that they were angels), he asked God to wait until he finished hosting them. The *midrash* utilizes the word *adonay,* which according to the plain meaning of the verse refers to the three people, and then interprets it as addressing God (*Adonay* is also a designation for God)—asking that God wait:

> Rav Yehuda said in Rav's name: Receiving guests is greater than welcoming the Divine Presence for it is written, "And he said: My Lord(s) (*adonay*), if now I have found favor in your sight, pass not away" (Gen. 18:3). R. Eleazar said: Come and observe how the conduct of the Holy One, blessed be He, is not like that of mortals. The conduct of the mortals is such that an inferior person cannot say to the greater man, Wait for me until I come to you; whereas in the case of the Holy One, blessed be He, it is written: "My Lord(s), if now I have found favor in your sight, pass not away."[12]

God can and should wait, because God is the source of the command to feed the hungry and let the thirsty drink. God is the source of the command and precedes the command in time (in Levinas's terms: always from time past, who cannot be remembered because God is always there before me), but in the order of preferences nothing has preference over feeding the hungry person. Otherwise, this might lead to a reversal of the scale of values.

Levinas moves on:

> "If a man offends another man, Elohim reconciles...but if the transgression is against God...." The sentence is said by the great priest Eli admonishing his sons. Unworthy priests, they seduced the women who came to the Tabernacle and took an undue share of the offerings of the faithful. "My children, stop doing this," Eli said to them, "if a man does wrong to another man, God will forgive, but if the fault is toward God, who will intercede?" But the fault of Eli's sons seems to be toward men. The injury done to God, then, is the abuse of power that the very person put in charge of safeguarding the principles slides into. Who will be able to intercede? Who can intervene? In the name of what Law? Those who are given the responsibility of applying the Law reject the Law and turn the scale of values upside down. (*NT* 22)

Here Levinas attempts to assimilate the concept of God discussed at the beginning of the lesson. The verse quoted in the argument between R. Abbahu, who represents the opinion of the Mishna, and Rabbi Joseph Bar Helbe, on the question of whether one is indeed required to ask the forgiveness of the offended person, recognizes the offense against people as an offense against God. Before Eli speaks to his sons, we are given details of their transgressions against human beings. But Eli treats these offenses as transgressions against God. Hence, Eli's words in the verse are interpreted as enhancing the arguments made by Levinas, whereby any offense against another person is also an offense against God. All transgressions between people have within them a component of transgression against God, and an offense against God is first and foremost an offense against one's capacity to choose goodness (an internal offense).

Another type of transgression committed by human beings against God is also indicated here—the abuse of power. Governmental authorities and leaders are responsible for guaranteeing the rights of those subject to their rule and for seeing that their needs are met. Taking advantage of this authority to serve oneself at the expense of these values is an abuse of power and an offense against the social establishment. The social establishment, responsible as it is for the well-being of those subject to it, is a manifestation of divine authority, and therefore any offense against it is an offense against God. The damage done is irreparable. Furthermore, a priest who performs a ritual commandment but in the process inflicts harm on people represents the most serious reversal of values. Rituals cannot be separated from the moral behavior of their practitioners.

From all the above we can conclude that the vertical and horizontal dimensions are indeed not identical but are nonetheless interrelated. If left alone, the horizontal dimension is destined to fail under pressure, as it is incapable of arousing the self from its sameness toward the Other; and the vertical dimension alone is destined to become involved in a dangerous distortion of values, as it is intended to turn us toward each other. By basing his words on the Mishna and interpreting it in order to contend with this topic, Levinas is conveying an implicit message, namely, that this idea is not only his but is also a fundamental cultural conception. But his infallible consistency in this matter is what makes the moral content of his hermeneutics its major feature.

I would like to continue discussing this matter through the concept of "holiness," a distinctly religious concept. Holiness can be an essential feature of an object, time, place, or person, and in such cases, it results in a certain conduct toward that which is holy. In contrast, holiness can be perceived as an ideal that poses a set of demands attempting to generate the holiness of an object, time, place, or person. For example, we may ask whether the holiness of the Sabbath is a given, a part of its essence, and human beings are only required to honor it; or we may ask whether human beings sanctify the Sabbath through their acts, such as by saying the *Kiddush* or refraining from work. Is holiness a given or do human actions create holiness? Who sanctifies the holy, God or humans? This question has far-reaching religious and ethical implications. These two extreme conceptions, as well as intermediate ones, are evident throughout generations of Jewish thought.[13] What does Levinas have to say on this matter?

At the beginning of his lesson "Desacralization and Disenchantment" (*NT* 136–60),[14] Levinas speaks of "holiness, that is, separation or purity" (141). But even earlier, in his subheading, he distinguishes between two concepts that in both French and English share the same meaning. Annette Aronowicz, who translated his *Nine Talmudic Readings* into English, used the word "holy" for one and "sacred" for the other.

Levinas tries to distinguish between two types of holiness of which only one seems desirable. "Sacred" designates a numinous holiness, that is, a given quality. Those endowed with this quality are expected to serve as a medium of direct contact with God and of merging with the Divine. In his opinion, the sacred bears great similarity to sorcery and to various types of sleight of hand. It strives to eliminate the difference between the self, the Same, and the transcendent Other and to transform them into one totality. Moreover, it creates an illusion of sanctification that might lead to a shirking of social responsibility. In other words, the sacred is an attempt to connect with the vertical dimension in isolation from the horizontal dimension, and for this reason it is dangerous and inappropriate. The thought that it is possible to connect to God, to eliminate God's transcendence without relating to the human other, is an illusion and contradicts God's "separation and purity," that is, God's holiness: "The numinous annuls the links between persons by making beings participate, albeit ecstatically, in a drama not brought about willingly by them, an order in which they are lost.... The Sacred that envelops me and transports me is violence" (*DF* 14). If so, what is holiness in the positive sense, in the sense of "separation and purity"? First of all, it is an attitude that retains the separateness of people and God, of the Same and transcendence: "It is a great glory for God to have created a being capable of seeking Him or hearing Him from afar, having experienced separation" (15).

But second, and more than this, it has to do with the forging of human relationships: "This is the origin of the idea whereby human relationships constitute in a certain respect the most supreme religious act. Independent of any manifestation of ritual religiosity, even without any religious unification in the narrow sense of the word" (*UH* 118). Levinas does not often use the word "holy" (or "holiness") in a positive sense. He seems to worry about the similarity between holiness and the sacred. Nonetheless, and in order to further understand his approach, we can see in his lessons how he relates to objects designated holy in the interpreted texts. I will offer three examples.

The lesson "Model of the West" discusses, among other things, the shewbread (bread placed in the Tabernacle and in the Temple), and the Mishna describes the ritual of the weekly replacement of this holy bread in detail.

> The bread in question, *Lehem hapanim,* is translated as "Shewbread." Translating these words literally, one should say: "bread of faces." Why "bread of faces"? Rashi says: bread which has two faces because of the shape in which it is baked, these faces being turned toward the two sides of the sanctuary.[15] According to Ibn Ezra—who is probably less pious than Rashi, but has also said some extraordinary things—"bread of faces" is the bread which is always before the face of God.[16] I think the two interpretations are not dissimilar. What should bread before the eyes of God do, if not look at men? What other purpose should it have, if not to feed men? The horizontal direction of the look is the completion of the look descending from above. I know that "horizontal" and "vertical" are terms which are currently being discussed in the search for the meaning of the religious. The two directions, I believe, orientate the same movement.... Let us also emphasize that the bread in question is not originally communion bread: it is first and foremost the bread of the starving, and only by being such is it, perhaps, communion bread. (BV 18–19)

The holiest bread, placed in the holiest place, is holy because it is the bread of human beings, because it, so to speak, looks at the faces of human beings. It serves as a constant reminder to those seeing it that they must see to the food of hungry people, and it is ultimately eaten by the priests. "God's dominion" is the turning of one person toward another. This is the meaning of holiness according to the *midrash* offered by Levinas. The holiness of a place or of an object has to do with the manner in which it turns people toward each other. It is a challenge more than a quality, a task to be accomplished. The Temple, including its vessels and rituals, is holy because it directs people toward each other. The vertical dimension is never separate from the horizontal dimension, and exegesis is always required to extract the Torah's ethical meaning, because its ultimate aim is to form an improved society.

In the lesson "Damages Due to Fire," Levinas interprets a passage in Tractate Bava Kamma (60a b), which cites a list of instructions for times of crisis and hardship. Levinas writes:

> No escape into isolation! Watch out for the peace of private worship! Beware of dreams in an empty synagogue!
> "There is a *baraita*: If there is an epidemic in a city, one should not go to the house of prayer alone, for it is there that the angel of death keeps his implements; this is true, however, only in the case where schoolchildren

do not read Scriptures there and where there are not ten people to pray (together)."...

Not to seek refuge in the artificial peace of synagogues and churches! We have already spoken about this. Except if life is not absent from them, if children are learning Scriptures there and if prayer proceeds there from a collectivity. No lull in solitude. I do not know what Clausewitz would think of the thesis that arms are stored in synagogues which do not engage in public worship and in holy places which are not also schools. But that is undoubtedly where ideologies, oppositions, and murderous thoughts are born. If there are children who read Scripture, the murderous engines of the inner life lose their explosive force. (*NT* 193)

A holy place, even a synagogue, that contains no people might become sacred in certain circumstances. The empty holy place allows us to imagine holiness in isolation from people, and therefore, it is an illusion—a lethal ideology or thought. It is not possible to connect or to draw close to the holy directly through devotion, even fanatically, in the absence of other people. An idea that is not directly associated with the faces of people easily deteriorates into an ideology that sanctifies in its name even the loss of human life. The presence of people emphasizes the separateness of the holy, its otherness, and its power to command one to turn toward these people. In this respect, the presence of children causes the murderous engines to lose their force. When the face of the child that is encountered stands against the desire to save the world at any price in the name of a sanctified ideal, this face may be capable of reinstating the human, non-absolute dimension within one's consciousness. The sanctified can once again become holy.

Holiness is derived from the prayer of people praying together and from children studying. Any ritual act or object that has no intrinsic stipulation or intention to direct one to assume responsibility for the other person is merely a manifestation of the sacred and not of holiness. Can we go even further and say that observing a religious or ritual commandment as a purpose unto itself, rather than as an intention to obey a command that directs me to the face of the Other, is not an act of holiness and belongs to the realm of the sacred?

In the lesson "Cities of Refuge," which discusses the holiness of Jerusalem, Levinas speaks of "the impossibility for Israel—or according to Israel—of religious salvation without justice in the earthly city. No vertical dimension without horizontal dimension. An unavoidable stage-of-justice for all elevation.... There is no other access to salvation than that which passes through the dwelling place of men" (*BV* 38). The holiness of Jerusalem is not in heaven, detached from earth. There can be no religious peace without justice, and there can be no holiness without peace. Speaking of Jerusalem's holiness without relating to its human reality is meaningless. The holiness of Jerusalem is "the hope of a science of society, and of a society, which are wholly human" (52). Jerusalem must serve as an example of a city in which, more than in any other, justice is carried out.

In all these examples, holiness is not merely a given feature.[17] It exists only if it serves an interpersonal purpose. The bread is holy because it is the bread of people and is supposed to remind us of the duty to care for the hungry. The synagogue is holy if groups of people pray or study there. Jerusalem is holy if it teaches and exemplifies how social justice is realized in cities. And as we have seen, the Torah is holy because it teaches us all of these things.[18] Since the purpose of the Torah is to convey this message, Levinas is completely consistent in translating any religious or theological term that might seem to refer only to the vertical dimension as having significance for human relationships as well.

This approach is not compatible with the plain meaning of the text. Similarly to holiness, love of God, fear of God, and worship of God may be perceived as foci of the divine command, as concepts with religious and not necessarily ethical content. With regard to fear of God, Levinas expounds: "'The unique treasure of the divine treasury is the fear of God' (Brachot 33b).... The fear of God which reveals itself concretely as the fear for the other person.... But the possibility of adhering to this total and unique alterity—that is, of bearing witness through this obedience to Highness would define and justify the humanity of Man, and describe his freedom" (*BV* 96).[19] Fear of God is not fear of a supreme, external force; rather, it is fear for the fate of the other person for whom I am responsible. In this way, worship of God is also understood as obedience to the divine command that directs me toward the other person. One's attitude to God is an attitude to the other person, and Levinas often speaks of the attitude to the other (*l'autre*) in reference to both God and human beings. This ambiguity is intentional. My attitude to the other person is an expression of my attitude to God. The former derives from the latter. They depend on each other and are inseparable.

This is a demythologization of the concept of God. We know nothing about God, and such an abstract conception of divinity is incompatible with the plain meaning of the stories and descriptions of a personal God as they appear in the Scriptures. Since we know nothing about God, the only significance that can be attributed to anything said about Him is through the human-moral context. This is what Levinas calls "a religion of adults" (*NT* 15; cf. *BV* 3–10; *DF* 11–23). In this context, it is worthy to note that he approaches the question of divinity from another direction as well, that is, through the concept of the "trace" that he uses in his later writings. When he says that the ethical command is heteronomous, that the face of the other person is a revelation or it is an encounter with transcendence, when he claims that beyond ontology is that which is beyond being—what does he mean, what is he talking about? His answer is "God." But the face of God is never revealed; it is not possible to know God directly, but only to follow God's traces. In this context, Levinas often mentions the revelation to Moses in the cleft of the rock, when he asks to see God and God answers: "You will see my back but my face shall not be seen" (Exod. 33:23). These traces, preceding all time in time, always from a past that cannot be remembered, are those revealed in the face of the other person and in the Scriptures as commands, and lead to that which is beyond.

People are exposed to religious concepts that have ethical goals through the study of Torah: "Man, therefore, learns humanity of the fear of God through the Torah. The study of the Word of God thus establishes or constitutes the most direct relation to God, perhaps more direct than the liturgy" (*BV* 97). On this matter Levinas does not refrain from far-reaching statements:

> In the light of this, I wonder whether there are not aspects in Judaism which indicate the "rationality" of a reason less turned upon itself than the reason of philosophical tradition. For example, there is the primordial importance in Judaism of the prescriptive, in which the entire Revelation (even the narrative) is formed according to both the written teaching (the Pentateuch) and the oral teaching. Or the fact that the revealed is welcomed in the form

of obedience, which Exodus 24:7 expresses in the phrase: "All that the Lord has spoken we will do, and we will listen to it." The term evoking obedience here ["we will do"] is anterior to that which expresses understanding ["we will listen"].... It is an obedience, rather, which can be traced back to the love of one's neighbor: a love without eros, without self-complacency and, in this sense, a love that is obeyed, the responsibility for one's neighbor, the taking upon oneself of the other's destiny, of fraternity. The relation with the other person is placed at the beginning! (146; cf. *ITN* 58–59)

Discussing the essence of Jewish rationalism, unlike Greek rationalism, Levinas repeatedly asserts that everything contained in the Written Law and the Oral Law is in fact a call for obedience to a command to assume responsibility toward the other person. This is how he perceives the Torah, and this directs his interpretation at life and at human relationships.

The rituals of the Day of Atonement, the shewbread in the Temple, the holiness of Jerusalem, and the significance of the State of Israel—all these are interpreted by Levinas as having distinct ethical meaning, and these are only a few examples. This is the essence of his hermeneutical enterprise. He attests to this and realizes it. Indeed, this orientation is evident in a great many rabbinic *midrashim*, but there are also many *midrashim* with other orientations. The prominence of this orientation within Levinas's philosophy and its constancy identify the connection between ethics and metaphysics, between religion and morality, as a major feature of his hermeneutical works.

The Text Has Universal Meaning

The universal meaning that Levinas finds in the text is another unique feature of his hermeneutics. The uniqueness of the People of Israel versus other nations is a topic frequently discussed in the Bible and in the Talmud. The People of Israel are designated *am segulah*, a treasured people, and this has many halakhic and moral implications. The plain meaning is that, since the People of Israel are a chosen people and they alone were given the Torah, the laws of the Torah, both ritual and social, apply only to them. For example the ban against giving loans with interest says: "You may charge interest to a foreigner, but don't charge interest to your relatives" (Deut. 23:21). Is Israel's uniqueness manifested primarily in its essential difference from other nations, thus translating into a system of privileges, or does it mean an extra commitment and responsibility as a result of Israel's mission within the nations? On this question different opinions are already evident in rabbinic literature,[20] and it has served as grounds for dispute throughout the history of Jewish thought and halakhic rulings.[21] The attitude of Levinas to this issue is complex:

> Here are some indications as to the extent of the other man's right: It is practically an infinite right. Even if I had the treasures of King Solomon at my disposal, I still would not be able to fulfill my obligations. Of course, the Mishna does qualify this. In question of the other man, who descends from Abraham, Isaac, and Jacob. But do not become alarmed. We are not in the presence of a racist idea here. I have it from an eminent master: each time Israel is mentioned in the Talmud one is certainly free to understand by it a particular ethnic group which is probably fulfilling an incomparable destiny. But to interpret in this manner would be to reduce the general principle in the idea enunciated in the Talmudic passage, to forget that Israel means a people who has received the Law and, as a result, a human nature which has reached the fullness of its responsibility and its self-consciousness. The descendants of Abraham, Isaac, and Jacob are human beings who are no longer childlike. Before a self-conscious humanity, no longer in need of being educated, our duties are limitless. Workers belong to this perfect humanity, despite the inferiority of their condition and the coarseness of their profession.... The heirs of Abraham—men to whom their ancestor bequeathed a difficult tradition of duties toward the other man, which one is never done with, an order in which one is never free. In this order, above all else, duty takes the form of obligations toward the body, the obligation of feeding and sheltering. So defined, the heirs of Abraham are all the nations: any man truly man is no doubt of the line of Abraham. (*NT* 98–99)[22]

A "racist" reading of the text (i.e., understanding it in its plain meaning) reduces its meaning and also its implications—and that is why Levinas rejects this reading. This is his own moral decision. As one who was persecuted on racial grounds during the Holocaust he is unwilling to accept a worldview based on such concepts. He completely rejects any racial or essentialist way of thought. For this purpose, he makes use of classical midrashic methods, such as those with the formulations "Do not read...rather" (*al tikrey...ela*), "Maybe...but the Torah says" (*yachol...talmud lomar*), "I have only...but the Torah says...in any case" (*Ein li ela...*

talmud lomar…mikol makom), which address the plain meaning of the text only in order to then refute it and show that its real intention is different.[23] Levinas systematically and consistently interprets any such reference to the People of Israel as having implications for all humanity, as bearing a universal message. In the section quoted above, he repeats his statement that the term "the descendants of Abraham, Isaac, and Jacob" has no genetic significance and does not confer any privileges. It is a universal term with ethical meaning that applies to people who accept the law of the Torah that commands them to assume infinite responsibility for the other person. Anyone who accepts these obligations is a descendant of Abraham, Isaac, and Jacob.

The reference to the Torah and to Judaism as bearing a message for all humanity and having a universal mission is not unique to Emmanuel Levinas. What makes this approach a unique feature of his *midrashim* is his manner of systematically and consistently explaining any expression of ethnic particularism, any appearance of the word "Israel" and the like, as having an ethical-universal meaning:

> The manner in which I read the Talmudic text (a manner I have not invented, for it was taught to me by a prestigious master[24]) consists in never giving the word "Israel" only an ethnic sense.… The notion of Israel designates an elite, of course, but an open elite and an elite that is defined by certain properties that concretely are attributed to the Jewish people. This enlarges every perspective opening on to the Talmudic texts and helps us once and for all to get rid of the strictly nationalist character that one would like to give to the particularism of Israel. This particularism exists, as you will see, but it certainly has no nationalist sense. A certain notion of universality is expressed in the Jewish particularism. (*DF* 83)[25]

In this comment Levinas does not specify the meaning of the uniqueness, of this particularism, but he rejects the ethnic-national option both in content and as a methodical principle of interpretation. The uniqueness of the People of Israel stems from certain qualities that they endeavor to embrace and adopt, qualities that can characterize people who are not Jewish by origin as well.

What are the contents of Jewish uniqueness? It has a mission toward the entire world: "The navel indicates the Sanhedrin. Is it not true that the Sanhedrin protects the entire universe?…The universal meaning of the court: it protects the universe. The universe subsists only because of the justice made in the Sanhedrin. The role of Judaism, of which the Sanhedrin is the center, is a universal role, a deaconry in the service of the totality of being" (*NT* 78). The content of this mission consists of justice: "To accept the Torah is to accept the norms of a universal justice. The first teaching of Judaism is the following: a moral teaching exists and certain things are more just than others. A society in which man is not exploited, a society in which men are equal... The very contestation of moral relativism. What we call the Torah provides norms for human justice" (66). If so, Israel's universal mission is an excessive commitment to justice and to bringing biblical "norms for human justice" to all humanity. The Torah teaches that "everything I know of God and everything I can hear of his word and reasonably say to Him must find an ethical expression" (*DF* 17). The ethical content of the Torah is also the meaning of Israel's universal mission.

On the personal level, when I encounter the face of the other person I am commanded to regard the other through a heteronomous command that precedes all time, all consciousness, and all rational analysis. I am responsible for providing for the other's needs. On another level, the appearance of a "third party," that is, an additional other, requires justice, which requires a limiting of the first other's infinite rights for the benefit of additional others. Justice is a uniform set of norms that guarantees minimum rights for all people, and the realm in which it is realized is the state. But within the state is "the internal contradiction of the State subordinating some men to others in order to liberate them" (*BV* 184). In this realm Judaism also has a major role in teaching that which is "beyond the State" (*BV* 183), that is, a political existence that limits its aggressiveness toward the individuals that comprise it, a state aware of its arbitrariness stemming from uniform norms dictated to everyone. A state that is in the service of humanity, of each person as a separate individual with his or her own rights, is a utopia with horizons outlined by Judaism. Justice might be arbitrary and violent if not limited by compassion and mercy, by ethics, which is superior to politics (see *BV* 177–87; *ITN* 92–108; *TI* 212–15; *EN* 103–22).

All of these are messages conveyed by Judaism, and Levinas is convinced that they are intended for the entire world, for anyone ready to hear the voice and the command, even though their wording appears to be directed at a concrete group of people: "A message addressed to all humanity! Thought through to its conclusion, this particular ceremony[26] of a people whose members can look upon one another, a concrete community capable of being taken in at a gaze, permits the whole of humanity to be included in the legislation in whose name this pact has been concluded.... Right from the beginning, the society which aspires to intimacy between twelve tribes looking at one another, this society of a community, is already present to the whole of humanity, or opens on to the whole humanity" (BV 75). On the one hand there is a defined community, whose members see each other face-to-face—not only in the concrete sense but also in the metaphorical sense of seeing each other's needs and taking responsibility. On the other hand, there are the implications of this model for the conduct of all humanity. The vision that Levinas identifies in the Torah is a vision of all humanity conducting itself as a community, one with face-to-face relationships. Reinforcement of the community constitutes a universal model, but this message requires the example of the specified model in order to materialize. This is the meaning of Israel's uniqueness. It serves as a model for all humanity, demonstrating a constant tension between the unique and the universal, between the communal-specified and that which pertains to everyone.

Despite its universal appeal, Jewish uniqueness has not waned. This is evident first and foremost in Levinas's interpretation of Jewish texts—of the Talmud,[27] with an interpretation that has distinct hermeneutical features, that is, a deep connection to the uniquely Jewish textual tradition. Other contents comprising this uniqueness are the commandments: "The ritual law of Judaism constitutes the austere discipline that strives to achieve this justice" (DF 18). The commandments direct one's consciousness and bring it to a state of unconditional obedience, to a heteronomous commitment. These skills are the sound foundation of ethical behavior. Ethics can, indeed, be attained without them; however, the commandments reinforce and enhance discipline as well as the capacity to comply with commands that have nothing to do with persevering in one's being. The observant Jew can serve as an emissary, an example, and a model for all other people. Levinas does not relinquish the decisive role of *halakha* in Judaism. This may surprise those who recognize him primarily as a great "universal" philosopher, one whose perception of Judaism is "enlightened" and free of ritual commandments that to modern, rational, and self-conscious people may seem old-fashioned and worthless. It also does not make things easy for secular Jewish humanists who have no trouble identifying with the universal ethical messages conveyed by Levinas but do not abide by Jewish law and tend to make light of it. The universal mission at the heart of this uniqueness, however, its ulterior motive, forms an integral part of his halakhic perception.

Another component of the Jewish people's uniqueness is what Levinas frequently calls "holy history" or "Passion", the torments of the mission. Jewish fate is entangled in a history of suffering and persecution, which escalate whenever the world's humaneness is overcome by barbarism. Levinas wrote about Jewish fate in the Holocaust: "Their suffering, common to them and to all the victims of the war, received its unique meaning from the racial persecution which is absolute, since it paralyses, by virtue of its very intention, any flight, from the outset refuses any conversion, forbids any self-abandonment...touches the very innocence of the being recalled to its ultimate identity" (*DF* 12).[28] Being a nation that refuses to be judged by history, a nation that avoids or has been prevented from assimilating among other nations, is the unique fate of the Jewish People. Among all the different types of suffering, this has reason and meaning. When barbarism threatens to overcome the world, the Jews—by virtue of their very being and due to their traditions—are living reminders of an alternative that consists of ethical values. They are a live testimony to the commands of the Torah. Jews, precisely because of their unique fate, bear a message for all humanity. Thus, their unique features have universal meaning.

The universality of the message stems from a uniqueness that does not disappear within this universality. The Jewish People have not faded away within a humanity that embraces the values of ethics and humanism. They have remained distinct, a distinction that is a reminder to all humanity. To conclude, I shall quote another section in which Levinas emphasizes this tension, here explaining the ethical meaning of the destruction of the Temple: "The ultimate distinction between good and evil on the social and political plane would stem from the possibility, for a social and political order, of coexisting with the ethical demands of Israel. We must not speak here, prematurely or lightly, of nationalism. The Temple of Jerusalem in Jewish thought is a symbol which signifies for the whole of humanity; it is not simply a national institution" (*BV* 63). The destruction of the Temple is an act that has moral significance for all humanity. It was an attempt to erase the universal message brought by Israel to all nations. Although it is a concrete building serving as a spiritual center of one specific nation, it has meaning for all humanity.

Another aspect of this issue is evident in that which Levinas calls "translation into Greek." His *midrash* of the Talmud, directing readers to current issues, was written in the language of twentieth century Western intellectuals. The Talmud is in Hebrew and Aramaic and thus unintelligible to most of his students and listeners. Moreover, its manners of expression, the symbols that appear therein, its logic that often seems cumbersome and strange, and its ambiguously motivated redaction—all of these impede the study of the Talmud. But Levinas believes that the Talmud bears relevant meanings and messages for all people, and not only for Jews. In order to make these messages more accessible, he expounds the Talmud—translates it into rational language, into philosophical concepts and the language of Western culture. In the lesson "The Translation of the Scripture" (*ITN* 33–54), he says:

> It is the spiritual trial, for the tradition of Shem, of welcoming the speech of Japheth,[29] while at the same time exalting the genius particular to the oral Torah (despite the nineteenth century's denial of it) in its infinite richness of new meaning, brought out in the rabbinic reading of the Scripture; the challenge of bringing to the common civilization (whether for the purpose of joining or of judging it) the Greek expression of that creative thought and life. Greek expression, i.e. like that of our academic language of the Western world—even if the latter's unbiased intelligence sometimes runs the risk of remaining naïve and there may be something missing in its "clear and distinct ideas." A spiritual trial for the tradition to open the tents of Shem for Japheth; tents in which, according to the *midrash,* the study of the Torah takes place. (51–52)

Translation into Greek is a matter of both form and content. The style employed is Western-academic or rational and makes use of modern philosophical concepts. This course of action is essential although it uncovers and stresses a certain naïveté of the translated text (the Talmud) versus philosophical writing, as well as its unsystematic manner, for it is not obliged to define and distinguish every statement and does not engage in conceptualizations. Theoretically, this is an old-fashioned, irrational text dealing with petty, obsolete problems. This, at least, is what strikes many intelligent and enlightened people not accustomed to Torah study. They are quick to judge the difficulties involved in studying the Talmud as a flaw in the text. But Levinas believes that these writings are important for "joining or judging common civilization." They add missing content and voices to Western culture and thus can not only rejoin it as a universal, common denominator but can also judge it as a culture which, by virtue of its focus on the Same, is not sufficiently aware of the Other.[30] Levinas's writing in general, as well as his commentary on the Talmud, which is so foreign to customary Western intellectual discourse, has at its foundation the wish to further enrich Western culture from another source. The Talmud, when translated to a language more comprehensible to Western people, teaches an openness to and awareness of the Other, an infinite responsibility toward the Other, ethics; this stands in contrast to Western culture, with its invariable emphasis on totality or the self (which sometimes converge). In Western culture the Other was never accorded a proper, correct place, not even a place corresponding to reality, whereas the Torah in general and the Talmud in particular focus on the Other and responsibility toward the Other as their point of departure.

The significance of translating the Talmud into "Greek" is also discussed in "The Pact" (*BV* 68–85), a lesson that interprets a talmudic passage describing various pacts between the People of Israel and God, of which one segment was quoted above:

> "And afterward they brought stones and built the altar and plastered it with plaster. And they wrote thereon all the words of the law in seventy languages, as it is written *ba'er hetev* [very clearly]" (Sotah 32a). What was a question of writing is now a question of language! This third version of the pact...is proclaimed in seventy languages. A message addressed to all humanity....This transition, then, from Hebrew to the universality which I call Greek is quite remarkable. It is the formula *ba'er hetev*, "very clearly," recommending the clarity and distinction of Scripture, which begins to signify complete translatability. The process of liberation and universalization must

therefore be continued. We have not yet finished translating the Bible. The Septuagint is incomplete. Nor have we finished translating the Talmud. We have hardly begun. (74, 75)

When Levinas translates a talmudic passage into French and teaches it in a language that is comprehensible not only to his audience but also to anyone who reads French, and when his interpretation suggests universal meaning and teachings—all this is done in order to influence reality. The pact between the transcendent and the human is not only the legacy of the People of Israel; it is also a pact with all humanity. The universal teaching here is that communal society, proper society, is one of responsibility and mutual assistance, a society in which people "not only live side by side rather than face to face" (69).

In contrast to essentialist doctrines in which national (or racial) particularism serves as the justification for innate structured superiority, Jewish singularity, its special features and chosen status—according to Levinas—does not entail privileges but only means more commitment and more responsibility toward all humanity. Nonetheless, does not this very notion of particularism constitute a root, an ancient foundation, from which other theories of chosen people are then generated? Might the very term *am segulah,* attesting as it does to a self-concept of chosenness, even if it bears the meaning of being on a mission, also carry a sense of superiority with all the negative, dangerous potential of such a recognition? Even the concept of chosenness as a mission has at its heart a foundation of dangerous arrogance and pride. Nevertheless, the idea that the People of Israel bear a message for the world, one that cannot be voiced without them—a message that requires me as a member of this people to maintain highly critical, moral self-expectations, having a consciousness that requires constant self-examination—is an important and basic component of my self-concept. I believe that it should have an effect on Israeli reality, even in the midst of amoral political situations such as occupation. I would like to retain this significant element.[31]

At any rate, the idea that the Torah aims to teach something universal, that the singularity of Israel is not essentialist but, rather, is a challenge with moral contents, and that these messages must be translated to be understood by all humanity—is a fundamental conception in the hermeneutics of Levinas from which he does not deviate.

The Rationalism of the Talmud

A basic assumption of Levinas in his talmudic readings, which constitutes another feature of his *midrash,* is that the Talmud is a rational text; therefore, it invites the commentator to use rational tools. Unlike the Bible, which is based on inspiration, on the prophecy that may originate from outside human beings, the Talmud is a discussion between people and the tool they use is logic. The *midrash* and halakhic rulings are generated using rules and laws through rational debate—through speech and persuasion.[32]

Utilizing rational tools to interpret the Talmud matches its underlying rational structure. This methodological principle permits a great deal of freedom, as rational discussions allow for multiple opinions that spar with each other on an equal footing until one party is convinced by the other. This is the commentator's intellectual freedom.

In this context it is interesting to note that Levinas interpreted few halakhic discussions—dialectical debates with a logical structure of their own—and chose instead to focus on aggadic passages, a genre with a very diverse character (e.g., stories, parables, but also disputes and debates) that is less distinctly rational. He explicitly attested to this distinction and to his choice in the introduction to his four talmudic readings (*NT* 3–11). He explained this choice both by his lack of proficiency in the Talmud, for which he frequently apologized in nearly all of his talmudic readings, and by the fact that aggadic passages contain more philosophy than halakhic debates, although not exclusively so:

> The Halakhah comprises those elements which, on the surface, concern only the rules of ritual, social, and economic life, as well as the personal status of the faithful. But these rules have a philosophical extension often concealed beneath questions of "acts to do" and "acts not to do," which were seemingly of immediate interest to the sages.... But "philosophy," or the equivalent of what philosophy is in Greek, that is, Western.... These are passages found side by side with the Halakhah and which are referred to as Aggadah.... In itself, this Talmudic text is intellectual struggle and courageous opening unto even the most irritating questions. (4; cf. 14, 121–22, 167; *NTR* 55–56; *ITN* 36–37)

Indeed, Levinas approaches the talmudic text as a philosopher, bringing with him all of his philosophical knowledge. This opens a new range of meaning; philosophical questions are aimed at the text, and attempts are made to uncover its rational meaning. On the one hand, this is a restrictive principle, as it focuses on certain aspects of the text; on the other hand, it opens previously unknown interpretive possibilities.[33] A philosophical approach to the text presents questions that originate not only from the personal world of a specific *darshan* but also from the philosophical issues occupying the commentator. This is the choice Levinas makes between several options he mentions—for example, the religious option (e.g., traditional exegesis, Rishonim and Aharonim, which usually focuses on halakha) and the mystical option (e.g., kabbalistic exegesis that searches the Talmud for ways of symbiotically connecting to God). Levinas continues an orientation evident in biblical exegesis. (Philo, Maimonides, Rav Saadya Gaon, and Samson Raphael Hirsch are prominent representatives of this interpretive orientation.) His exceptional contribution is evident in the use of this approach to specifically interpret talmudic passages, mostly of an aggadic nature, and in the content of his exegesis, strongly affiliated as it is with his philosophy.

Consider, for example, the lesson "The Temptation of Temptation" (*NT* 30–50).[34] This is a philosophical commentary on the Babylonian Talmud's description of the Revelation on Mt. Sinai and reception of the Torah, as it appears in Tractate Shabbat (88a–b). The passage offers a hermeneutical interpretation of the biblical description and stresses that the Torah was received under duress, under threat, and not freely. It also emphasizes the "We shall do" said by people of Israel, which preceded "We shall hear." This reverse order of action and comprehension, of obedience and learning, reflects a value, a model, an "angel's mystery."

Levinas further develops this idea. He presents the normal order of "We shall hear" and then, "We shall do," as the temptation of philosophy, which underlies Western culture. This culture appreciates only that which it understands and is capable of analyzing. Rational analysis is a necessary stage that precedes practical acts that are derived from its conclusions. This is not spontaneous but is a calculated attitude. "We want to know before we do... the temptation of temptation is, as we have already said, philosophy itself" (*NT* 34). And also: "But opinion... this unlimited and anticipatory indiscretion which constitutes knowledge... makes us forget the unsavory joy of knowledge, its immodesty, the abdications and incapacities peculiar to it. It makes us forget all that could, in times of great dangers and catastrophes, have reminded us of the Luciferian origins of this mobility and of the temptation to which this indiscretion responds" (34, 35).

Levinas alludes here to the incapacity of Western philosophy to prevent injustice in general and the Holocaust in particular. Overcome by the joy of knowledge and by the freedom to experience any idea without taking responsibility for its consequences, philosophy fails miserably in times of danger and catastrophe; it has no power to prevent them. In contrast, receiving the Torah constitutes obedience before rational analysis—"We shall do and we shall hear"—a culture of ethics and responsibility. It is an immediate, unconditional response to the other and the other's needs, before any calculation involving rationalism and comprehension: "One accepts the Torah before one knows it. This shocks logic" (42). Receiving the Torah presents the world with the option of unconditional openness to the Other, of overcoming the temptation of evil and the temptation of temptation, that is, the temptation to be tempted. The Torah offers an approach that is not predicated on comprehension but an attitude that has the potential for goodness (*bonté*). "The world is here so that the ethical order has the possibility to be fulfilled" (41). And he interprets the following homily accordingly:

> "And they stood at the foot of [*betachtit,* also: underneath] the mountain [Exod. 19:17]. R. Abdimi bar Hama bar Hasa said: This teaches us that God suspended the mountain above them like a barrel and said: If you accept the Torah, all is well, if not, here will be your grave" [Shabbat 88a].... Does freedom begin in a state of freedom?...This is a vicious circle....In the beginning was violence.... That the mind needs training suggests the very mystery of violence's anteriority to freedom, suggests the possibility of an adherence prior to free examination and prior to temptation. (*NT* 37, 38)

Freedom is an important value that has a prime place in all of modern Western thought, and the question of its validation has occupied philosophy from time immemorial. According to modern liberalism people are free to do as they wish, so long as they do no harm to others. This approach does not oblige one to prevent injustices that are caused to another by a third party. Such freedom, as a supreme value, implies that I can choose to refrain from intervening and to ignore a person who needs my help. Levinas is adamantly opposed to an approach that bases our entire system of values on freedom.

The Torah is a heteronomous law, and human beings are not autonomous legislators. The mountain forcefully suspended like a barrel is a symbol of the heteronomy of the law, indicating that freedom is preceded by obligation. Once the Torah, the Law, is received, people are free to choose whether to comply with it or not. That is the freedom they are given. Freedom always appears after the Torah and does not precede it. It is given as part of the definition of good and bad, obligation and law. This is the answer to the problem posed by the temptation of temptation: instead of experiencing all ideas and all experiences devoid of any commitment, people are under a forced obligation to the Torah, which turns them from themselves to the needs of the other.

I shall not get into a detailed discussion here; suffice it to say that in Levinas's *midrash* the issue of coercion, which might annoy any modern person who considers freedom as a supreme value, receives a new and surprising interpretation that is relevant to the world of his readers. Freedom based on itself is a logical failure, and it also lacks the necessary power to serve as a foundation of ethics, and therefore, is dangerous. Seeing things in this context allows contemporary readers to relate to the question of freedom from a new perspective.[35]

Levinas's commentary also links the two parts of the passage, which have no clear association. What is the connection between the statement of Rav Abdimi that the Torah was violently forced on Israel and the commendation of Israel's commitment and statement, "We shall do and we shall hear"? There appears to be good cause for the claim of the "unbeliever" cited in the passage: "People in a hurry for whom the mouth passes before the ears...you are always in a state of headlong haste. You should have listened in order to know whether you were able to accept, and if you were not able to accept, you should not have accepted" (*NT* 47). As interpreted by Levinas, the "unbeliever" well represents the problem of the temptation of temptation. At first, the unbeliever wishes to understand what is before him or her and only then, if the unbeliever so decides based on his or her understanding, shall act in complete freedom. But when I am confronted—not by an ontological or theoretical issue but by the human condition of an other who needs me—this approach makes it possible to ignore and disregard the cause of distress and even collaborate with it. The Torah takes a stand against this moral bankruptcy, the very Torah that is by nature a compulsion, accepted a priori as an attitude of commitment: "We shall do and we shall hear." "Here am I," ready to act even prior to analysis and comprehension, as a point of departure.

Such a philosophical interpretation is enriching in all respects: the passage is awarded philosophical meaning, philosophy learns something of which it was not aware before studying the Talmud, and people—the teacher, the writer, and the students hearing or reading—take part in the revelation, in the connection to the Torah's source of inspiration.

Levinas's philosophical writing and his talmudic commentary are closely affiliated; therefore, in order to understand the meaning of his commentary on a certain matter within the talmudic passage, it is often necessary to clarify its meaning through his philosophical thought. Although Levinas consciously separated his philosophical work from his Jewish writings, their common elements are fundamental and essential. Thus, for example, in the passage on damages due to fire,[36] the Baraita recommends remaining at home during an epidemic. Through familiarity with the meaning of the home in Levinas's early philosophy—as a place where one can become detached from the world, which is experienced as a foundation for the possibility of forging one's separateness, as the basis for the capacity to reply "Here am I"—it is possible to understand the full meaning he ascribes to the Baraita in his commentary and its association with the situation of Jews in World War II and in the Yom Kippur War. By revealing and explaining the philosophical meaning of concepts and themes that appear in the talmudic readings, these texts will presumably become accessible to all readers rather than only to professional philosophers. Unlike his philosophical writing, which requires extensive knowledge and professional tools, in his talmudic readings he appeals to an audience of intellectuals (in France basic philosophical concepts are taught in secondary school) who are not necessarily professionals in this discipline or Talmud scholars. The Torah invites any person to study it, as he repeatedly reminds us.

Another example of this matter is evident in the lesson "Model of the West" (BV 13–33),[37] where Levinas interprets a passage in Tractate Menachot. Every detail of the mishna, which describes a concrete ceremony, is given contemporary ethical meaning. The mishna presents persistence as the rationale for the operations described, while the talmudic passage chooses to focus on persistence per se, thus shifting its discussion from the work of the Temple to the study of Torah. Levinas adds another level of discussion to the issue of persistence and time and uses it to criticize Western culture. Instead of perceiving time as an abstract concept or a conscious structure he shows, in his interpretation of the passage, that time is an endless collection of moments that can be shaped and utilized for activities that turn the self toward the other person. Persistence is a dynamic effort to utilize time in order to shape a reality in which the other person is at the center of attention and intention. Methodologically, this lesson illustrates that it is possible to adhere to all components of the text and to its unusual structure as well, with the connection between its various parts enhancing comprehension of the content. Addressing the question of time and Western culture's attitude to time forms part of Levinas's fundamental and comprehensive criticism of this culture. Although he respects Western culture and does not reject it completely, he also emphasizes its limitations as a culture that is merely human and as a totality-oriented way of thought that has no room for the individual, for the infinity of each person. In contrast, the Torah, which issues to human beings a heteronomous command, a "trace of transcendence," is a source of thought that is "otherwise than being," a thought that centers on infinity.

The discussion of abstract philosophical questions from a perspective of concrete actions is particularly conspicuous in this lesson. In a manner evident elsewhere as well but maybe even more so here, the style of writing employed is well suited to the contents, with their criticism of the generalizing way of thought while interpreting concrete acts and symbols. On another level, Levinas's commentary corresponds with his listeners' and readers' sense of the world as members of Western culture who are strongly affected by the tyranny of time. The rate at which acts are performed and tasks are completed is accorded utmost importance. Output is the goal, and in our haste we do not always have the time to question their value and significance. Levinas shows them, and us, a conception that has time resuming its role as a means, with people assuming responsibility for developing the causes to which it is devoted—a thought-provoking conception.

This lesson might lead to another question: does Levinas, in exposing an essential weak spot in Western culture and in suggesting that the Torah indicates the correct attitude to this issue, believe that Judaism is immune to totalitarianism, that it cannot be understood as allowing mistreatment of another person? Levinas is well aware that Judaism is not a certified format for solving the problem of violence between people. He takes every opportunity to stress that Torah study never reaches completion, that it requires persistent studying together with other people. Continuous study of a law that emphasizes the needs of the other person might increase one's awareness of the other person. The persistence discussed in this lesson is also persistence in limiting the perseverance of one's being, a persistence in coping with self-satisfaction, which is a never-ending task.

The uniqueness of Levinas's talmudic commentary in this respect is particularly conspicuous when compared with two other methods. Talmud study in yeshivas that follow the Lithuanian model consists of exegesis that focuses on the logical structure of passages and centers on rational comprehension of the text. However, this type of study does not relate to questions that originate outside of the Talmud. Levinas follows the Lithuanian model in assuming that the Talmud is rational and that its study should utilize rational tools; however, he brings philosophical questions to it, and his commentary on its passages adds a discussion of these questions. Philological exegesis of the Talmud, customary in academic circles, is also rational in essence; however, it deals mainly with the history of the text, its language, form, and so on, and less with its content and messages. In any case, it remains objective toward the object of its research.[38] Levinas, in contrast, sees his interpretive role as expanding the meaning of the text's content. His interpretive *midrash* is philosophical, ethical, and seeks to influence the lives of his listeners and readers. This is an involved manner of study that takes a stand and assumes responsibility for its practical implications.

Levinas utilizes his basic assumption concerning the Talmud's rationalism to approach the passages and interpret them as a philosopher who is also a *darshan*. Torah and philosophy both evolve and expand as a result of this enriching encounter, in which the Torah is asked new questions and philosophy learns new values and content.

Editing the Talmudic Readings

The talmudic readings were written in an exceptional style. In the introduction to many of them Levinas defines the issue treated in his commentary and provides a short summary of his thoughts on the topic. Why is this not sufficient? Why does he insist on the intricate and sometimes confusing process of learning an entire passage with no skipping? What is the meaning of those sections he interprets that are not related to the topic of his lesson? What is the meaning of those of his comments that seem to have no connection to the conceptual sequence of his words? Most of the research on these readings consists of what Levinas would have called "thematic" writing—research that relates within the talmudic readings only to that which pertains to the topic of study. Such writing disregards significant parts of these talmudic lessons, treating them as mere decorations or as superfluous and therefore missing an important facet. Levinas insists on adhering to the sequence of the text he is interpreting. The thematic approach disregards both the sequence of the talmudic passage interpreted and the special sequence of the talmudic lesson itself.

In his lessons, Levinas adheres to the sequence of the passage he is interpreting and accepts all its components in their current form, as worthy of interpretation, while showing respect for the text and assuming that the effort to study it as it is will allow learners to discover aspects that are new to them. This does not mean that the text cannot be disputed or criticized, but it does assume that it was constructed thoughtfully and intentionally. The structure of Levinas's talmudic readings and their editing are meaningful as well. At times the lessons shift from interpretation of the Gemara's plain meaning to hermeneutical interpretations; nearly all the lessons discuss and deal with different questions, including topics that do not always appear to be related. The consecutive study process, which persists in asking why different issues are discussed in this context—such as, what is the association between the plain meaning of the text and its hermeneutical interpretations or those of tangential segments—makes it possible to uncover levels of content that might not have been revealed in any other reading. For in many cases, they are implicit and complex.

Levinas's talmudic readings. are an intricate fabric composed of different layers that are interwoven to form a contrapuntal texture; they contain exegesis of the selected talmudic passage, references to the topic of the colloquium at which the lesson was taught, methodological comments on the Talmud's *midrash* and exegesis, and often also references to additional topics that are problems that occupied Levinas as a commentator who is also a philosopher. Consecutive reading, one that takes its time with the text and follows all of its twists and turns, makes it possible to explore this multiplicity and to extract maximal meaning. It explores those places that appear to deviate from the topic or from the interpreted text, investigates and studies them and their accumulated effect, and thus, makes it possible to uncover the implicit theme.[39]

To illustrate the structure of the lessons and its significance I shall return to the talmudic lesson "Toward the Other," discussed in the first part of this chapter from a thematic point of view. In my initial interpretation I chose to place the lesson in the context of a topic that is occupying me—the relationship between religion and morality—and I composed a pertinent *midrash*. Now I shall examine the context and structure of the lesson in full. This lesson is built as a *petihta*. It begins from a "distant" text, a passage in Tractate Yoma dealing with the subject of repentance and the atonement mechanisms of the Day of Atonement. The passage appears to be only slightly connected to the topic of the colloquium at which the lesson was taught—namely, the relations between French Jews and the Germans in the 1950s and 1960s. Through this passage and its interpretation, however, Levinas lays the foundation for his treatment of the said topic, which is reached through the interpretation of another, more relevant passage in Tractate Yevamot.

Levinas refers to the question of forgiveness between Jews and Germans first and foremost as concerning human relationships, that is, one person versus another, offender versus offended, even when the offended is Jewish and the offender a Nazi. In his opinion, this is the right context for dealing with this painful matter. The extensive discussion of the passage in Tractate Yoma raises many insights as to the process of forgiveness and atonement between the offender and the offended. The process might continue ad infinitum; there is no mechanism that produces automatic atonement; and it depends on the good will and ability of the offender to go through a process of remorse and repentance on one hand, and on the offended allowing absolution and forgiveness, on the other. The only one capable of absolving the offender is the offended and this hinges on his or her good will. This is an important contention in the context of the colloquium's topic. If the offended dies, the offender has no chance of atonement. Moreover, interpretation of the stories in the passage emphasizes, together with the passage itself, the difficulties involved in utilizing the system of atonement suggested in the mishna. The significance of speech as a tool that connects people and the need to act in order to put an interpersonal process into motion are both elements that in the context of the Jewish attitude to the Germans contrast with the expectation that the survivors "continue with their life" or forget the past and the injustices that have been committed toward them.[40] People who have sustained emotional, financial, or physical harm are entitled to have someone talk to them, hear them, and perform additional operations to appease and compensate them. This is an important lesson that is relevant for any situation involving people who have been mistreated.

Further on in the lesson and through the passage in Tractate Yevamot, Levinas asserts, applying strict justice, that the Nazis or their descendants should have been nailed to rocks, as was inflicted on the descendants of Saul. This is the grave extent of inexpiable guilt. He also says, however, that the demand for retributive justice is cruel. It ignores the criminals' humane aspects and perpetuates the murderous cruelty of their deeds. In order to avoid perpetuating the circle of violence there is need for mercy and compassion—behavior beyond the letter of the law. Nonetheless, it must be emphasized that foregoing retributive justice is not the equivalent of absolution, atonement, or forgiveness. Foregoing the demand for retributive justice against the Nazis does not constitute absolution. That would be the exclusive prerogative of those offended toward those who offended them, after the latter expressed regret for their deeds, showed remorse, and repented. This is an infinite process and it is important to know that its results are not guaranteed, due to the internal damage to the murderers' soul, the damage to the sense of natural justice, and due to the predicaments that are possibly encountered by the victim when required to forgive—not to mention that so many of the offended were murdered, and thus, cannot grant absolution.

The many levels that comprise this statement are gradually revealed through interpretation of the texts chosen by Levinas and the links he forms between them. One level is interpretation of the text focusing on forgiveness, which lays the foundation for a discussion of the colloquium's main issue. By using modern philosophical language, Levinas extracts from the text a meaning that holds relevance for his world as well as a universal message for all people. On another level, he lays the foundations and exposes the principles of his unique interpretive-hermeneutical method, both its general principles (mainly in the introduction to the lesson) and the techniques used in this specific lesson (for instance, recognizing the context of a quoted verse as meaningful for understanding the content of the text, the need to involve people in the study process, etc.).

This consecutive reading also makes it possible to uncover, through its accumulated effect, the implicit theme mentioned above: every person and every situation demand specific attention. There is no day of reckoning, there are no universal processes, there are no unvarying rules of behavior. There are no guaranteed formulas. On another level, the explicit theme and the implicit theme sustain each other. Discussing the proper attitude toward the Germans as a human issue with no single correct solution, that must not force the victims to grant absolution and that cannot automatically absolve the guilty of their guilt—and yet at the same time is open to a process of atonement and remorse by those guilty of the crimes, notwithstanding their heavy guilt that will probably never be erased—all this emerges in all its complexity as a result of the interpretation but also of the recurring element that there is no day of reckoning. Reference to the explicit theme, in which those attending the colloquium have a personal stake, allows them to understand and maybe also identify with the implicit statement that interpersonal situations indeed require a great deal of caution and acceptance of otherness and of the uniqueness of each person. Beyond all this, the integral connection between the horizontal and vertical dimensions of Judaism also becomes evident—the connection between the ritual and the intention realized or illustrated through it, between the community and the individual. The Torah consciously and actively intervenes in the most sensitive interpersonal relationships. Torah study is aimed at analyzing these relationships on a deeper level, beyond their immediate emotional significance. Integrating the discussion on how to relate to the Germans within the context of forgiveness and atonement, justice and compassion, adds a whole new dimension that may enable movement and progress beyond the paralysis generated by the offense.

On an additional contemporary level, this lesson makes it possible to take a look at relations between Jews and Arabs in Israel. For instance, we may ask who is the offender and who is the offended in this relationship, and what is the responsibility borne by the offending party? We can try to check whether there are insurmountable obstacles on the way to atonement, resembling those mentioned in the stories featured in Tractate Yoma. Can such a discussion provide tools for coping with these obstacles? The idea that those offended need and are entitled to be appeased, to have their story heard and to be asked for forgiveness, might be helpful. Moreover, statements indicating that in the case of inexpiable crimes, it might be possible to forego retributive justice, which is not the equivalent of absolution yet avoids perpetuating the cycle of violence, are important in this context. An experience of studying this talmudic lesson in a mixed Jewish-Arab group generated many ideas and various answers to the questions I have asked here. It helped to initiate a painful conversation as well as an understanding that in the current circumstances, while the two sides are still constantly at each other's throat, a real process of atonement and absolution may not be possible. In my opinion, if Jewish Israeli society were to assume more responsibility in this matter, it might be possible to reduce the ongoing mistreatment of the Arab minority, and to begin a process of appeasement and rectification. But maybe this is only a dream.

I have not produced a consecutive interpretation as proposed, as all my attempts ultimately resulted in an awkward and ungainly text. Consecutive study of the text is most appropriate for oral learning, for conversation in a group, or for *beit-midrashic* study. So I will now propose principles and offer demonstrations of its outcomes.

This method of study, with its effort to follow the text, remain attentive to all its components and details, and search for added meaning in the context of the verses it quotes suits and serves both the explicit theme of Levinas's talmudic lesson and its implicit theme. A language that follows specific details of reality is aware of the uniqueness of every person, every situation, and every point in time—of different circumstances that require different approaches. This is not a formula for the ideal exegesis; rather, it is a suggestion for listening and opening up to different voices that reverberate within the written talmudic text and Levinas's exegesis.

The counterpoint structure of this *midrash,* its different levels, and the interwoven strands create a whole in which all components are elaborately interrelated. Only an attentive reading of Levinas's text in sequence, understanding the inner logic of those parts of his commentary that seem unrelated—which is a reading that does not hold on to the object of study but opens up to it with all of its otherness—allows one to uncover additional intrinsic levels that would not be revealed otherwise. All this is not meant to replace existing thematic readings but, rather, to join and supplement them. There is also a reflective dimension: the attitude to Levinas's *midrash* resembles his own attitude to rabbinic *midrashim* in the Talmud. And since we are speaking of the *midrash,* it makes sense to employ a similar method of interpretation on the various midrashic levels.

Apart from that which can be learned through consecutive study, such as the text's implicit messages, another matter comes to light. The *midrash* is generated in adaptation of its attitude to the interpreted text and the text's goals on the one hand, and its manner of study and interpretation on the other. Levinas is well aware of this principle, and in his method of interpretation he embraces and applies it, as he does other midrashic principles, to the Talmud. As we have seen, the form of the talmudic readings and the way in which they are written adapts midrashic principles to the circumstances of the *darshan.* These principles include adhering to the sequence of the interpreted text, calling attention to all its components, and creative use of midrashic principles while maintaining contact with reality and with the audience. Furthermore, the style of the talmudic readings, by appealing directly to the readers and inviting them to join in the act of interpretation, is an attempt to generate a closeness that is reminiscent of the face-to-face encounter. The writer is not conversing with himself.

Just as he appealed to his audience orally, he is appealing to the readers and learners through the text, among other things, by retaining these oral appeals in the written version.

All of this generates a unique written genre. Consecutive reading of the lessons demonstrates respect for this process. It applies to itself this attempt at adaptation of the form of interpretation to its contents, of the principles used in the interpretation to how they are taught. These lessons were not written as philosophical lectures, and although it is necessary to note the philosophical aspects and concepts raised within them, concentrating on these aspects to the exclusion of all others disregards the special character of the lessons and the aims and goals of their conscious form.

The idea of adapting the method of study to the text taught, form to content, and language to its purported message, is strongly associated with Levinas's attempts to adapt the form of his philosophical writing to its content. This issue— the tension between the content of the words, openness to the Other and otherness, and the conceptual, generalizing philosophical language used to express them—appears repeatedly in *Otherwise than Being*.[41] Jacques Derrida posed this question to Levinas as early as 1969 in "Violence and Metaphysics," and Simon Critchley, to offer one other example, raised it once again.[42]

In *Totality and Infinity* Levinas deals with ethics, with the breaking out of the Same toward the Other. Yet it is written in a language of generalizing concepts, a language well suited to dealing with the question of essence, and one that has no room for otherness. Its thought is linear, focused; it grasps its objects, defines, and analyzes them. The contents of the words, criticizing the totality of Western philosophy based as it is on ontological thought, are clearly incompatible with a language inadvertently tied up in the forms that serve this philosophy. In contrast, in *Otherwise than Being*, Levinas makes an attempt at performative writing, where style adapts itself to its content, very possibly in response to Derrida's criticism.

This is the problem: "We have been seeking the *otherwise than being* from the beginning, and as soon as it is conveyed before us it is betrayed in the said that dominates the saying which states it. A methodological problem arises here" (*OB* 7). And this is the proposed solution: "The *otherwise than being* is stated in a saying that must also be unsaid in order to thus extract the *otherwise than being* from the said in which it already comes to signify but *being otherwise"* (7). To unsay that which was written, to restrict its statements, to form spaces between the concepts and contentions, to preserve an ambiguity within the words, to unsay statements while they are being said, and to shift between different levels of language—all of these aim to open an expanse of *otherness* in the language. They seek to form a language that is not closed in on itself, a language where the object has a life of its own, a life that exists beyond the hold exerted by language. Opening the method of presentation in order to adapt words to content, which are an opening of the philosophical manner of thinking toward the Other, creates a type of discourse that deviates from what is customary in this discipline. The writing endeavors to open itself up to the Other, to invite interpretation, to avoid generalizations, and to maintain contact with the complexity of individual phenomena through its concepts. This language encompasses the order, rationalism, and clarity of philosophical discourse, but it does not grasp its objects; it leaves room for their uniqueness.

Although the language of the talmudic exegesis is incapable of encompassing Levinas's philosophy with all of its complexity, dimensions, and attitude to the philosophical tradition, it shows considerable compatibility between the contents of its words and their form. This language retains a space of otherness; reality in all its complexity is present. People who take a stand or who stand up for their beliefs are present and identified by name. The language of the Talmud is open to otherness;[43] the essence of this language is being commanded, and the command originates from the other. As stated, Levinas adapts the language of his lessons to talmudic language, which deals with concrete people and situations, and which accepts and finds room for the Other without generalizing. (In this matter the Talmud's choice to refrain from reaching a decision on most of the disputes cited is notable; the opinions are presented in their multiplicity, with no conclusion.) Its language contains, in its very essence, the space that the complex writing of *Otherwise than Being* aims to create.

Can the language and style of the talmudic readings be perceived as a more radical shift in this direction? Hermeneutical writing has in it something that facilitates even greater freedom, in this process of adapting form to content, than unsaid philosophical language. And if this were true, would it not be appropriate to try and create a similar form of study that would involve reading the talmudic readings themselves based on these same principles? How can the form used to study, speak, and write about them be adapted to the content of his teachings? Awareness of Levinas's principles of exegesis and of his effort to adapt the form and language of his talmudic readings to their content might lead to their utilization in learning and interpreting his talmudic readings, thus producing a form of study that is compatible with its content.

Levinas's Talmudic Lessons and the Contemporary *Beit Midrash*

The *midrash* generated by Levinas, with all its unique aspects, has much value for contemporary Jewish reality, both in the content that is emphasized and in the method of study that is suggested. The issue of the relationship between religion and ethics has implications for many aspects of life in Israel. On the one hand, Israel has no separation of church and state but, on the other hand, those who have been awarded the authority to operate religious establishments within the state tend to subject the prevalent ethical system to their interpretation of religion. In practice, it is often assumed that religion is superior to ethics even when the former contradicts the latter or when it is interpreted as contradictory; or it is even assumed that religion should define what is moral. Religious and secular people share this assumption and cooperate with it. Endless injustices are committed as a result. But the statement that a major part of Judaism does not accept this contradiction and, on the contrary, believes that the main essence of religion is to construct a fair and just society that shall attempt to rectify moral injustices, is extremely important in these circumstances. Levinas suggests that there is no reason to perceive the Jewish character of the State of Israel as incompatible with its morality. On the contrary, immoral acts are incompatible with Israel's Jewishness. He also shows and demonstrates the mechanisms that make it possible to resolve discrepancies between religion and ethics through the *midrash*. Of course, he is not the only one to do so. But his is an important voice in support of this approach, which in my opinion has had an insufficient impact on reality.

Levinas's attitude to Jewish perceptions of the relationship between uniqueness and universalism has practical implications for Israeli reality as well. Israel's laws follow a racist definition of Judaism: anyone born to a Jewish mother is considered Jewish. I shall not recount the current problems with Israel's conversion system, but even without getting into an extensive discussion it is clear that the many predicaments encountered by potential converts stem from an alienated approach to those attempting to join the Jewish People. Citizens' rights are abused and people are deported from the country and are incarcerated as a result of this definition. Levinas offers a completely different approach, one that identifies Judaism as a system of values where anyone committed to this system is considered one of the "descendants of Abraham, Isaac, and Jacob." Even if we do not accept Levinas's suggestion, attempts to examine the meaning of Israel's uniqueness in light of contemporary circumstances are clearly significant. It is important to explore different options than what is shaping Israeli reality at present.

In my opinion, the role of rationalism in interpreting Jewish texts in particular and the place of rationalism in Jewish culture in general are also issues of interest and meaning in current-day Judaism. Numinous holiness, which encourages people to eschew all responsibility for their deeds and decisions, seems attractive to many today, as does relinquishing one's freedom of thought and the tendency to rely on the guidance of rabbis and "luminaries," trips to the graves of the righteous, and more. The philosophy of Levinas urges a renewed debate on this issue as well.

Beyond all this, Levinas's *midrash,* affiliated as it is with the hermeneutical tradition of Torah study within which it was formed—but rooted in the commentator's basic premises, with no apologies and as a legitimate and even desirable part of the interpretation—is a model of what current-day pluralistic *batei midrash* can and should do. The declared pluralism of these *batei midrash* invites people with different worldviews and motivations to approach the interpretive process together and enrich each other. Learners are not expected to leave their world of values, opinions, feelings, and life experience outside the walls of the *beit midrash;* on the contrary, these serve as tools for producing interpretations of the text. Similar to Levinas—who approaches the text with his philosophical framework and informs his philosophy through the text's teachings—learners, each from their own discipline, are invited to contribute to the study process and to be informed by it. In this way, every learner creates unique *midrashim.*

A considerable number of these *batei midrash* have defined their specific orientation. For example, the *beit midrash* established by Hamidrasha at Oranim was originally intended to allow secular people unacquainted with the Talmud to connect to their cultural roots, on the assumption that theirs is not a sociological process of "teshuva" but, rather, a cultural process. Once this goal became less central, additional *batei midrash* were established by Hamidrasha, and in each of these the study process was intended to serve another goal as well. After the assassination of Prime Minister Yitzhak Rabin, joint study groups of religious and secular participants were instigated, called "Nigun" groups. The intention was to bring these people closer to each other and to facilitate a dialogue through joint study and in response to the polarized reality. Women studying at these *batei midrash* expressed a great deal of frustration with the status of both religious and secular women in Jewish culture. This led to study groups for women only, "Nigun Nashim," aimed at reanalyzing these sources from a feminist perspective and making it possible for women to better situate themselves within their culture. After the events of October 2000 a Jewish-Arab *beit midrash* was opened, allowing Jews and Arabs to study Hebrew and Arabic texts together in the same *beit midrashic* method and with the intention of forming contacts and meaningful dialogue between these groups in light of the violent occurrences.

Other *batei midrash* set themselves goals of connecting contemporary Israeli culture with its sources in Jewish texts (e.g., the art *beit midrash* at Hamidrasha, the *beit midrash* at Alma, etc.), connecting business people and influential figures to Jewish values of social justice and fair business practices (e.g., the *beit midrash* at Kolot), and more. Naturally, the founding purpose of every *beit midrash* affects both the choice of texts studied and the interpretations formed therein. The aim is not to acquire knowledge per se but to apply the Torah to the current context and to offer tools for dealing with reality. According to their basic perspective, Torah study and interpretation stem from existential problems and are meant to impact how we live our lives. Obviously, interpretation formed in a feminist *beit midrash* might have different emphases than interpretation of the same text in a *beit midrash* focusing on Jewish-Arab encounters. But "these and these are the living words of God" (Babylonian Talmud, Tractate Eruvin 13b).

As in any *midrash,* this form of Torah study does not seek a single truth; rather, it constitutes a creative conversation with the text, desiring and aiming to influence and to be influenced by it.

Just as Levinas creates unique *midrashim* as a result of his personality and life circumstances, each *beit midrash* creates unique *midrashim* of its own according to its emphases. And within these emphases the multiple voices of the different learners are discernable and are not lost within the totality.

All of this is taking place in practice. In my opinion, contemplating Levinas's commentary makes it possible to understand and analyze the principles underlying this reality, to understand their significance, to observe how this study method is adapting itself to its goals with the aim of maintaining and enhancing the process. This cultural development is an adequate and important response to current Israeli Jewish circumstances. And Levinas can not only be a welcome "guest" at these *batei midrash,* but he can also be a creative and thought-provoking model of what they can and should be.

Afterword

What is the proper way to summarize a study process that will never reach its conclusion, of texts that shall forever remain open to renewed consideration and interpretation from new perspectives? Obviously, these are not conclusions but rather some thoughts.

Any attempt to study Levinas's talmudic readings is analogous to entering a hall of mirrors: The biblical verses were expounded by the Tannaites, whose words were expounded by the Amorites. This produced the Talmud, expounded by Levinas, who invites learners to create their own homiletical readings, thus forming an interpretation of an interpretation of an interpretation.

The multiple levels of the text are also multiple voices. People from different periods, places, and contexts encounter each other between the lines. In this way Abraham might encounter R. Akiva, Descartes encounters Abaye, Hegel encounters Plato and R. Meir, and Moses encounters Heidegger. All of the above also encounter students of the text through

Levinas's commentaries, each bringing to these encounters their own world, questions, thoughts, and unique personality.

Also present in these lessons and affecting the style in which they were written are convergences of philosophy and Talmud, Written Law and Oral Law, tradition and renewal, interpersonal relationships and relationships of people and God, content and form. The interpretive tools are adapted to the aims and content of the exegesis, and we have seen the significant correspondence between the various features of Levinas's interpretive method and those of the *midrash*. In addition to the research they have prompted, the talmudic readings of Levinas invite and demand consecutive and attentive consideration using midrashic tools resembling those utilized to study the Talmud. In this way, by conversing with the learners' realities, other dimensions of these lessons can be uncovered.

I can testify that when teaching these lessons orally within different groups this method proves creative and stimulating. Every renewed contemplation of a talmudic lesson in the order it was written reveals additional meanings and new dimensions. Regretfully, I have yet to find a proper way of transcribing such study sessions without yielding an ungainly and unreadable product. This volume offers interpretive principles, examples of readings, and suggestions of my interpretations in the here and now, often generated in a process of study and teaching involving colleagues and students.

I am happy to be constantly involved in studying these lessons. Thanks to their dynamic character and the infinity of the inspiration contracted within the letters, repeated study of the lessons at other points in time, and with other people, shall produce additional understandings. Have I managed to adapt my writing to the contents of my words and to the object of my investigation? I have done my best to open up to the interpreted text, to let it draw me out of the Same in both thought and deed.

My first encounter with the talmudic readings of Levinas was joyful and enthusiastic. At the time, I felt that these texts facilitated a real and meaningful debate on the most burning issues within the framework and language of my cultural heritage. As I probed deeper into the lessons this feeling became a certainty. The talmudic readings of Levinas address major questions for contemporary Jewish existence through unfearful Torah study and hermeneutics. Even the "Torah from heaven" narrative is not excluded from the discussion; on the contrary, it is examined as an unsettling question for those who do not believe in the myth. Jewish existence after the trauma of the Holocaust, current-day relationships between Jews and non-Jews, the State of Israel and its meaning for Jewish and universal life, the relationship between science and religion, religion and politics, religion and morals—all of these are discussed by Levinas in his lessons in an original and challenging manner. One does not necessarily have to agree with him; nonetheless, his voice is important among all the others. Considering the Jewish options currently available in Israel, in the midst of what appears to be a deep ethical crisis—growing religious radicalism, Messianic nationalism, violent capitalism, egocentric sectarianism, shameless racism, nationalist and male chauvinism, increasing violence, a lack of boundaries on all levels and in all spheres of life, with humanistic Judaism marginalized as far out or naïve—the Jewish conception presented in these talmudic readings offers a basis for serious and meaningful discussion.

I must admit my interest is in promoting the Jewish approach stressing the other person (both Jewish and non-Jewish, male and female) and our responsibility toward him, as proposed by Levinas, in twenty-first century Israel. For example, it is intriguing that according to Levinas, who takes a view prevalent in the Bible, as well as among the sages and other Jewish thinkers (Benamozegh, Herman Cohen, and Rosenzweig, to mention a few), the much publicized conflict between the "Jewish state" and the "democratic state" may in fact be less acute then popularly portrayed in Israeli politics and in the media. Perhaps we could discern how these two value systems complement and even supplement each other, if we could only manage to clarify the meaning of the expression "Jewish and democratic state" and its implications. A Jewish state does not necessarily mean indifference toward all non-Jews; on the contrary, it extends the commitment to "loving the stranger, the orphan, and the widow" to all weak persons in society. Jewish communities have always seen and thought of themselves as committed to their proper social conduct. Can this commitment be transposed to the level of political thought? Furthermore, maybe the holiness of the land, far from being considered a given quality worthy of martyrdom, should be construed as a challenge and a demand for human civility toward each other on this land. Accordingly, dispossessing people and appropriating their property is a grave Jewish prohibition.

Levinas proposes that all these questions be debated through renewed study of Jewish sources, revealing the meaning of these sources and their treatment of problems currently occupying Jews—that is, through *midrash:* "Jewish wisdom is inseparable from a knowledge of the biblical and rabbinical texts; the Hebrew language directs its reader's attention towards the true level of these texts, which is the most profound level of Being" (*DF* 250). Levinas's engagement in a relevant interpretation of talmudic passages derives from what he grasps as an existential Jewish need. In his talmudic lessons at the colloquia of Jewish intellectuals he attempted, by means of illustrations, to convince his listeners that the Talmud is completely applicable to the problems that concern them, that its contents are universal, and that although it appears to be an outdated text it can be understood otherwise, as timely and challenging. Does the notable apologetic element in his method stem from his (almost desperate) wish to convince these assimilating Jews to resume their study of Jewish sources? It seems so. But this does not detract from the conclusion that he offers an effective Jewish method, one well rooted in tradition, for coping with existential questions that occupy Jewish intellectuals.

In the current Jewish-Israeli circumstances, Levinas's call for a return to Jewish sources is propitious, and his commentary demonstrates a possible way of responding to this call. As Hebrew speakers and readers, Israelis have the advantage and the privilege of being able to study the Bible and rabbinic sources in their original language.

Understanding the text as suggested in these talmudic lessons proposes a humanistic Judaism that remains relevant for current times. This course of action dares to touch upon modern contemporary issues, and that is its distinction. It will not be considered as such if treated as a one-time incident of extraordinary creativity, one characterized by surprising audacity but foreign to our very being and culture. Moreover, Levinas invites us to join this virtual or actual *beit midrash,* to continue expounding the Torah, always in the knowledge that it is a never-ending pursuit:

> The words of the Torah are not a debt, because a debt can be settled, whereas here we are faced with something which is always to be settled. In

his commentary, Rashi introduces here the most original category of our text; to the overabundance of the blessing he adds a beyond of duty, which is not a mere setting free from duty. The Torah is a permanence because it is a debt that cannot be paid. The more you pay your debt, the more in debt you become; in other words, the better you see the extent of what remains to be discovered and done. (*BV* 30)

NOTES

NOTES TO INTRODUCTION

1. This does not imply that Levinas's philosophical writings are to be considered Jewish philosophy. Levinas did not define himself as a Jewish philosopher and most of his writing does not deal with Jewish thought. Nonetheless, many of the ideas in his philosophical writings are indeed evident in his talmudic commentary and his philosophical theories are inspired by Jewish sources. Much has been written about the complex relationship between the two parts of his works. Similar to most scholars who have studied his talmudic readings, such as Catherine Chalier, Daniel Epstein, and Simon Critchley, I view his works as forming a whole although, as stated, distinguishing its different parts. On the interrelations between the philosophy and the talmudic commentary of Levinas see Catherine Chalier, "Levinas and the Talmud," in *The Cambridge Companion to Levinas,* ed. Simon Critchley and Robert Bernasconi (Cambridge: Cambridge University Press, 2002), 100–18.

2. Scholars who have considered Levinas's talmudic writings in-depth include Richard Cohen, Jacob Meskin, and Annette Aronowicz in English; Catherine Chalier, David Banon, and Schmuel Trigano in French; Ze'ev Levy, Ephraim Meir, Daniel Epstein, Hanoch Ben-Pazi, Shmuel Wygoda, and myself in Hebrew.

3. See, for example, Eliezer Schweid, "Jews in Israel and in the World: Identities Moving Apart," in *Who Is a Jew Today? Symposium on Jewish Identity,* ed. Maya Leibowitz, Ariel-Joel David, and Moti Inbari (Tel Aviv: Yediot Aharonot, 2005), 114–26.

4. See Franz Rosenzweig, "Upon Opening the Jüdische Lehrhaus," in *On Jewish Learning,* ed. N. N. Glatzer (Madison: The University of Wisconsin Press, 1955), 95–102.

5. Ibid., 98.

6. See Tova Ilan, "Pluralistic Batei Midrash as a Discourse of Identity," in *Heart's Furrow,* ed. Avraham Shapira (Tel Aviv: Hakibbutz Hameuhad, 2006), 190–200 [Hebrew]; Yoram Verete, ed., *Learning the Learning: The Beit Midrash* (Jerusalem and Tivon: Mandel and Hamidrasha Oranim, 2008) [Hebrew]; Ruth Calderon, "On Torah Study," *Alpayim* 18 (1999): 161–66 [Hebrew].

7. Researchers of the talmudic readings tend to focus on the relationship between these lessons and Levinas's philosophy and see this as a deeply fundamental connection. The philosophical ideological aspect of the talmudic readings is strongly stressed in most of these writings. See Annette Aronowicz, "Teaching Levinas's

Talmudic Commentaries: The Relation of the Jewish Tradition to the Non-Jewish World," in *Paradigms in Jewish Philosophy,* ed. Raphael Jospe (Madison, NJ: Fairleigh Dickinson University Press, 1997), 280–89; David Banon, "Lévinas, penseur juif ou juif qui pense," *Noésis* 3 (1999): 27–45; Richard A. Cohen, "Humanism, Religion, Myth, Criticism, Exegesis: Translator's Introduction," (*NTR* 1–46); Lawrence J. Kaplan, "Israel under the Mountain: Emmanuel Levinas on Freedom and Constraint in the Revelation of the Torah," *Modern Judaism* 18, no. 1 (Feb. 1998): 37–46; Jacob E. Meskin, "Critique, Tradition and the Religious Imagination: An Essay on Levinas' Talmudic Readings," *Judaism* 47, no. 1 (Winter 1998): 90–106; Jacob E. Meskin, "Toward a New Understanding of the Work of Emmanuel Levinas," *Modern Judaism* 20, no. 1 (Feb. 2000): 78–102; Samuel Moyn, "Emmanuel Levinas's Talmudic Readings: Between Tradition and Invention," *Prooftexts* 23, no. 3 (2003): 338–63; Daniel Epstein, "Introduction" and "Afterword," in Emmanuel Levinas, *Nine Talmudic Readings* (Jerusalem: Schocken, 2001) 7 8, 255 61 [Hebrew]; Hanoch Ben Pazi, "Call to Responsibility" (doctoral thesis, Bar-Ilan University, Ramat Gan, 2003) [Hebrew]; Hanoch Ben-Pazi, "The Talmudic Readings—Philosophy or Religious Interpretation," *Da'at* 67 (Winter 2000): 117–43 [Hebrew]; Zev Harvey, "Levinas on Innocence, Naivete, and Boorishness," *Da'at* 30 (1993): 13–20 [Hebrew]; Ze'ev Levy, "The 'Greek' Dimension in Rabbinical Writings and Particularly in the Talmudic Legends," in *The Other and Responsibility* (Jerusalem: Magnes, 1997), 161–67 [Hebrew].

8. See Shmuel Wygoda, "The Jewish Philosophy of Emmanuel Levinas" (doctoral thesis, Hebrew University, 2003) [Hebrew], particularly in comparison to different contexts: philosophical interpretation of the Talmud, modern hermeneutical theories, and current-day customary methods of studying Talmud; Annette Aronowicz, "Les commentaires talmudiques de Lévinas," *Cahiers de l'Herne—Emmanuel Lévinas* (Paris: Editions de l'Herne, 1991), 368–77; Annette Aronowicz, "Translator's Introduction" (*NT* ix–xxxix); Gil Bernheim, "A propos des lectures talmudiques, entretien," *Cahiers de l'Herne—Emmanuel Lévinas* (Paris: Editions de l'Herne, 1991), 352–65; Perrine Simon-Nahum, "Une 'herméneutique de la parole': Emmanuel Lévinas et les Colloques des intellectuels juifs," in *Emmanuel Lévinas, philosophie et Judaïsm,* ed. Danielle Cohen-Levinas and Schmuel Tigano (Paris: In Press Editions, 2002), 255–71; Shmuel Wygoda, "A Phenomenological Outlook on the Talmud: Levinas as Reader of the Talmud," *Phenomenological Inquiry* 24 (Oct. 2000): 117–48.

9. See *OB* 7, 97, 100, 155–57, 170, 181, 192n18. See also Simon Critchley, *The Ethics of Deconstruction: Derrida and Levinas* (West Lafayette, IN: Purdue University Press, 1992). This is one of the major topics discussed in the book.

10. When quoting sections that have already been published in English I have used the existing translations, with some corrections when these seemed essential in view of the original.

11. On this Levinas writes: "It is doubtful that a philosophical thought has ever come into the world independent of all attitudes or that there ever was a category in the world which came before an attitude" (*NT* 15).

12. The voices of my teachers and friends at the *beit midrash* of Hamidrasha at Oranim are always present in the pages of this work, between the lines.

Notes to Chapter 1

1. The etymology of the term is a commonly researched topic that has not been resolved. See Menachem Elon, *Jewish Law*, vol. 2, trans. Bernard Auerbach and Melvin J. Sykes (Philadelphia: Jewish Publication Society of America, 1994), 239; Ofra Meir, *The Story as a Hermeneutic Device* (Tel Aviv: Hakibbutz Hameuhad, 1987), 11–18 [Hebrew]; Yona Frankel, *Midrash and Aggadah* (Tel Aviv: Open University Press, 1996), 26–40 [Hebrew]; Avraham Shapira, *The Light of Life in Ordinary Days* (Tel Aviv: Am Oved, 1996), 304 [Hebrew]; Marc Hirshman, "Aggadic Midrash," in *The Literature of the Sages, Second Part*, ed. Safrai Shemuel (Royal Van Gorcum: Fortress Press, 2006), 109–13.

2. Elon, *Jewish Law*, 240; Hirshman, "Aggadic Midrash," 115; Meir, *The Story as a Hermeneutic Device*, 19; Frankel, *Midrash and Aggadah*, 53; Gershom Scholem, *Explications and Implications* (New York: Schocken Books, 1971), 184–86 [Hebrew].

3. See Ephraim Elimelech Urbach, *Collected Writings in Jewish Studies* (Jerusalem: Magnes, 1999), 704 [Hebrew]; Meir, *The Story as a Hermeneutic Device*, 33; Frankel, *Midrash and Aggadah*, 225–26; Yom Tov Lipman Zunz, *Gottesdienstliche Vorträge der Juden* (Frankfurt am Main: J. Kauffmann, 1892), 1; Shapira, *Light of Life*, 304–05. Jacob Neusner objects to this approach and states that the Mishna is revolutionary in refraining from direct reference to the biblical text and that the Mishna formed the basis for rabbinic literature, while all the *midrashim* and the Talmuds are merely an attempt to reconcile and link the Mishna and the biblical text. See, for example, Jacob Neusner, *How Judaism Reads the Torah* (Frankfurt: Peter Lang, 1993), 17–18; Jacob Neusner, *Midrash in Context: Exegesis in Formative Judaism* (Philadelphia: Fortress Press, 1983)

4. This proves, in my opinion, that the midrashic technique was known to the Mishna and was not devised at a later stage.

5. Some scholars, among them Michael Fishbane and Yair Zakovitch, are of the opinion that there is an inner biblical *midrash* that anticipates the rabbinic *midrash*. In contrast, rabbinic literature scholars, such as Marc Hirshman, claim that despite indications of the midrashic method in the Bible, this is not *midrash* per se. In my opinion, this conflict derives, at least to a certain degree, from the wide and narrow definitions of the *midrash:* Hirshman embraces a narrow definition of the *midrash* and its formative features as a distinct work of the sages, while Fishbane and Zakovitch use a wider definition. I tend to agree with the wider definition, which perceives the *midrash* as a major determinant of Jewish culture over the generations, with its constantly changing forms. Its roots are in the Bible, and it has continued to develop and shape Jewish language until the present, which is worthy of study and reflection. See Michael Fishbane, *Biblical Interpretation in Ancient Israel* (Oxford: Oxford University Press, 1985), 281–91; Yair Zakovitch, *Introduction to Inner Biblical Interpretation* (Even Yehudah: Rekhes, 1992), 9–11, 131–35 [Hebrew]; and Hirshman, "Aggadic Midrash," 126–27.

6. See Melila Hellner-Eshed, *And a River Flows from Eden* (Stanford, CA: Stanford University Press, 2009), 189–202.

7. Texts showing that the sages are aware of the fact that they are not dealing with the author's intention are classics currently studied by countless scholars and commentators. Some examples include "The Oven of Achnai," Bava Metzia 59b; Moses

in Rabbi Akiva's Study Hall, Menahot 29b; and "Who Has Gone above, Has Returned [and Reported]?," Makot 23a.

8. Gadamer's hermeneutical theory clearly strongly resembles the attitude of the *midrash* to the interpreted text. See also: Michael Avraham, "Between *Iyun* and Research: Hermeneutics of Canonical Texts," *Akdamot* 9 (2000): 161–78 [Hebrew]; Daniel Boyarin, "Essays in Midrashic Hermeneutics: The Episodes of the Manna and the Quail in the Mekhilta," *Iyunei Mikra Uparshanut* 3 (1993): 41–52 [Hebrew]; Hanoch Ben-Pazi, "On Speech in Written Texts and on the Written in Speech," *Dimuy* 28 (Summer 2006): 36–48 [Hebrew]; Hanoch Ben-Pazi, "As Strings on Wood—Scriptures and Their Reading according to Levinas," *Akdamot* 16 (2005): 33–63 [Hebrew]; Almut S. Bruckstein, "Hermeneutics and Jewish Philosophy," in *Historiosophy and the Science of Judaism,* ed. Michael Mack and Yoram Jacobson (Tel Aviv: Tel Aviv University Press, 2005)]), 67–91 [Hebrew]; Shmuel Wygoda, "The Jewish Philosophy of Emmanuel Levinas," (doctoral thesis, Hebrew University, 2003), 216–35 [Hebrew]. Wygoda claims, and justifiably so, that Levinas's talmudic readings are based on a hermeneutic theory very similar to that of Gadamer, although Levinas does not mention Gadamer at all in his writings. In my opinion this similarity is true of the *midrash* in general and of the rabbinic *midrash* in particular. See Ze'ev Levy, *Hermeneutics* (Tel Aviv: Poalim and Hakibbutz Hameuhad, 1986), 9–29, 83–173, 254–82 [Hebrew].

9. David Halivni claims that the *midrash* is very close to the theory of deconstruction, both due to its reference to the text as having many meanings and due to the absolute dependence of the text on the interpretive act. Both methods have a common dimension, but in my opinion the attitude of the commentator to the text in the *midrash* assumes that the text is also a teacher and that it demands something of the commentator. The status of the text is higher than that defined by the theory of deconstruction. This issue requires further study. See David Weiss Halivni, *Peshat and Derash* (New York: Oxford University Press, 1991), 158–62; Hirshman, "Aggadic Midrash," 129; Frankel, *Midrash and Aggadah,* 60–61; Joshua Levinson, *The Twice-Told Tale* (Jerusalem: Magnes, 2005), 29–60 [Hebrew]. Thanks to Jonathan Cohen, who helped me elucidate these insights by discussing them with me.

10. Ruhama Weiss, *Committing my Soul* (Tel Aviv: Yediot Aharonot, 2006), 11 [Hebrew].

11. See also Gershon G. Scholem, "Revelation and Tradition as Religious Categories in Judaism," in *The Messianic Idea in Judaism* (New York: Schocken, 1971), 284–87.

12. See Joseph Heinemann, *Aggadah and Its Development* (Jerusalem: Keter, 1974), 11 [Hebrew]; Hirshman, "Aggadic Midrash," 115–17; Frankel, *Midrash and Aggadah,* 37–50; Zunz, *Gottesdienstliche Vorträge der Juden,* 21–24. [Hebrew]

13. Cited in Hirshman, "Aggadic Midrash," 115.

14. Bamidbar Raba 10:8.

15. A very similar interpretation of the same verse appears in another context in a different version: "Freedom from the Angel of Death. R. Nehemia said: freedom from the kingdoms, and the Rabbis said: freedom from suffering" (Shir Hashirim Raba 8:4). There the context of this *midrash* is different and therefore its meaning is different too.

16. This is how Zunz describes the development of the rabbinic *midrash,* as it perceives itself, as replacing the prophecies. Zunz, *Gottesdienstliche Vorträge der Juden,* 22–24; and see Frankel, *Midrash and Aggadah,* 62–64; Scholem, "Revelation and Tradition," 284–92. According to Zakovitch and Fishbane there is an inner-biblical *midrash* and the midrashic method was formed even before the end of the prophetic era. See Zakovitch, *Introduction to Inner Biblical Interpretation,* 9–11, 131–35; Fishbane, *biblical Interpretation in Ancient Israel.* However this makes no difference for the process of development described. This portrayal also shows a transition from that which purports to be direct communication with God to open exegesis that declares itself as such, as a way of learning God's will, a process that increased as unmediated contact with God waned.

17. The first mishna in the Tractate Avot exhibits how the transmission of authority and the Torah skipped from a line of prophets to Members of the Great Assembly (*Anshei Knesset Hagdola*) and thence to other sages who were not prophets.

18. Babylonian Talmud, Tractate Makot 23b.

19. See Heinemann, *Aggadah and Its Development,* 9; Ze'ev Levy, *Hermeneutics,* 10, 18, 26; Frankel, *Midrash and Aggadah,* 33.

20. For example, medieval *pshat* commentators compare their innovative approaches to interpretation of the Torah to rabbinic *midrashim.* At the end of Ibn Ezra's introduction to his biblical commentary he writes,

> The fifth among these ways, the foundation of my commentary upon them stays; and it is right in my eye, before God's face on high. His awe alone I savor; in the Torah, I will never show favor. I will explicate each word's grammar with all my strength ... because *drash* does not make the way of *pshat* mistaken, for the Torah has seventy faces which we may awaken. Only when it comes to teachings, laws, and decrees, if the verse has two reasons which may please, and the one reason relies on the scribes' expertise, for they are all righteous, we need no guarantees, we will doubtless rely on their truth, with strong hands and ease. God forbid that we may involve ourselves with Sadducees.

See R. Avraham ibn Ezra, part II, etzion.org.il/vbm/english/archive/parshanut/14parshanut.htm. The Rashbam as well stresses that "A verse cannot depart from its plain meaning" (Gen. 1:1; 37:2). Nonetheless, he also says: "The *midrash* of our sages and their laws and traditions handed down from the first sages is a basic foundation" (Lev. 13:2). Accordingly, we can find formats such as: "According to the *pshat*...but the sages interpreted" (Exod. 21:28) and "This is the interpretation of our sages, but the plain meaning" (Exod. 24:4).

21. This is based on the research of Isaak Heinemann, *The Methods of the Aggadah,* 96–154 [Hebrew]; Frankel, *Midrash and Aggadah,* 124–78. In rabbinic times several attempts were made to characterize the rules used to interpret the Torah. These rules are directed mainly at the *midrash halakha:* Hillel's seven rules (Tosefta, Sanhedrin 7:11) and R. Yishmael's thirteen rules (Sifra, Leviticus, Proem). There is also a Baraita in the name of R. Eliezer son of R. Yose Haglili, with a list of 32 rules for producing *midreshei aggadah.* It appeared in the Vilna Edition of the Babylonian Talmud at the end of the Tractate Berachot. See also Levy, *Hermeneutics,* 25–29; Marc-Alain Ouaknin, *The Burnt Book,* trans. Llewellyn Brown (Princeton, NJ: Princeton University Press, 1995), 70–72.

22. Heinemann, *Methods of the Aggadah,* 15–18.

23. "The organic way of thinking does not subjugate the tangible to the rational the way scientific thought does" (ibid., 15).

24. Ibid., 96, 148; Meir, *The Story as a Hermeneutic Device,* 27–28; Neusner, *How Judaism Reads the Torah,* 18–23; Frankel, *Midrash and Aggadah,* 39.

25. Much has been written about the "life situation" (*Sitz im leben*) of the *midrash,* and there is a dispute between those who claim that the main context was a public sermon in the synagogue (see Heinemann, *Aggadot and Their History,* 12; Joseph Heinemann, *Public Sermons in the Talmudic Period* (Jerusalem: Bialik, 1971), 8–11, and Zunz, *Gottesdienstliche Vorträge der Juden,* 164–69), and those who situate the *midrash* in the *beit midrash,* among the Torah scholars (for example, Frankel, *Midrash and Aggadah,* 90–93). Meir summarizes this topic (Meir, *The Story as a Hermeneutic Device,* 26–27). Hirshman forms a type of synthesis between the different opinions (Hirshman, "Aggadic Midrash," 122–24; Marc Hirchman, "What is the Place of *Midreshei Aggadah* and Who Are 'Ba'alei Ha'aggadah'?," *Talmudic Research* 3 (2005): 190–203. In any case, this does not affect the current discussion—the practical aim of the *midrash.* This discussion also does not affect the assertion that the *midrash* constitutes oral study written down after the fact. Whether it took the form of a public sermon or of a debate in the *beit midrash,* the initial act of study was oral.

26. Frankel describes the format of the *midrash* as follows: the plain meaning of the verse, the homiletical interpretation of the verse, the new (explicit) idea, and the general latent idea (Frankel, *Midrash and Aggadah,* 52).

27. Babylonian Talmud, Tractate Shabbat 88a.

28. Babylonian Talmud, Tractate Berachot 61a.

29. See, for example: Neusner, *How Judaism Reads the Torah,* 7–10; Frankel, *Midrash and Aggadah,* 683–84. This is also a major claim of Joseph Heinemann's book *Public Sermons in the Talmudic Period.*

30. An example of an error that occurred at an early stage, apparently when still in the oral form, appears in Mishna Kiddushin 1:7. The version that appears in the Mishna and in the Babylonian Talmud does not make sense, because it contradicts well-known laws and the Babylonian Talmud devotes a discussion to this matter (Babylonian Talmud, Tractate Kiddushin, 29a). The Talmud forms a *midrash* on the Mishna to solve the conflict stemming from its current wording. However the same *mishna* appears in the Jerusalem Talmud, Kiddushin 1:7, 61a, in a clear and plain form that creates no problems. Another version of the same law appears in the Tosefta, Kiddushin 1:11, in another more comprehensible form. The Babylonian Talmud seems to have based its study on an erroneous version, being unaware of the version of the Jerusalem Talmud. Such errors can be presumed to have occurred in the process of oral study rather than in the process of copying the Talmud, which can be checked and corrected.

31. See, for example, Heinemann, *Public Sermons in the Talmudic Period,* 11–12.

32. One distinct well-known example is the Laws of Chanukah that appear in the Babylonian Talmud, Tractate Shabbat 21b–24a, further to the discussion of "With what may one kindle and with what may one not kindle." The associative connection between the discussion of legitimate materials for kindling Sabbath candles and Chanukah candles led to the placement of the topic in this tractate.

33. Heinemann, *Methods of the Aggadah*, 15–18.

34. See Babylonian Talmud, Tractate Makot 10a for the entire matter; see also Berachot 63b; Taanit 7a; and Jerusalem Talmud, Nedarim 11:1, 42c.

35. Hirshman, "Aggadic Midrash," 108, 118–20; Meir, *The Story as a Hermeneutic Device*, 34; Frankel, *Midrash and Aggadah*, 61–62, 124, 144; Zunz, *Gottesdienstliche Vorträge der Juden*, 154.

36. Frankel, *Midrash and Aggadah*, 80.

37. Meir, *The Story as a Hermeneutic Device*, 29.

38. Heinemann, *The Methods of the Aggadah*, 96, 134, 144; Zunz, *Gottesdienstliche Vorträge der Juden*, 161.

39. Heinemann, *The Methods of the Aggadah*, 154.

40. Babylonian Talmud, Sanhedrin 71a.

41. For more on this matter see Moshe Halbertal, *Interpretative Revolutions in the Making* (Jerusalem: Magnes, 1997), 59–67. [Hebrew]

42. Bereshit Raba 21:10.

43. Similarly, *midrashim* that state, "If it had not been written it would be difficult to say this thing, and the mouth could not utter it" are theologically bold aggadic *midrashim* whose attitude to the text is far from that of the plain meaning. They use the text to convey a message that contradicts the plain meaning of the verse.

44. The research distinguishes between collections of *midrashim* arranged in this way and called "interpretive" from collections of homilies that focus on a single subject and are arranged by the first verse of each homily. See Meir, *The Story as a Hermeneutic Device*, 20–21.

45. Another consequence of this approach, which does not relate directly to the *midrash* as method, but to the redaction of the Mishna and the Gemara, is the many controversies portrayed in them with no final ruling. All the multiple options are presented.

46. Babylonian Talmud, Tractate Eruvin 13b.

47. Frankel, *Midrash and Aggadah*, 146.

48. Ibid., 160.

49. See Meir, *The Story as a Hermeneutic Device*, 33; Frankel, *Midrash and Aggadah*, 148–60.

Notes to Chapter 2

1. *Illéité* is a word devised by Levinas. Literally translated, it means "He-being." This word emphasizes God's absolute otherness.

2. See also Epstein, "From Ithaca to Ethics," in Levinas, *New Talmudic Readings*, 113–15 [Hebrew]; Ben-Pazi, "As Strings on Wood," 34–36, 40–41 [Hebrew].

3. Not incidentally, Levinas published a book entitled *Of God Who Comes to Mind* (see also *EN* 219–22).

4. Here Levinas follows Descartes, *Meditations on First Philosophy*, III, §22–24.

5. See *TI* 33–35, 149; Catherine Chalier, *La trace de l'infini: Emmanuel Levinas et la source hébraïque* (Paris: Cerf, 2002), 45–46.

6. Chalier, *La trace de l'infini,* 107–39. Levinas also depicts biblical prophets through their political role, as critics of politics in the name of values that are beyond politics. I will not refer to that here. See also Hanoch Ben-Pazi, "As Strings on Wood," 33–63.

7. Chalier, *La trace de l'infini,* 113.

8. Ibid., 111.

9. Moses Maimonides, *Guide for the Perplexed,* 2nd ed., trans. M. Freidlander (1904), III, 51, www.teachittome.com/seforim2/seforim/the_guide_for_the_perplexed.pdf.

10. It is possible to see how Levinas challenges any attempt to identify him as either a Jewish-religious thinker or a philosopher with an essentially secular theory, as various Israeli scholars are now suggesting. It is precisely the complexity of his attitude that precludes a one-dimensional understanding of his work. In his theories, Levinas challenges both the humanistic secular system of values and the Jewish Orthodox system, which would accept the theological contents of the Scriptures in their simple form. This is a schematic presentation that Levinas strives to undermine in all of his philosophical and Jewish endeavors. My refusal to treat Levinas as merely a European philosopher or a Jewish religious thinker is based on the approaches of scholars such as Catherine Chalier and Simon Critchley. Hanoch Ben-Pazi and Annette Aronowicz also hold this approach.

11. For more on this point, see chapter 6.

12. The danger of a worldview that includes no atonement for acts committed is demonstrated, among others, in the story of Elisha ben Avoya. When he hears that he cannot atone for his deeds, Elisha loses all restraint and allows himself to sin (Babylonian Talmud, Hagiga 16a–b).

13. The word "saying" is a translation of the French term *dire* and the word "said" of the term *dit.* These terms are explained further in the section entitled "Connection to the Origins of Language—Inspiration."

14. This is an extensive subject that I shall not discuss here. See, for example, *TI* 82–101; *GCM* 152–71.

15. Er is a war hero, related to have died and then reawakened to report what he had seen in the other world. Plato speaks of the lessons this story teaches about life and human choice.

16. Levinas provides the following footnote on spirituality: "It is in this sense certainly that the prophet Amos (3:8) attributes his prophetic gift to his very hearing: 'The Lord God has spoken, who would not prophecize?' But watch out for the false prophets! More prudently then Amos, the greatest of the prophets [Moses], in Numbers (11:27), learning that 'Eldad and Medad prophecize in the camp,' wishes that all men accomplishing their anthropological essence ('all the people of God') could prophecize. This is a vow and a prayer like the liturgical formula cited above ["Give us our part in your Torah"]. Men must have teachers, schools, philology and History. But the danger of false prophets is certainly not reason enough to remain troglodyte" (*NTR* 77n27).

17. For more on the essence of language, inspiration, and their relationship see *OB* 140–52, 165–72; Emmanuel Levinas, *En découvrant l'existence avec Husserl et Heidegger* (Paris: Vrin, 1949), 261–330; *HO* 9–44; Edith Wyschogrod, *Emmanuel Levinas: The Problem of Ethical Metaphysics* (New York: Fordham University Press, 2000), 141–75; Michael Eskin, *Ethics and Dialogue* (Oxford: Oxford University Press, 2000); Jeffrey

Dudiak, *The Intrigue of Ethics: A Reading of the Idea of Discourse in the Thought of Emmanuel Levinas* (New York: Fordham University Press, 2001).

18. Levinas is alluding here to the content conveyed by the Scriptures, that is, their ethical meaning. I discuss this in greater detail in chapter 3.

19. See *BV* 114–15; *NT* 36–48; *ITN* 64–65; Henri Atlan, *Les Etincelles de Hasard: Athéisme de l'écriture* (Paris: Seuil, 2003), 2, 409; Hanoch Ben-Pazi, "On Speech in Written Texts and on the Written in Speech," 117–43 [Hebrew]. On the inspiration at the basis of all written language, and on the connection between philosophy and prophecy, see Catherine Chalier, *L'inspiration du philosophe: "L'amour de la Sagesse" et sa Source Prophétique* (Paris: A. Michel, 1996).

20. There are many examples of this interpretive method. See *NT* 21–22, 62–69, 77–82, 98–99, 113–14, 165, 185–86; *BV* 25–27, 37–38, 77–78, 83; *ITN* 15–16; *NTR* 92–93.

Notes to Chapter 3

1. See also *DF* 24–26, 161, 213–14. This is one of the main topics of the entire book.
2. For more on holiness see the first part of chapter 7.
3. For an example of this attitude of the *midrash* to the biblical verses, which occupies Levinas who stresses its hermeneutical orientation, see *NT* 18–20.
4. Rivka Lubitch, "The Midrashim of Dina," in *If You Do Not Know*, ed. Yoram Verete (Tel Aviv: Hakibbutz Hameuhad and Hamidrasha, 2005), 94 [Hebrew].
5. See also Aronowicz, "Translator's Introduction," *NT* xviii–xix.
6. For more on the relationship between youth, renewal, and time, see *TI* 282–83. The years that have elapsed since the lesson was taught, with their accelerated processes of globalization, only enhance the relevance and acuity of these issues.
7. For a more in-depth discussion of the structure of this lesson, see below, in the section "The Relationship between Exegesis and Reality."
8. See also *BV* 103, 123; *DF* 68; *NT* 5–6, 60–61; *NTR* 47–48, 63.
9. On this see Uwe Bernhardt, "Le statut de la théorie chez le dernier Lévinas," *Cahiers d'Études Lévinassiennes* 1 (2003): 185–201; Eli Schonfeld, *The Wonder of Subjectivity* (Tel Aviv: Resling, 2007), 20–29 [Hebrew].
10. The biblical commentary of Paul Ricoeur also focuses on the relationship between the text, the world, and the commentator. He writes: "I define 'symbol' as any structure of signification in which a direct, primary, literal meaning designates, in addition, another meaning which is indirect, secondary, and figurative, and which can be apprehended only through the first." Paul Ricoeur, *The Conflict of Interpretations* (Paris: Seuil, 1969), 12. See also the above discussion on the punishment of excision in chapter 3; *BV* 15–19; *NT* 16–17, 22; *ITN* 61–62.
11. See also *NT* 7–9. In these texts, Levinas also refers to the philological method (*NT* 91–93, 108–09, 111; *BV* 54–55).
12. See also *ITN* 64, where Levinas claims that focusing on the historical aspect instead of hearing the word of God in the Scriptures may be idolatry (a theme I also discuss at the beginning of this chapter). And see Samuel Moyn, "Emmanuel Levinas's

Talmudic Readings: Between Tradition and Invention," *Prooftexts* 23, no. 3 (2003): 338–63.

13. For more on this approach and its goals, see Menachem Kahana, "Talmudic Research in the University and Traditional Study in the Yeshiva," *Bechavlei Masoret Utmura* (Rehovot: Kivunim, 1990), 113–42 [Hebrew].

14. Indeed, I experienced this when teaching one of Levinas's talmudic readings before a respectable forum of Talmud scholars. His words were rejected by some of the participants as unfounded, arbitrary, and so forth.

15. See above and also Shmuel Wygoda: "Le maitre et son disciple," *Cahiers d'Études Lévinassiennes* 1 (2003): 164–72. Levinas's approach to interpreting the Talmud is discussed in this article as differing from the Brisker approach and from the philological approach.

16. See, for example, chapter 6. Strong criticism of these approaches can be found in the following section: "And is the hand just a hand and not also a certain imprudence of spirit that seizes a text savagely, without preparation or teacher, approaching the verse as a thing or an allusion to history in the nakedness of its vocables, without regard for the new possibilities of their semantics, patiently opened up by the religious life of tradition? Without precautions, without mediation, without all that has been acquired through a long tradition ... which is the opening up of horizons through which alone the ancient wisdom of the Scriptures reveals the secrets of a renewed inspiration. Touched by the impatient, busy hand that is supposedly objective and scientific, the Scriptures, cut off from the breath that lives within them, become unctuous, false or mediocre words, matter for doxographers, for linguists and philologists" (*ITN* 24). This is a criticism of philology in the language of the symbol. The impurity of the hands becomes relevant for a completely current matter.

17. The original sentence is a wordplay in French: *"Parfait dans un monde mal fait ou dé-fait."*

18. This section refers to the interpretation of a section of the Mishna, which appears in Tractate Menachot 99b–100a, that deals with the table located in the Temple and the shewbread placed upon it.

19. Here Levinas utilizes a play on words: in French the word for "end"—*fin*—sounds like the word for "hunger"—*faim*.

20. See Genesis 42:6.

21. See Levinas's early book, *Time and the Other,* trans. Richard A. Cohen (Pittsburgh: Duquesne University Press, 1987); and later essays under the heading "Death and Time" (lessons from 1975–76), in Levinas, *God, Death and Time,* trans. Bettina Bergo (Stanford, CA: Stanford University Press, 2000), 7–119; "The Ethical Relation and Time" in *TI* 220–52; Richard A. Cohen, "Responsible Time," *Cahiers d'Études Lévinassiennes* 1 (2003): 39–53; Manuel Weill, "Le temps dans la pensée d'Emmanuel Lévinas" (master's degree thesis, Paris X Nanterre, 1999).

22. See, for example, *DF* 72–78, 85–86; *NT* 54, 103, 108–09, 166, 172–73; *BV* 42, 44, 108, 124, 136, 209n6.

23. See Abraham Weiss, *On Research of the Talmud* (New York: Feldheim, 1955), 3–108 [Hebrew]; Shulamit Waller, *Women and Womanhood in the Talmudic Narratives* (Tel

Aviv: Hakibbutz Hameuhad, 1993), 16–19 [Hebrew]; Shamma Yehuda Friedman, *The Chapter Hiring a Craftsman* (New York: The Jewish Theological Seminary of America, 1997), 7–23 [Hebrew]; Mordechai Anshel Tenenblatt, *The Formation of the Babylonian Talmud: A Historical and Textual Study* (Tel Aviv: Dvir, 1972) [Hebrew]; Noam Zohar, *Secrets of the Rabbinic Workshop* (Jerusalem: Magnes, 2007), 1–7, 123–51 [Hebrew].

24. There are two deviations from this rule: In the lesson "Toward the Other" he skips two of the four stories brought in Tractate Yoma 87a and states that this is due to a lack of time (*NT* 22); "Messianic Texts" is an interpretation of several passages in Tractate Sanhedrin, where the original order of appearance is not maintained (*DF* 59–96).

25. "Biblical wisdom is inseparable from *Midrash*, the fruit of centuries of spiritual life forming a chain of tradition in which thought is at once transmitted and renewed.... Writing is intimately bound to an "oral Torah," at once preliminary and renewing.... The Jewish reading is anything but unbiased, although here being a biased reader means, not sterility of dogmatic prejudices, but the possibilities and risks of a thought transcending the given; and probably the extraordinary trace of Revelation leaves in a thought that, beyond the vision of being, hears the word of God" (*ITN* 51). See also *NT* 7–8, 75; Catherine Chalier, *Lévinas: L'utopie de l'humain* (Paris: Albin Michel, 1993), 26.

26. What does Levinas mean by "Jewish reading"? Historical and philological interpretations do not appear to be included in this definition. Perhaps Levinas identifies "Jewish reading" with the *midrash*.

27. The connection to the interpretive tradition takes place through the teacher's instruction and through the text, the Talmud. On the teacher's role, see section "Study-oriented Conversation and the Bounds of Freedom" in chapter 6.

28. Yariv Ben-Aharon and Eli Alon, *Exposure and Coverage in Language—C. N. Bialik, A Treatise* (Tivon: Machberet Shdemot, 1997), 3 [Hebrew].

29. See for example, Yariv Ben-Aharon, *The Legend of Pumbedita*, (Tivon: Machberet Shdemot, 2000) [Hebrew]; Ari Elon, *Alma Di* (Tel Aviv: Yediot Aharonot, 2011) [Hebrew]; Yoram Verete, ed., *Studying the Study: The Beit Midrash* (Jerusalem and Oranim: Mandel and Hamidrasha, 2008), 15–50 [Hebrew]; Admiel Kosman, *Men's Tractate* (Jerusalem: Keter, 2002) [Hebrew]; Admiel Kosman, *Women's Tractate* (Jerusalem: Keter, 2007) [Hebrew]; Ruth Calderon, *The Market, The Home, The Heart: Talmudic Legends* (Jerusalem: Keter, 2001) [Hebrew].

Notes to Chapter 4

1. Babylonian Talmud, Tractate Kiddushin 40b and elsewhere.

2. This is reminiscent of Gadamer's hermeneutic theory, with its reference to the "fusion of horizons" between the commentator and the text, where both the commentator and the text expand their horizons following this encounter. Levinas does not mention Gadamer.

3. Levinas stresses this point as a significant bone of contention with Martin Buber who perceives dialogue as a symmetrical, equal relationship (*PN* 39–43, 46–47).

4. The first part of the book *Totality and Infinity* deals with this topic extensively. It disagrees fundamentally with other philosophical theories, mainly Heidegger's ontology. See also *HO* 49–52.

5. For more discussion of this lesson, see chapter 6.

6. As I write these words, in the midst of a doomed battle against an economic plan that will only worsen the economic aggression and disparity within Israeli society, I feel that I myself am their target—sitting at home and writing a book instead of taking a more active part in the struggle.

7. See also "The Name of a Dog, or Natural Rights" (*DF* 151–53).

8. See also Simon Critchley, "Five Problems in Levinas's View of Politics, and the Sketch of a Solution to Them," *Political Theory* 32, no. 2 (2004): 172–85.

9. On the meaning of Zionism see, for example, *BV* 160, 177–95; *DF* 216–20; *NT* 51–69. The talmudic lesson "Promised Land or Permitted Land" (*NT* 51–69) is also another distinct example of the association between text and reality. In it Levinas deals with the meaning of the State of Israel and the political and moral attitude of Western intellectuals toward Israel, in the context of the biblical affair of the explorers.

10. His analysis of the murderous events at Sabra and Shatila in an interview with Shlomo Malka published in *Les nouveaux cahiers* 18 (1982/3): 1–8, indicates this tension between seeing the terrible reality, which contradicts all humanism and certainly any ideal of ethical politics, while not losing the sense of judgment and the wish to do good, influence, and improve. His assumption is that IDF soldiers were not really aware of what was happening in the camps, and therefore they are not guilty but rather (only) responsible, and he emphasizes the vigorous public protest in Israel that led to the establishment of an investigation committee, as an example of introducing ethical criticism in politics.

11. Jonah Frankel, *Midrash and Aggadah*, 52–53 [Hebrew]. See also Elimelech A. Halevy, *Values of the Aggadah and of the Halakha* (Tel Aviv: Dvir, 1982), 19 [Hebrew]. Marc-Alain Ouaknin writes that every talmudic passage contains an implicit question that is not congruent with its explicit content, and emphasizes that this matter is part of the essence of the Talmud as an "open" text that withstands any attempt to render it closed through exhaustive interpretation (Ouaknin, *The Burnt Book*, 82–95). Ruth Lorand claims that exegesis is in essence compliance with the presumption that the text contains an implicit message that the exegesis must reveal. See Ruth Lorand, *Aesthetic Order: A Philosophy of Order, Beauty and Art* (London: Routledge, 2000), 130–34.

12. See also *GCM* 70–72 where, among other things it says: "The responsibility for the other...comes to me prior to my freedom."

13. Freedom and heteronomy are discussed at length in the talmudic lesson "The Temptation of Temptation" (*NT* 30–50). See also chapter 6.

14. As in many places in the philosophy of Levinas, here too he focuses on the desirable more than on the current. The role of intellectual, religious, political, and social leadership is to shape a just society free of violence. And as in other cases, here the desirable also serves to judge current reality.

15. Babylonian Talmud, Tractate Berachot 61a. First are *midreshei aggadah* on the verse, "Then the Lord God formed man" (Gen. 2:7), and only then is there an aggadic sequence that opens with *midrashim* on the verse, "Then the Lord God made a woman

from the rib" (Gen. 2:22). The structure of the talmudic passage recognizes the order of the Creation as presented in chapter 2 of Genesis, which differs from that presented in chapter 1. Levinas enhances what is implicit in the passage.

16. Much has been written on this topic. See, for example: Ze'ev Levy, *The Other and Responsibility* (Jerusalem: Magnes, 1997), 204–19 [Hebrew]; Hanoch Ben-Pazi, *Call to Responsibility* (doctoral thesis, Bar-Ilan University, 2003), 259–96 [Hebrew]; Ephraim Meir, "The Dimension of the Feminine in Levinas's Philosophy," *Iyun* 43 (1994): 145–52 [Hebrew]; Catherine Chalier, *Figures du féminin, lecture d'Emmanuel Lévinas;* and chapter 5, note 8.

17. See Hanoch Ben-Pazi, "On Territories and the Holy Land in Levinas's Thought: Questions for Zionism," *Iyunim Bitkumat Yisrael* 17 (2007): 123–54. [Hebrew]

Notes to Chapter 5

1. Levinas does not give a reference for this citation. I assume that it is from Midrash Tehilim 92.

2. Paul Ricoeur also emphasizes this aspect of exegesis. See for example: Ricoeur, *The Conflict of Interpretations,* ed. Don Ihde (Evanston, IL: Northwestern University Press, 1974), 16–17; André Lacocque and Paul Ricoeur, *Penser la Bible* (Paris: Seuil, 1998), 15 [French].

3. This is one of the central topics in the philosophy of Levinas discussed in *Totality and Infinity,* which offers a philosophical alternative to the concept of totality. The current discussion will be a superficial one, limited to its context.

4. See also Marie-Anne Lescouret, "After You: Ethical Challenges in Real Life," in *Levinas in Jerusalem,* ed. Joelle Hansel (Jerusalem: Magnes, 2007), 94 [Hebrew].

5. Franz Rosenzweig, *The Star of Redemption,* trans. Barbara E. Galli (Madison: University of Wisconsin Press, 2005), 11–12.

6. On the need to maintain one's privacy, including one's feelings and pains, versus inclusion in total and violent methods of thought, see also *NT* 18–19. On the relationship between this approach and postmodernism with its ethical motivations, see Simon Critchley, *The Ethics of Deconstruction: Derrida and Levinas* (West Lafayette, IN: Purdue University Press, 1992).

7. See also chapter 2.

8. I choose here to disregard the gender problematics involved in identifying women with the intimate. Levinas was not a feminist. The talmudic lesson cited demonstrates this clearly. At the moment I am focusing on another matter. And see chapter 4, note 16. See Tina Chanter, ed., *Feminist Interpretations of Emmanuel Levinas* (State College: Pennsylvania State University Press, 2001; Hanoch Ben-Pazi, "Rebuilding the Feminine in Levinas's Talmudic Readings," *Journal of Jewish Thought and Philosophy* 12, no. 3 (2003): 1–32.

9. The concept of "idolatry" appears in the lesson "Toward the Other" (*NT* 17) as one of man's transgressions against God, with no explanation. In the lesson "Contempt for the Torah as Idolatry" (*ITN* 55–74), idolatry is defined as a futile attitude to the Torah, an attitude that objectifies it without any interpretive conversation, and without

allowing those who sanctify it to be taught anything about their ways of life. In this context, the lesson "Desacralization and Disenchantment" (*NT* 136–60) also comes to mind, where Levinas deals with the difference between real holiness and sorcery and other types of fictitious sanctity. For an interpretation of this lesson, see Wygoda, *The Jewish Philosophy of Emmanuel Levinas*, 236–70 [Hebrew].

10. The very choice made by Levinas to pursue philosophy, a philosophical language, is in fact a choice to live within this culture, albeit in conversation with it and in resistance to some of its components. An example of an explicit manifestation of his approach is provided by the lesson "The Translation of the Scripture" (*ITN* 33–54), where he deals with the uniqueness of Greek culture versus other cultures. He also distinguishes between the Greek language and Greek wisdom whose achievements are splendors (*BV* 26–29).

11. This is an implicit argument with Heidegger who speaks of authentic existence as a life of observation, a life that in the language of the current text takes place behind the woman while relinquishing the domain of the lion. It is interesting to note the fact that the second part of *Totality and Infinity* deals entirely with the primacy of the home and of intimacy as an essential condition for going out to that which is beyond, to meet the Other. Levinas's interpretation here appears to express a change of position on this topic, as presented in *Otherwise than Being*, where there is no self that precedes responsibility. First, there is the other person and the responsibility for him or her, and only then is there a self that responds to the other. In the concepts proposed here, first there is the lion, and only then is there the woman behind whom one can walk.

12. For other examples of interpretive freedom see the following: the meaning of the names of the Messiah (*DF* 85–88); the use of a symbol from the text to reflect the process it goes through versus its audience (*NT* 18–20, 46–47); the choice to interpret the designation *Rakhamana* (Merciful), which is most common in the Talmud, as bearing special meaning in the context of the discussion on war (98–99, 127, 129–34, 183); the "leap" from the personal home to the State of Israel as a national home (190–91); lending relevant meaning to calculations that seem strange and unintelligible (*BV* 18–19, 65–85); the meaning of "Torah from heaven" (*ITN* 58–61); the meaning of the change of Sarai's name to Sarah (86); a *midrash* on the meaning of negative commandments with their role in limiting the perseverance of being (*NT* 61); and others.

13. On the meaning of impurity of the hands, which constitutes another example of interpretive freedom, see also *ITN* 38 and in chapter 3, note 16.

14. For another example where the plain meaning of the text receives a meaning related to Levinas's philosophy, see the lesson "Beyond the State in the State" (*NTR* 79–107), in which the story about Alexander the Great and the sages is charged with the complex meaning of the relationship between politics and ethics.

15. See the section "Pluralism and Interpretive Freedom" in chapter 1.

16. See also *NT* 24–25, 31, 32, 44, 48, 55, 61, 63, 66, 72, 75, 81, 103, 112, 125, 140–41, 174, 182; *DF* 81–82; *BV* 15, 21, 28; *ITN* 32, 60. In all these places Levinas explicitly mentions members of the audience and their words or opinions.

17. Another example of quoting and referring to another text is the letter quoted in the lesson "Judaism and Revolution" (*NT* 115–16).

Notes to Chapter 6

1. Ze'ev Levy, "Religion and Ethics in the Thought of Emmanuel Levinas," in *Between Religion and Ethics,* ed. Daniel Statman and Avi Sagi (Ramat-Gan: Bar-Ilan University Press, 1993), 65–74 [Hebrew]; Shlomo Malka, "Yisrael Salanter and Emmanuel Levinas: Wisdom of the World," in *Levinas in Jerusalem,* ed. Joëlle Hansel (Jerusalem: Magnes, 2007), 178–84 [Hebrew]; Catherine Chalier, "'Dieu de notre côté': Emmanuel Lévinas et R. Haim de Volozin," *Journal of Jewish Thought and Philosophy* 14, nos. 1–2 (2006): 175–92; Richard Cohen, "God in Levinas," *Journal of Jewish Thought and Philosophy* 1, no. 2 (1992): 197–221; Benjamin Gross, "Language et discourse religieux dans l'oeuvre d'Emmanuel Levinas," *Revue de Théologie et de Philosophie* 135, no. 4 (2003): 299–312; Asher Horowitz, "By a Hair's Breadth: Critique, Transcendence and the Ethical in Adorno and Levinas," *Philosophy & Social Criticism* 28, no. 2 (2002): 213–48; Claire Elise Katz, "Before the Face of God One Must Not Go with Empty Hands: Transcendence and Levinas' Prophetic Consciousness," *Philosophy Today* 50, no. 1 (2006), 58–68; Jeffrey L. Kosky, *Levinas and the Philosophy of Religion* (Bloomington: Indiana University Press, 2001); William Large, "God and the Philosophy of Emmanuel Levinas: a Nietzschean Response," *Literature and Theology* 14, no. 3 (2000): 335–49; David Novak, "Emmanuel Levinas and Ethical Monotheism," in *Ethical Monotheism, Past and Present: Essays in Honor of Wendell S. Dietrich,* ed. Theodore M. Vial and Mark A. Hadley (Providence, RI: Brown University Press, 2001), 240–58; Michael Purcell, *Levinas and Theology* (Cambridge: Cambridge University Press, 2006); George Salemohamed, "Levinas: From Ethics to Political Theology," *Economy and Society* 21, no. 2 (1992): 192–206; Edith Wyschogrod, *Emmanuel Levinas: The Problem of Ethical Metaphysics* (The Hague: Martinus Nijhoff, 1974).

2. See Pat J. Gehrke, "The Ethical importance of Being Human: God and Humanism in Levinas's Philosophy," *Philosophy Today* 50, no. 4 (2006): 428–36, which attempts to define the complex relationship between ethics and theology in the philosophy of Levinas. Yeshayahu Leibowitz takes a completely opposite approach to this matter. As he sees it, religion and ethics are two unrelated spheres that are irrelevant for each other, although both are important. An act is considered religious or moral in accordance with the intention of its practitioner (who performs the act for religious or moral reasons), and it cannot be both religious and moral concurrently. See Eliezer Goldman, "Religion and Ethics in Leibowitz's Thought," in Statman and Sagi, eds., *Between Religion and Ethics,* 107–13.

3. See "A Religion for Adults" (*DF* 11–23); Purcell, *Levinas and Theology,* 60.

4. This is the topic of the entire book. Significant parts of *Entre Nous* deal with it as well.

5. Levinas bases this conception on the prophets and cites Isaiah 58 at length, the *haftorah* read on the Day of Atonement (*BV* 4–6), as well as Jeremiah and Amos (123), to mention only a few examples.

6. Maimonides, *The Guide of the Perplexed,* I.54.

7. For a reference to the topic of repentance (*le pardon*) and its association with time in the philosophical writings of Levinas, see *TI* 282–85.

8. See also *DF* 24–26, 54–55; *NT* 81–84; *BV* 77–79; Joëlle Hansel, "The Meaning of Religious Practice: a 'Pre-Talmudic' Text of Emmanuel Levinas," in Hansel, ed., *Levinas*

in Jerusalem, 1–7 [Hebrew]; Shmuel Wygoda, "In the First Skies of the Garden of Eden," in Hansel, ed., *Levinas in Jerusalem,* 185–215 [Hebrew]; Richard Gibbs, "Blowing on the Embers: Two Jewish Works of Emmanuel Levinas: A Review Essay," *Modern Judaism* 14 (1994): 99–113; Peter Atterton, Matthew Calarco, and Joëlle Hansel, "The Meaning of Religious Practice by Emmanuel Levinas: An Introduction and Translation," *Modern Judaism* 25 (2005): 285–89. Hanoch Ben-Pazi, "The Innocence of the Righteous Shall Guide Them: Talmudic Casuistry as a Halakhic Alternative, on Criticism of the Ideological Dimension of Halakhic Tradition in the Philosophy of Levinas" (unpublished) [Hebrew]. I am grateful to Hanoch for letting me read the article.

9. Interestingly, at present the Reform Movement tends to acknowledge this problem indicated by Levinas and a significant trend toward returning to a more halakhic orientation is evident, as arising from the Statement of Principles for Reform Judaism (Pittsburgh, May 1999), which says among other things: "We are committed to the ongoing study of the whole array of *mitzvot* and to the fulfillment of those that address us as individuals and as a community. Some of these *mitzvot,* sacred obligations, have long been observed by Reform Jews; others, both ancient and modern, demand renewed attention as the result of the unique context of our own times." Available at ccarnet.org/rabbis-speak/platforms/statement-principles-reform-judaism (accessed Apr. 12, 2014).

10. Levinas does not appear to have any pretense of describing reality but only of indicating the fundamental level as he sees it. The fact that, in practice, observance of the commandments is not always directed at proper human relationships, and that the moral meaning of various commandments has become lost in time (the commandment of *Shmita* is probably the most distinct example that comes to mind in this context), is not discussed here.

11. "Virile" perhaps in the sense that in the philosophical tradition, a distinctly patriarchal tradition, rationalism was identified with masculinity (as were other "positive" concepts). Masculine (virile) rationalism is totalitarian at its basis. Levinas objected to this tendency of philosophy.

12. Babylonian Talmud, Tractate Shabbat 127a. See also Rashi, Genesis 18:3, beginning from "and he said: My Lord(s), if now", Babylonian Talmud, Tractate Shvuot, 35b; Rashi, beginning from "That too is holy" (Tractate Shvuot, 35b); *BV* 124–25. See also David Hartman, *A Living Covenant: The Innovative Spirit in Traditional Judaism* (Woodstock, VT: Jewish Lights, 1997), 31. Referring to this same *midrash,* he reaches nearly the same interpretation as Levinas.

13. See, for example, Avinoam Rosenak, "Journey Following the Thought of A. I. Kook and Yeshayahu Leibowitz," in *Wisdom by the Week* (Jerusalem: Van Leer, 2012).

14. On the attitude of Levinas to sanctity, see Shmuel Wygoda, "Sanctity as Ethics in Light of the Philosophical Thought of Emmanuel Levinas," in *Wisdom by the Week;* John Caruana, "Levinas's Critique of the Sacred," *International Philosophical Quarterly* 42, no. 4 (2002): 519–34.

15. Rashi on Exodus 25:29: "Therefore, it is called 'the bread of faces' because it has faces looking in both directions—toward the sides of the house from here [in one direction] and from there [in the other direction]."

16. Ibn Ezra on Exodus 25:30: "In the simple meaning it is called 'the bread of faces,' by reason of the explanation that it is after Him."

17. On the holiness of the Torah, see also chapter 3. On this point it is interesting to note the similarities and dissimilarities between Yeshayahu Leibowitz and Levinas. Both think that holiness is not a given quality and that it is necessary to act in order to sanctify the holy. The difference between them, however, remains vital and sharp with regard to the dependence or independence of the vertical on the horizontal. For more on this subject see Michael Fagenblat, "Lacking All Interest: Levinas, Leibowitz, and the Pure Practice of Religion," *Harvard Theological Review* 97, no. 1 (2004): 299–312.

18. The concept "in the image of God" (*betzelem Elohim*) may constitute another example of how Levinas connects the vertical and horizontal dimensions. See *BV* 151–67; Shlomo Malka, "Israel Salanter and Emmanuel Levinas: Wisdom of the World," in Hansel, ed., *Levinas in Jerusalem,* 178–84 [Hebrew]; Chalier, "Dieu de notre côté," 175–92.

19. See also *BV* 109–10, 123–24; *NT* 92–93; *HO* 49–53, 63–64; *OB* 93–94; *EI* 91–92.

20. See Marc Hirschman, *Torah for the Entire World* (Tel Aviv: Hakibbutz Hameuchad, 1999) [Hebrew].

21. For distinct (but partial) examples from Jewish thought, see R. Yehuda Halevy, *The Kuzari: In Defense of the Despised Faith,* trans. N. Daniel Korobkin (New York: Rowman and Littlefield, 1998), I, para. 95; Maimonides, *The Guide of the Perplexed,* III.51; Rav A. I. Kook, *The Lights of Holiness* (Orot Hakodesh) (Jerusalem: Mosad Harav Kook, 1939), para. 13, 45 [Hebrew]; R. Elijah Benamozegh, *Israel and Humanity,* trans. Maxwell Luria (Mahwah, NJ: Paulist Press, 1995), 237–48. The only one I found who rejects the very presumption of *segulah* is Hartman, *A Living Covenant,* 3–4.

22. See also Catherine Chalier, "Levinas and the Talmud," in Critchley and Bernasconi, eds., *The Cambridge Companion to Levinas,* 106–11; Annette Aronowicz, "Teaching Levinas's Talmudic Commentaries," 287.

23. For detailed discussions of this type of example see Moshe Halbertal, *Commentary Revolutions in the Making: Values as Interpretative Considerations in Midrashei Halakhah* (Jerusalem: Magnes Press, 1997) [Hebrew]; Chana Safrai and Avital Campbell-Hochstein, *Women Out—Women In* (Tel Aviv: Yediot Aharonot, 2008) [Hebrew]

24. This is a reference to Mr. Chouchani, Levinas's Talmud teacher, whom he often mentions and for whom he expresses his deepest respect in his talmudic readings.

25. See also *DF* 93–96; *NT* 113–16, 164, 191; *BV* 83–85, 123; *ITN* 81–82, 88; *NT* 114–15.

26. This is the ceremony of the blessings and the curses on Mt. Grizim that appears in the Pentateuch in Deuteronomy 27 as well as in Joshua 7. The Talmudic lesson from which this quotation was taken deals entirely with this ceremony, as portrayed in Tractate Sotah 37a–b.

27. For many years Levinas also taught a weekly lesson on the portion of the week with Rashi; but these lessons, taught on Sabbath mornings, regretfully remained "Oral Torah."

28. The term "Passion" is used in the context of the last days of Jesus. The suffering of Jesus in these days has a function of atonement and constitutes a mission on behalf

of all humanity. Using this of all terms to denote the role of Judaism in the world is a polemical, anti-Christian device. In this context, Levinas often quotes Isaiah 53 (a chapter identified by Christians as describing Jesus): "Surely he took up our infirmities and carried our sorrows" (*DF* 4). See also *BV* 3–4; Levinas, "Being Jewish," trans. Mary Beth Mader, *Continental Philosophy Review* 40, no. 3 (2007): 205–10.

29. This is a paraphrase and *midrash* on Noah's blessing to his son: "May God enlarge Yefet; he will live in the tents of Shem" (Gen. 9:27), a verse that appears further on in the passage that Levinas interprets in this lesson. Shem represents Judaism and Yefet represents Greece, that is, Western culture, and in particular, philosophy.

30. On the relationship between philosophy and prophecy in the thought of Levinas, and how the Scriptures can be a source of additional inspiration or thought for the philosophical tradition, see *BV* 13–33; Chalier, *La trace de l'infini*, 112–21.

31. See also Elisabeth Goldwyn, "The Universal Mission of Judaism in Emmanuel Levinas' Philosophy," *Iyunim Bitkumat Israel* 18 (2008): 79–98. [Hebrew]

32. An explicit illustration of this is evident in a story that appears in the Babylonian Talmud, Tractate Bava Metzia 59b, known as "The Oven of Akhnai." When R. Eliezer fails in his efforts to convince his colleagues using logical means, he tries to use magical forces, including a voice from heaven. This method is completely rejected by the sages who claim that "it is not in heaven," which is reinforced by the principle that "the ruling follows the majority." In other words, only a human majority convinced by logical means may determine the halakha.

33. For examples of the choice to focus on philosophical questions and of the innovation manifested in this choice, see *NT* 127; *BV* 39–40; *ITN* 36–37, 58.

34. For further considerations of this lesson see Epstein, "From Ithaca to Ethics," in Levinas, *New Talmudic Readings*, 111–15 [Hebrew]; Warren Zev Harvey, "Levinas on Temimut, Naiveté and 'Am-Ha-Artsut," *Daat* 30 (1993): 13–15 [Hebrew]. Lawrence Kaplan, "Israel under the Mountain: Emmanuel Levinas on Freedom and Constraint in the Revelation of the Torah," *Modern Judaism* 18, no. 1 (Feb. 1998): 36–44; Annette Aronowicz, "Teaching Levinas's Talmudic Commentaries: The Relation of the Jewish Tradition to the Non-Jewish World," in *Paradigms in Jewish Philosophy*, ed. Raphael Jospe (Madison, NJ: Fairleigh Dickinson University Press, 1997), 280–89.

35. In his philosophical writings, Levinas discusses the topic of freedom at length and develops this element of establishing its basis outside of human beings in the institutions of government, law, and transcendence. See *TI* 45, 82–86, 143, 164, 200–01, 223–25, 238–46, 251–52, 270–71, 279–80, 302–04; *OB* 10–11, 53, 59, 76, 88, 122–24, 137–38, 147–49. And see chapter 4.

36. Bava Kamma 60a, which Levinas discusses (*NT* 178–97; cf. *TI* 130–35).

37. For an interpretation of this lesson, which follows the sequence of the text, see Jacob E. Meskin, "Critique, Tradition and the Religious Imagination," 97–106.

38. See Menahem Kahana, "Academic Talmudic Research and Traditional Yeshiva Studies," 113–42 [Hebrew]. See also chapter 4.

39. See chapter 4.

40. The Rwandan and South African truth and reconciliation commissions, known as "restorative justice," were established for this purpose.

41. See, for example, *OB* 7, 12, 100, 155–57, 170–71, 181–82, 192n18, 193n36.

42. Jacques Derrida, "Violence and Metaphysics," in *Writing and Difference,* trans. Alan Bass (Chicago: University of Chicago Press, 1978), 79–153; Critchley, *The Ethics of Deconstruction: Derrida and Levinas* (West Lafayette, IN: Purdue University Press, 1992), 7.

43. See also Simon-Nahum, "Une herméneutique de la parole: Emmanuel Lévinas et les Colloques des intellectuels juifs," in *Emmanuel Lévinas, philosophie et Judaïsm,* ed. Danielle Cohen-Levinas and Schmuel Tigano (Paris: In Press Editions, 2002), 256–59.

Index

Abaye, 45, 188
Abbahu, R., 152, 154
Abdimi bar Hama bar Hasa, Rav, 22, 24, 172
Abraham, 20, 153, 188; descendants of, 162, 163, 186
absolution, 179, 180, 181
abuse of power, 154–55
aggadah. See midrash aggadah
Akiva, R., 88, 138, 139–40, 188
Amorites, 188
ancient texts, 16, 26, 61, 62–63; and the present, 85, 96
anxiety, 108–09
Arabic texts, 187
Arabs and Jews, 101, 102, 181, 187
Aristotle, 37, 75
Atlan, Mrs., 135
atonement, 106, 152–53, 180–81, 202n12, 211n28
authentic literature, 44–45

Babylonian Talmud, the, 40, 67, 83, 171, 200n30; tractates of, 140, 200n30, 212n32; Vilna Edition of, 131, 199n21. *See also* Talmud, the; tractates
Bamidbar Raba, 16
baraitas, 65, 71, 107, 157, 174, 199n21
batei midrash (houses of learning), 4, 102, 128; pluralistic, 4–5, 9, 63, 137, 186; publications from, 86
bat kol, 46. *See also* heavenly voice

beit midrash, 8, 57, 66, 116; contemporary, 185–88; and dialogue, 130; of Hamidrasha at Oranim, 131, 187, 197n12; Jewish-Arab, 187; "Nigun Nashim," 66, 187; Rosenzweig's, 4
Bereshit Raba, 30
Bialik, Chaim Nachman, 86
Bible, Holy, 38; Amos in, 202n16; Cain and Abel in, 20, 28–29; David in, 80; descendants of Abraham, Isaac, and Jacob in, 162, 163, 186; Deuteronomy, 27, 211n26; Ecclesiastes, 38; Exodus, 90–91, 161, 172, 210n15, 211n16; Genesis, 66–67, 207n16, 212n29; Golden Calf in, 16, 17; Isaac in, 20; Isaiah, 53, 212n28; Job in, 38, 114; Joseph in, 80; Joshua, 211n26; *midrash* and, 197n5; Mikraot Gedolot edition of, 86; Moses in, 16, 22, 33, 160, 188; Numbers, 69, 202n16; Old Testament of, 84; Psalms, 55–57, 98; Samson in, 103; Samuel in, 103, 104; Scroll of Esther in, 38, 126–27; Song of Songs, 38, 82; and the Septuagint, 169; stories in, 11–12, 38, 48; the stubborn and rebellious son in, 28; translating of, 169; unity of the, 19–20; and verses and *midrash*, 16–17. *See also* Abraham; Mt. Sinai, Revelation on; Pentateuch, the (written teaching); Talmud, the; tractates
biblical exegesis, 85, 171

Index

biblical text, 20, 61, 192, 197n3
biblical verses, 13, 18, 81, 152, 189; commitment to, 28–29; interpretation of, 47, 49, 58; *midrash* and, 16, 17, 203n3
Brisker method, 78

calamity, 90–92, 107, 114
Chouchani, Mr., 131, 135, 162, 163, 211n24
colloquia of Jewish intellectuals in France, 60, 67–68, 82, 83, 192; "Damages Due to Fire," 91; "Forgiveness," 93; "Jerusalem the Single and the Universal," 94, 97–100; "Judaism and Revolution," 93; oral delivery at, 132; "Le Pardon," 140; participants of the, 62, 180; "The Temptation of Temptation," 94; theme of, 73, 89, 103, 106, 109; topic of, 178, 179, 180; "The Youth of Israel," 67–70, 83, 103, 105
commandments, 37, 39, 111, 113–14, 145; different types of, 146–49; and human relationships (*ben adam lahavero*), 139, 146–47; "Israel" and, 165; at Mt. Sinai, 19, 22, 35–36; negative, 208n12; observing, 100–01, 142, 210n10; religious, 11–12, 20, 147, 158; ritual, 140, 142, 149–51, 155, 158, 166
commentators, 76, 89, 129; and freedom, 54, 170; as individuals, 116–17, 119–20; and interpretation, 66, 85, 130; the Maharsha, 135; medieval, 199n20; multiple, 115–21; and renewal, 90–91; and text, 13–15, 43–44, 83–84, 93, 198n9, 205n2
community, 111, 137, 147, 151, 181
concepts, 6–7, 24, 73–81, 211n18
conversation, 93, 128–37
court of law, 40–41, 46
Creation, 30–31
crisis, 157–58
Critchley, Simon, 183

darshan (learner), 16, 37, 43, 44, 74; and commentary, 29, 67, 102–03, 121; as interpreter, 39–51; interpretive freedom of, 19, 27, 66; Levinas as, 124, 176–77; preoccupation of, 22, 89, 91; and text, 29–30, 78, 116, 128, 139; and the Torah, 14–15; world of, 67, 76, 97, 171, 182
darshanim, 19, 21, 27, 135
Day of Atonement, 3, 73, 144–47, 150
Derrida, Jacques, 14, 183, 198n9
Descartes, René, 75, 188
drashot (homiletical interpretations), 13
Dreyfus, Theo, 135

Eleazar, R., 153
Eliezer, R., 212n32
epistemology, 17, 18, 80
eschatological, the, 80, 118, 119
ethics, 99, 101, 118, 155; Bible and, 84–85; and the metaphysical, 142, 161; religion and, 2, 140, 185; and theology, 141, 209n2; Torah and, 39, 128
excision, 40–41, 42, 43, 46–47
exegesis, 53, 63–64, 77–78, 176; and the Bible, 84, 85; and dialogue, 129–30; homiletical, 58, 62; Levinas and, 68, 119–20, 171, 185; purpose of, 55, 88, 139–61; and text, 90, 92; various personalities of, 116–17
existents [*étants*], 119
explorers (*parashat hameraglim*), 110, 206n9
external and internal, the, 5, 151

face of the Other, 158, 164
face-to-face encounter, 75, 108, 165
feminist perspective, 109, 110, 128, 187. *See also* women
forgiveness, 73, 93, 146, 148, 181; between offender and offended, 178, 179; a set date for, 144, 150, 151
Frankel, Jonah, 102
freedom, 17, 24, 41, 110, 206n13; interpretive, 27–30, 85, 121–37, 180,

208n12, 208n13; Levinas and, 104–05; as a value, 172–73
French Jews, 73, 93, 106, 125, 178–81
French language, 169

Gadamer, Hans-Georg, 14, 30, 198n8, 205n2
Gemara, the, 18, 40, 46–47, 96, 122, 201n45; and the Babylonian Talmud, 90–91; and forgiveness, 151, 152–53; Levinas and, 69–70, 77; and mishna, 40, 201n45; and the Nazirate, 71–72; *pshat* (plain meaning) of the, 127, 177
gematria (assigning numeric values to Hebrew letters), 19
Germans, 73, 93, 106, 178–81
globalization, 95, 203n6
God, 33, 139–40, 141–42, 149, 159–60
Golden Calf, Sin of the, 16, 17
grace, saying, 69–71, 72
Greek gods, 123
Greek language, 167–68, 208n10; Pentateuch translated into, 77; as philosophical, 62, 170
Greek thought, 123, 161, 167, 208n10
Grossman, Vassily, 135
gzeira shava (verbal analogies), 19

halakha (Jewish law), 2, 11–12, 165, 170–71, 212n32; *aggadah* and, 106, 107; Talmud's integration of, 78; tractate of, 69. *See also* halakhic; *midrash aggadah*; *midrash halakha*
halakhic: authority, 128; discussions, 78, 79, 170; implications, 161; instance, 74; orientation, 210n9; perception, 166; rulings, 162, 170, 199n21; system, 149; techniques, 13; text, 78; thought, 78; way, 126
Hanania ben Gamliel, R., 40, 42
Hanassi, Rabbi Judah, 151
Hassidic leaders, 25
havruta (partnership), 130, 131
heavenly voice (*bat kol*), 46, 47, 48

Hebrew language, 2, 61, 167, 168, 190, 192; holy, 121; numeric values assigned to letters in (*gematria*), 19; texts in, 187
Hegel, Georg Wilhelm Friedrich, 119, 152, 153, 188
Heidegger, Martin, 188, 208n11
Heinemann, Isaak, 20
Hellenism, 123, 124
hermeneutical theory. *See* Gadamer, Hans-Georg
Hillel, the Elder, 138, 139–40
Hirsch, Samson Raphael, 171
history, 77–78, 79, 81
holiness, 64, 155–59, 109, 111–13, 211n17
Holocaust, the, 1, 62, 73, 172; reactions to, 4, 92, 162; trauma of, 2, 114, 162, 166, 191
holy bread, 157, 159. *See also* shewbread
Holy History, 126–27, 166
Holy One, 153
holy place, 158
Holy Scriptures, 52, 127
Holy Spirit, 46
holy text, 13, 16, 87, 116, 129, 139; and commentator, 3, 93, 117; and reality, 23–24; in written form, 25
homiletic: *drashot* (homiletic interpretations), 13; exegesis, 58, 62; *petihta* (homiletic introduction), 73, 178. *See also* midrash
human relationships (*ben adam lahavero*), 139, 156, 159, 161, 178; and God, 141–42, 149
hunger, 72, 74, 80, 95, 204n19; and saying grace, 69–71
hungry, 70, 80, 81; duty to feed the, 105, 153–54, 157, 159

Ibn Ezra, 157, 199n20, 211n16
ideas, 11–12, 89, 102, 103
identity, 2, 45, 46, 48, 80; closed, 113; of commentators, 117; individual and infinite, 119, 166; Jewish, 4–5, 59, 63

idolatry, 123, 124, 125, 147, 203n12; concept of, 64, 207n9
il y a, the, 108
individual, the, 113, 116, 118, 119, 123
infinite, the, 35, 36, 68
inspiration, 36, 44, 46–47, 48, 115; and origins of language, 51–59
intellectuals, 106, 107
interpretations, 9–11, 128–29, 183, 198n9; multiple, 115–21; philosophical-allegorical, 26
interpretive freedom, 27–30, 121–28, 180; examples of, 208n12, 208n13
interpretive tradition, 47, 205n27
Iranians, 125
Isaac Luria, R. (the Holy Ari) of Safed, 25
Ishmael, R., school of, 138
Israel, 110, 126–27, 167, 185; meaning of, 2, 162, 163; mission of, 162, 164; present-day, 107. *See also* Levinas, works by, "The Youth of Israel"; People of Israel
Israelis, 125
Israelites, 22

Japheth, Shem and, 167
Jeremiah ben Elazar, R., 23
Jerusalem: and cities of refuge, 94, 98; colloquium entitled "Jerusalem the Single and the Universal," 94, 97–100; holiness of, 72–73, 100–02, 158–59, 161; symbolic meaning of, 57; in the Talmud, 140, 200n30; Zionism and, 99
Jewish identity, 4–5, 169, 191, 197n5
Jewish intellectuals. *See* colloquia of Jewish intellectuals in France
Jewish language, 121, 197n5
Jewish law, 69, 109, 145, 200n32. *See also* halakha
Jewish Orthodox system, 202n10
Jewish People, 166, 186
Jewish texts, 13, 165, 192, 205n26
Jewish thought, 1, 101, 155, 161, 195n1

Jews: and Arabs, 101, 102, 181, 187; and Germans, 106, 179; Reform, 149, 210n9
Johanan, Rabbi, 122, 123
Jonatan, Rabbi, 91
Jose b. Hanina, R., 26, 105
Joseph, R., 42–43, 48
Joshua b. Levi, R., 18, 42
Joseph bar Helbe, R., 151–53, 154
Judaism, 84, 85, 160, 180, 192; and ethics, 148, 185, 186; *halakha* in, 165; Levinas and, 140, 61; Reform, 149, 210n9; renewed, 62–63, 68; revised, 13, 106; role of, 164, 212n28; and totalitarianism, 176. *See also* Levinas, works by, "Demanding Judaism," and "Judaism and Revolution"
Jüdische Lehrhaus (Free House of Jewish Learning), 4
justice, 36, 41, 164, 179, 181

Kant, Emanuel, 104

labor camps, 95
labor laws, 57
language, 24, 29, 53, 92, 123–24, 182–84; of concepts, symbols, and examples, 73–81, 204n16; "Exposure and Coverage in Language," 86; interpretive, 19, 31; Levinas and, 6–7, 74–76, 80, 111; and the Mishna, 12, 14; origins of, 51–52; philosophical, 62, 68–69, 180, 183, 108n10; religious, 113–14; revelation and, 120; talmudic, 7, 74–75, 184–85; the text and, 68, 124; theological, 34, 141; and totality, 113, 183; and Western philosophy, 6; written, 51–52, 203n19
Levinas, works by: "And God Created Woman," 109, 121–25; "As Old as the World?" 81–82; "Beyond the State in the State," 208n14; *Beyond the Verse*, 133; "Cities of Refuge," 57, 72–73, 76, 94–102, 109, 158–59; "Contempt for

the Torah as Idolatry," 63–66, 207n9; "Damages Due to Fire," 91, 102, 106–07, 157–58, 174; "Demanding Judaism," 140; "Desacralization and Disenchantment," 155, 208n9; essay on Jewish exegesis, 133–34; exegetical writing, 132; "For a Place in the Bible," 126–27; "Judaism and Revolution," 55–57, 93, 208n17; "Messianic Texts," 205n14; "Model of the West," 111–13, 156–57, 175–76; "The Name of God according to a Few Talmudic Texts," 133; *New Talmudic Readings*, 133; *Nine Talmudic Readings*, 155; *Of God Who Comes to Mind*, 141; "On Religious Language and the Fear of God," 113–14; *Otherwise than Being*, 183, 184, 208n11; "The Pact," 110–11, 168–69; "Promised Land or Permitted Land," 110, 206n9; "Revelation in the Jewish Tradition," 133; talmudic lessons, 133–37, 170, 176–77, 185–88, 190–91; talmudic readings, 1–4, 6–10, 31–32, 60–67, 93–94, 177–85; "The Temptation of Temptation," 62, 94, 107–09, 171–74, 206n13; *Totality and Infinity*, 106, 112, 141, 183, 206n4, 207n3, 208n11; "Toward the Other," 73–74, 106, 135, 140–42, 178, 205n14, 207n9; "The Translation of the Scripture," 167–68, 208n10; "The Will of God and the Power of Humanity," 39, 133–34; "The Youth of Israel," 67–70, 83, 103, 105
Lubitch, Rivka, 66–67

Maharsha, the, 135
Maimonides, 37, 142–43, 171
manslaughter, 94–98, 100–02
Meir, R. Ephraim, 195n2
metaphysics, 73, 76, 140, 142, 161; and desire, 36; "Violence and Metaphysics" (Derrida), 183

midrash (homiletical exegesis), 3, 92, 136–37, 198n8; definitions of, 11–12, 197n5; and life, 21–24; "life situation" (*Sitz im leben*) of the, 200n25; and methods, 19–21, 67–73, 87, 162–63, 182; and oral instruction, 25–26; and prophecy, 17–18; rabbinic, 138, 197n5, 198n8, 199n20; and the text, 15–17, 102. *See also* midrash aggadah; midrash halakha; midrashim, the; midreshei aggadah
midrash aggadah, 6, 11, 18, 19, 106, 107, 170
midrash halakha, 11, 18, 19, 28, 90–91; and rules, 199n21
midrashic methods, 19–21, 67–73, 87, 162–63, 182
midrashim, the, 197n3, 201n43; collections of, 26, 201n44; *tannaitic*, 12, 25, 138
midreshei aggadah, 199n21, 206n15
Mikraot Gedolot, 131
Mishna, the, 42, 154, 155, 162, 200n30; and atonement, 144–45, 150–52, 179; and excision, 40, 43; and the midrashic, 12, 197n4, 201n45; and the Nazirate, 69, 71, 103–04; oral, 25–26, 200n30; and persistence, 112, 175; and rabbinic literature, 197n3; redaction of, 201n45; and repentance, 145–46; and shewbread, 156–57.
See also tractates
mitzvah of Torah study, 20
mitzvot (sacred obligations), 147, 210n9
morality, 150, 161
Mt. Sinai, 39–40; commandments given at, 19, 22; Revelation on, 24, 33–34, 49–50, 58–59, 108, 160, 171

Nachman, Rav, 127
Nahman ben R. Hisda, R., 22–23
Nazirate, the, 67, 69, 71, 72; Samuel and, 103, 104; and Samson, 105
Nazism, 95, 106, 149, 179
Nehorai, Rabbi, 103

Nerson, Dr., 135
New Age culture, 124

obligation, 24, 109, 173
offense against others, 150
ontology, 34, 39, 49, 113, 119, 183; and being, 160; ethics and, 118, 141; Heidegger's, 206n4
Oral Law, 25, 33; and Written Law, 15, 111, 115, 161
oral teaching, 25–26, 131–36, 160–61, 167
organic thinking, 20–21, 200n23
other, 35–36, 39, 45, 92; female, 122; the Nazirate and, 72; in relationship, 96, 141–42, 146, 159–60; responsibility for, 85, 92–93, 104, 111, 140, 208n11; and the Same, 49, 51, 168, 183; and Self, 128, 155. *See also* face of the Other
otherness: God's absolute, 201n1; transcendental, 113–14. *See also* face of the Other

Patriarchs and Mt. Sinai, 19
Pentateuch, the (written teaching), 38, 131, 160, 211n26
People of Israel, 161, 163, 168, 169. *See also* Israel
persistence (*tamid*), 111–12, 175, 176
pesharim, 26
petihta (homiletic introduction), 73, 178
Philo of Alexandria, 13, 171
philosophy, 7, 107, 172, 174, 211n30
pitra, 19
plain meaning (*pshat*), 11, 15–16, 142, 159–63, 177. *See also pshat* (plain meaning)
Plato, 48, 118, 188, 202n15
politics, 2, 99
poverty, 72, 95
practice, 88–89
prayer, 3, 13, 113, 140, 145; house of, 61, 125, 157, 158; Levinas and, 142, 202n16
prophecy, 18, 48, 50, 58, 202n6, 211n30

pseudoepigraphy, 26
pshat (plain meaning), 11, 15–16, 26–27, 102, 103, 199n20. *See also* plain meaning (*pshat*)
public life, 124–25, 151

Rabba, and Scroll of Esther, 126
rabbinic literature, 120–21, 129–30, 139–40, 162, 197n5. *See also midrash; midrashim*, the; Mishna, the; Tosefta, the; Talmuds, the
Rabin, Yitzhak (prime minister), 187
racial persecution, 166
Rashi (commentator), 135, 157, 210n15
rational analysis, 170, 171, 172, 176
rationalism, 108, 186, 210n11
reality, 71–72, 74, 108; text and, 89, 94, 102–03
religion (*dat*), 139; "for adults," 144, 160; and ethics, 2, 140, 159, 185; and morality, 152, 161, 178
religious commandments, 11–12, 20, 147, 158
religious language, 113–14
remorse, 145, 179, 180
repentance (*le pardon*), 209n7; and Day of Atonement, 178; internal component of, 150; and the other, 140; ritual commandments and, 151; and ritual order (*seder ha'avodah*), 3; a set date for, 144; Talmud and, 21
Resh Lakish, 55–57
responsibility, 104, 108–11, 126, 143, 161
revelation, 120, 129, 139, 142; concept of, 34–36; contents of, 38–39; the *darshan* and, 39–51; transcendence of the, 36, 65. *See also* Mt. Sinai, Revelation on
ritual, 76, 155, 161, 181; commandments, 140, 142, 149–51, 155, 158, 166. *See also* Day of Atonement
Rosenzweig, Franz, 4, 118

Saadya Gaon, Rav, 171
Sabbath, the, 20, 155

sacred, the, 64, 156, 158; and obligations (*mitzvot*), 210n9
sages, 89, 117, 128, 140–41, 197n7; Levinas and, 37, 67, 135; Members of the Great Assembly, 199n17; of the Talmud, 69, 81, 85; and "the Torah has seventy faces," 27, 58, 59, 115, 199n21
said (*dit*), 44, 51–52, 68, 183–84, 202n13
Same, the, 48–49, 101, 141; and Other, 51, 155–56, 168, 183
Samuel Bar Nahmani, R., 91
Sanhedrin, the, 82, 163–64. *See also* Tractate Sanhedrin
sayer, and the said, 44
saying (*dire*), 36, 51–53, 57–58, 183–84, 202n13; the said (*dit*), and the text, 68
Scriptures, 78, 127, 136, 139, 167, 168–69, 204n16; relevance of, 79–80, 158. *See also* Holy Scriptures
Second Temple, 3, 12–13
Self, the, 128, 155, 156
shewbread, 113, 156–57, 159, 161
Shimon ben Pazi, R., 22–23, 28–29
Shmuel, 126–27, 195n2
smichut parshiot, 20, 71
Soloveitchik, R. Chaim, 78
speech, 51–52, 179. *See also* Oral Law; said (*dit*)
Spinoza, Baruch, 90
State of Israel, 99, 110, 161, 185, 206n9
state, the, 122–24
stranger, widow, and orphan, the, 39
study, 65, 78, 81, 88–89, 107; -oriented conversation, 130–31, 132, 136
symbols, 68, 86, 95, 175, 208n12; language of, 73–81, 113, 204n16; Ricoeur and, 203n10; various, 57, 122, 167, 173

Talmud, the, 21, 50, 106, 112, 143; attitude toward, 133–34; Bible and, 84–86, 90, 161; and cities of refuge, 98–100; commentaries on, 34, 38–39, 59, 140–41; commentator and, 54–55, 84, 117, 127–28; Gamliel and, 42; and heavenly voice, 46–48; holiness of, 66; and Israel, 161–63, 206n9; Jerusalem, 140, 200n30; language of, 74–76, 167–69; Levinas and, 133, 165, 167; Levinas's philosophy and, 195n1, 195n7; midrashic methods and, 73, 198n8; Mishna and, 26, 197n3; and the Nazirate, 69, 72, 105; as an "open" text, 27, 58, 59, 115, 199n21, 206n11; philosophy and, 105–07, 114, 168, 190, 196n8; R. Joseph and, 42–43; Rabbi Joseph bar Helbe and, 151; rationalism of, 170–77; and reality, 75–79, 89–90, relevance of, 122, 167, 192; Resh Lakish and, 57; and revelation, 58, 108; study methods and, 130–36, 149; study of, 4, 81–83, 96–97, 103; teaching and, 204n14, 205n27; translating, 167–69; women and, 4, 109, 123. *See also* Babylonian Talmud, the; Levinas, works by; tractates
Talmuds, the, 12, 25–26, 197n3
tamid (persistence), 111–12, 175, 176
Tannaites, 188
tannaitic midrashim, the, 12, 25, 138
Tarfon, R., 88
Temple, the, 112, 157, 166–67
Teshuvah, 148, 150, 151
text, 19–20, 77, 86, 117, 192; and commentator, 43–44; context of, 82, 83–84; *darshan* and, 29–30, 78, 116, 128, 139; interpretation of, 7–8, 93, 182; and the Other, 45, 137; and reality, 89, 94, 102–03; and universal meaning, 161–77. *See also darshan*, and text; Gemara
theodicy, 92
theology, and ethics, 141
time, 79–81, 90; as central theme, 104, 105, 113; persistence of, 111–12, 175; and study process, 130–31
Torah, 14–20, 42–45, 60–63, 96–101, 111–16; *beit midrash* and, 9, 192;

conversation and, 26, 31–32, 131–32, 188, 190–91; and discussion, 129–30, 175–77, 207n9; and ethics, 128, 142, 157, 159–60, 172; "has seventy faces," 27, 58, 59, 115, 199n21; hermeneutical tradition of, 186; holiness of, 63–67, 139, 159, 211n17; law of, 57, 162–63, 164, 166, 173; midrash and, 6, 13, 74, 199n20; Nazirate as portrayed in the, 69; of Israel, 72; oral, 167, 205n25, 211n27; and the Other, 80, 96, 168; and reality, 89, 187; and relationships, 161, 165, 181; revelation and, 33–34, 39–40, 171; sages and, 42–43, 56, 140, 199n17, 202n16; source of, 38, 44; study of, 3–5, 37, 88–89, 109, 126, 134, 137; values of, 145, 169; way of the, 129; women and, 102

Tosefta, the, 25, 200n30

totalitarianism, 91, 92

totality, 117–19, 168

"trace": concept of the, 160; of God, 36; "of transcendence," 175

Tractates, 69, 132; Avot, 25, 199n17; Bava Kamma, 90–91, 157–58; Bava Metzia, 55–57, 212n32; Berachot, 114, 121–25, 199n21; Kiddushin, 200n30; Makot, 133; Megillah, 38, 126–27; Menachot, 175–76, 204n18; Nazir, 68, 69–70, 72, 103; Sanhedrin, 28, 81–82, 205n14; Shabbat, 62, 94, 140, 171, 200n32; Sotah, 211n26; Yevamot, 73, 178, 179; Yoma, 73, 144, 151–52, 178–79, 181

tradition, 1, 3, 4, 25, 31, 56, 106; and design, 86; of duties toward the other man, 162; and exegesis, 171; and heavenly voice, 46; and innovation, 13, 15, 16, 125, 131; interpretive, 12, 47, 84–85, 130, 205n27; Jewish, 31, 59, 61, 166; knowledge of, 130–31; and midrash, 6, 8–9, 13, 87, 199n20, 205n25; oral, 132; philosophical, 160, 184, 210n11, 212n30; rabbinic, 80; and religiosity, 43, 204n16; and renewal, 35, 190; of Shem, 167; of silencing women, 67; talmudic, 85, 90; of Torah study, 31, 129, 165, 186; value of, 104. *See also* Levinas, works by, "Revelation in the Jewish Tradition"

transcendence, 36, 40–49, 58, 133, 175; and freedom, 212n35; of God, 156; relationship with, 58–59, 169; voice of, 44, 45, 47

transcendent, the, 7, 34, 141, 142, 169; dictation, 65–66, 120; Other, 37, 113–14, 156; source, 40–42, 58–59, 65, 126, Torah, 39

transgression, 147–48, 150, 152–53, 154

truth, many faces of, 120–21

unsaying (*dédire*), 7

verses, 19, 90–91, 93, 189, 204n16; call out "Interpret me," 44, 66; context of, 81–83, 86, 180, 182; interpretation of, 42–44, 115–16, 134, 198n15, 199n20; *midrash* and, 30, 48, 121, 100; plain meaning (*pshat*) of, 102, 152–53, 199n20, 200n26, 201n43. *See also* biblical verses

violence, 41, 120, 156, 176, 191; circle of, 172, 179, 181; and control, 47; and just society, 206n14; and poverty, 95; totalitarianism and, 6, 91, 106; "Violence and Metaphysics" (Derrida), 183

voice: of commentator, 119–20; heavenly (*bat kol*), 46, 47, 48; multiplied, 117, 136–37; of otherness, 126; of revelation, 129; of transcendence, 44, 47

Western culture, 111, 167, 168, 175, 212n29; attitude toward Israel in, 206n9; and humanism, 148–49; and Judaism, 123–24; and philosophy, 171–72, 183

women, 67, 102, 187, 207n8; as symbol, 122–23; and the Talmud, 4, 109, 123. *See also* feminist perspective
workers' rights, 55–57
World War II, 92, 174
writing, 44, 52, 53, 160; and other, 46, 184; and written language, 51–52. *See also* Pentateuch, the (written teaching)
Written Law, 15, 111, 115, 161

Yehuda, Rav, 153
yeshivas, 4, 78, 130, 176
Yom Kippur, 144, 145, 150–51
Yom Kippur War, 91–92, 174
Yosef, Rav, 127
youth, 67–69. *See also* Levinas, works by, "The Youth of Israel"

Zionism, 99
Zohar literature, 13, 138